Publisher's Note

Because the Chaco War and its antecedents aroused such bitter controversy, partisans of Bolivia or of Paraguay have seldom found basis for agreement. It is no mean distinction, therefore, that the foremost Paraguayan and Bolivian experts in the United States have consented to endorse the impartiality and accuracy of this book. In so doing, both the eminent former Paraguayan diplomat, banker, statesman, and scholar Pablo Max Ynsfran and the fast-rising young scholar, teacher, author, and Bolivian specialist Charles W. Arnade have sought to place the Chaco War in historical perspective. Each has succeeded admirably, as the Preface and Foreword attest.

The Conduct of the Chaco War

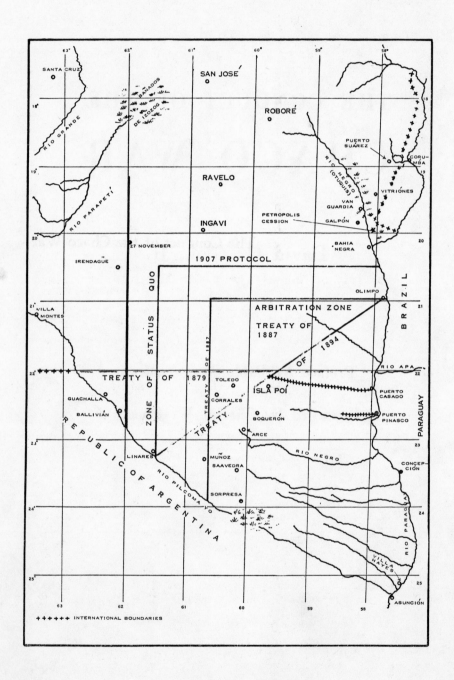

THE CONDUCT OF THE
CHACO WAR

David H. Zook, Jr.
United States Air Force Academy

Preface by Pablo Max Ynsfran

Foreword by Charles W. Arnade

ERRATA

The Conduct of the Chaco War

Page 118, note 17, line 8—for *Infantry* read *Infanteria*
Page 130, line 32—*for* incedibly *read* incredibly
Page 140, line 35—*for* Argentine *read* Argentina

TO

Patricia and David, III

PREFACE

Time enough has already passed since the Chaco War to state that posterity is now beginning to weigh, with a fair degree of accuracy, its significance in the context of Latin American history, and to pronounce its judgment. The dust has settled, passions have cooled sufficiently, outstanding actors and witnesses have spoken, archives have disclosed most of the crucial facts of the long diplomatic disputes and of the origin of the military clash, old issues have lost their bitterness, and the whole controversy can be viewed in a comparatively clearer perspective. In the light of these considerations, it is an act of justice to say that Captain David H. Zook, Jr. has written a book which voices the impartial verdict of posterity.

Although the work of a military man, *The Conduct of the Chaco War* is by no means a purely military account and appraisal of the struggle in which Bolivia and Paraguay were engaged from 1932 to 1935. On the contrary, Captain Zook analyzes the political and diplomatic aspects of the war with as much skill, method and care as the development of the campaign in the field. The two sides of the problem are so intimately interwoven in his narrative that neither can be properly understood without the other. His book, therefore, is of considerable interest not only to the student of wars but also to the political thinker, and even to anyone trying to discern the inner mechanism responsible for the interrelation of human thought and action.

With the first thoroughly integrated review of the Chaco War ever written in any language, Captain Zook makes a contribution which in all likelihood will place him among the highest authorities on the subject. In the preparation of this brilliant piece of historiography he has overlooked no important publication relative to the Bolivia-Paraguay controversy, has conducted many personal inquiries with living protagonists of the drama, and acquainted himself with all the pertinent material. A professional air officer himself, he approaches his topic with a keen technical mind entirely devoid of any national preconception that might otherwise have colored his opinons and conclusions. In general one must take with caution any history of the Chaco War written by the nationals of the two former contenders; such is not the case, however, concerning *The Conduct of the Chaco War.*

All major wars are commonly the outcome of causes which may be divided into two groups: distant and immediate. The former supply the explosive ingredient, and the latter the spark. In the Chaco War, as in almost every other serious international collision among South American countries, the distant causes derived from the ill-defined boundary lines that separated the administrative sections of the Spanish Empire in colonial times. Bolivia and Paraguay disagreed as to the line of demarcation between the Governorship of Paraguay and the Audiencia of Charcas in Upper Peru (today Bolivia). In proportion to the growth of the two countries, so grew also the difference of opinion about their territorial rights. With ever increasing intransigence they pressed their contentions until they reached a point where no compromise was possible. This hopeless impasse led to the Chaco War. Neither country would give ground because any concession would entail national shame. Then came the spark that set off the conflagration.

The penetration of the Chaco by Bolivia with small military posts called *fortines*—first constructed along the Pilcomayo River, in a southeast direction, and later turning north toward the center of the territory—induced Paraguay to build similar posts of its own as a barrier of contention. Facing each other over long stretches, the *fortines* were potential troublemakers, especially after 1920, when Bolivia intensified its penetration. Bolivia felt that without actual occupation its case would appear weaker than that of Paraguay—which was in possession of sizeable expanses of the Chaco since colonial times—and to strengthen its position inaugurated the policy referred to above. But the Paraguayan countermeasures were to be expected, and once both countries embarked upon this military competition, the Chaco controversy dragged ominously toward a military denouement.

A single imprudent shot from one *fortín* could provide the spark to detonate the powder keg.

It seems clear that Bolivia underestimated the determination of Paraguay to oppose force with force if confronted by a situation that would endanger its occupation of the Chaco. As a substantial part of the Paraguayan economic life depends upon the Chaco, the loss of this area would have meant an amputation which the country probably could not have survived. For a country so vitally bound to a piece of land, it was obvious that no sacrifice would be too great to preserve it. Bolivia, on the other hand, looked upon the Chaco as a sort of future colonial addition, not as an organic member of the nation itself. Paraguay was inferior to Bolivia in some important respects—mainly in population and financial capacity—but in the event of a major conflict over the Chaco, the Paraguayans would necessarily fight to the death.

Bolivia apparently did not realize this. Early in 1905 a Bolivian Foreign Minister, Sr. Claudio Pinilla, had warned his government not to ignore Paraguay's willingness to protect its position in the Chaco with the utmost determination. "Paraguay," wrote Sr. Pinilla, "is neither too strong to be feared nor too weak to be despised." Perhaps the Bolivian statesmen who followed Sr. Pinilla had not precisely disregarded his meaningful remark, but, at any rate, they acted as though the steady penetration of the Chaco would not be resisted to the point of war. This assumption implied too much reliance on the Paraguayan weaknesses; in other words, it was miscalculation.

So we see that human affairs, unfortunately, tend sometimes to fall into an inexorable drift which no reason will stop. And this was what happened in the Chaco. In *The Conduct of the Chaco War*, Captain Zook shows the tragedy in its true and regrettable light.

PABLO MAX YNSFRAN

The University of Texas

FOREWORD

Bolivia and Paraguay are among Latin America's poorest countries. They are also the most colorful. They are a piece of this earth soaked in violence and their histories read like tales full of fantasies. In the first half of this century these two nations, molded by fury, clashed over border disputes. Restraint was impossible and a vicious war, the Chaco War, developed. It was South America's greatest armed conflict. It was a true war by Americans called Bolivians against Americans called Paraguayans. History will say that it was one of the most useless wars. But nations like Bolivia and Paraguay, whose way of life had been a continued emotional outburst, could hardly have shed these tempers to solve their disputes peacefully.

The Chaco War does constitute a crucial event, if not the most crucial, in Bolivian history. It represents a somewhat lesser episode in Paraguayan history. Bolivia lost the War even though she had a superior army. The defeat shook the conscience of the country and laid the basis for the great social upheaval of the 1950's, which became the second social revolution in Latin America. Victorious Paraguay entered a period of complacency which cemented her traditional eighteenth-century pattern of Latin American politics and social order. Consequently today Paraguay stands as the lone country in South America that has not followed an accelerated pace of progress. *Caudillismo* still prevails in Paraguay. Loser and victor alike must look to the Chaco War as the initial generator of the present situations of their respective countries. The Chaco War must be impartially sketched and presented in Latin American history, in Paraguayan history, and in Bolivian history.

The history of Bolivia fades to obscure origins. The Incas conquered what is today's Bolivia in the thirteenth century. But far before that time a great empire flourished, whose mysterious remains are exemplified by Tiahuanaco. The Incas called the region Kollasuyo and imposed their language, Quechua, on the natives. In 1535 the first Spaniards appeared and by 1538 the first Spanish city, La Plata, later known as Chuquisaca or Sucre, was founded. In 1545 stupendous silver deposits were discovered in Potosi. Soon this important province of the great Spanish Empire, already steeped in history and by now named Charcas, became a most valued colony.

The systematic exploitation of the mines by the Spaniards created a rigid social system which leveled the natives into cheap labor. An administrative apparatus was set up. The *audiencia* located in Chuquisaca became the political and judicial unit of Charcas with nearby Potosi the economic pivot of the province. As one moved away from the Chuquisaca-Potosi core, in whatever direction, the standard of Spanish colonization declined and remoteness increased. No one really knew where the borders of Charcas lay. This fact was rather unimportant at the time but it did contain the seeds for border disputes of the future when each of the Spanish administrative units would achieve independence. One of the boundary controversies of the then distant future became the Chaco War.

It was in Charcas, a region of sharp contrast where harmony and compromise vanished before the ruggedness of the terrain and the boiling blood of its people, that the first rumblings against the Spanish master were heard. In 1809 the rebellion erupted, but not until 1825 did Charcas achieve independence as the Republic of Bolivia. All the problems of the colonial period and many more were given to the new nation. Independence meant the end of the Spanish bureaucracy with its paternalistic policies. The *criollos* took power; dominated by a narrow-minded provincialism, they failed to solve the many social problems.

Bolivian history became a bloody bout between the ins and the outs; all members of the ruling class. Little or no attention was given to the multifold problems of the nation. Lack of transportation facilities and ethnic differences made the faraway areas along the boundaries easy prey for conquest by nations surrounding Bolivia. Often these regions tended to gravitate away from Bolivia at their own volition, looking with more favor toward the next nearest national capital. The impossibility of determining the colonial boundaries of Charcas enhanced this centrifugal movement. Bolivia began to lose claimed sovereign territory to each nation that shared borders with her. The gravest loss was her Pacific seacoast to energetic Chile. This irreparable loss was due, more than anything else, to Bolivia's languor since she was absorbed in petty politicizing, neglecting her *litoral*. Although many good, honest and forceful men emerged in Bolivia, none was able to solve the two main problems: to provide social equality and justice to everyone and thereby break the corrupt rule of the *criollo* aristocracy, and to consolidate the nation into one national unit.

Unquestionably, when in 1884 Bolivia was forced to relinquish her coast to Chile, the conscience of the nation was shaken. She began a period of deep social, political and geographical reorientation. An era of boom was in the making that took an eastern and southeastern direction. Bolivia's weakest, most ineffectual and least known neighbor, Paraguay, had also lost a terrible war, against Brazil, Argentina and Uruguay. Her future lay to her northwest in the Chaco. A clash of both frustrated countries was inevitable. It blossomed into full war in 1932. This was the Chaco War. History previously has failed to give us an impartial sketch of this conflict.

Captain Zook in his *The Conduct of the Chaco War* is the first scholar, author and military expert to provide us with a thoroughly acceptable study of the subject. An excellent military account, this book also dwells on the diplomatic as well as the political aspects of the Chaco War. It constitutes the best and most impartial survey of the Chaco War to this date. Captain Zook has examined the entire historiography of the War and therefore has acquired a most definite knowledge of all pertinent sources. In the true fashion of scholarship he has sifted these sources, many of them very partisan, and created a first-rate book that is not only unbiased but extremely readable.

It is possible that Captain Zook will be accused, more likely by Bolivian partisans, as having given Paraguay a preferential treatment. But Zook has told the truth. Bolivia's conduct in the War was full of bungling followed by more maladroit actions. Many of the young generation of Bolivians, witnesses and veterans of the War, realized this. In the prison camps of Paraguay they laid the basis of new political, social and economic movements. Today

these men are in power, destroying the old order. It was the re-
volting conscience of the Chaco War that created modern Bolivia.

Captain Zook's *The Conduct of the Chaco War* is one of the
most important books on Latin American history to come into
print recently. I believe it to be a must for the student of Latin
America.

CHARLES W. ARNADE
The University of Florida

ACKNOWLEDGMENTS

In writing this book, I have incurred debts of gratitude to numerous kindly persons. The preliminary studies were accomplished under Dr. Lawrence F. Hill, well-known Professor Emeritus at The Ohio State University, warm friend and patient critic, to whom I must express my thanks and profound admiration. Professor Emeritus Warner F. Woodring has ever encouraged me to an extent he may never realize. During the research phase the sympathetic consideration of Colonels John R. Neal and Clarence Wilson, and of Major Edward Kelly, was invaluable. The personnel at the Bancroft Library were most helpful in making available their facilities.

Thanks are due to Brigadier General Robert F. McDermott, and to Lieutenant Colonels Wilbert H. Ruenheck, John A. Kerig, and Eldon Downs for their encouragement. Colonels Carlos José Fernández and José A. Ortiz (Paraguayan Army retired) provided information available only in their files or memories.

To my distinguished and kind colleagues, Charles Arnade and Pablo Max Ynsfran, I owe sincere and humble gratitude not only for their obvious contributions to the book, but for saving me from many errors. Without the assistance of my good friend, Elizabeth A. Tollmann, the work would contain more editorial errors than is now the case. Above all, of course, there is my wife, who over a period of four years has typed and retyped seemingly endless notes, pages, and chapters, who has performed errands at libraries, who has kept our little son from using my notes in play, and yet has remained devoted to my undertakings.

To all of these, I offer sincere thanks.

THE AUTHOR

CONTENTS

MAPS

MAPS

INTRODUCTION

Of all American conflicts, the Chaco War is the most enigmatic. So many misconceptions and mistaken ideas have grown up that refuting them individually would be an endless task. Even the name of the war has been perverted because many are unsure of its geographic setting.

The fighting occurred in the Chaco Boreal, that portion of the Gran Chaco which lies north of the Rio Pilcomayo. The generalized term Gran Chaco, when applied to the conflict, is therefore a misnomer. Westward to about 59° the region consists of extensive palm groves, high pastures, and small woods. Beyond there was not a town or place, however attractive the name, that was anything but a collection of mud huts. In the extreme west along the Andes the land is fertile, moist, and covered with forests. The intervening area consists of arid desert, often clothed with thick scrub and brush. Here the juice of cacti replaces water, and blood-sucking insects swarm by the millions. When during the months of the southern summer the rains come to this land, the rough roads turn to quagmires; during the dry season the fine, powdery soil rises in great lingering clouds.

No war is devoid of lessons, either professionally for the military man, or generally for the historian and student of human affairs. As the hemisphere's greatest struggle since the American Civil War, the Chaco conflict is indeed of great importance. The diplomatic contention which preceded and accompanied the war stresses the basic necessity for vigorous and forceful defence of a national position. This is not only a right, but also a duty of every state, regardless of its size. That in such a contest victory goes to him who best applies the full resources of his country is axiomatic, but it is brilliantly retold in the Chaco story.

Lying between the global struggles of our century, the Chaco War derived inspiration from the one, and in some cases pointed up lessons for the next. Appropriate then as now was the need for adequate preparation to enable the armed forces to support the policy of the nation. The result of neglecting the real essence of military power in favor of undue economy converts the military into a façade, incapable of aggressive, decisive action. Only by unrestrained application of the total resources of the state can victory be assured.

The lessons of World War I—particularly the superiority of defensive firepower and the vital necessity of trucks for strategic mobility—were re-emphasized in the Chaco. The return of genuine maneuver to warfare marked General José Félix Estigarribia as a precursor of Field Marshal Erwin Rommel. Yet, this was an infantry war. The terrain made it so. From necessity cavalry fought on foot; tanks proved of little value; artillery was less useful in the jungle than mortars; aircraft were poorly employed for lack of doctrine.

As in every conflict, the qualities that differentiate a great commander and leader, whether civilian or military, from an ineffectual opponent are lucidly revealed. Seldom in the history of warfare, however, have such extremes of quality faced one another as upon the obscure fields of the Chaco Boreal. The characteristics which distinguish the soldiers of some lands above those of others contrast brilliantly. Palpably, the soldier of a free country, energetic and capable of individual initiative, is infinitely the superior of the politically, socially, and racially submerged product of an oligarchical dictatorship. The feats performed by soldiers in the midst of the most exhausting privations are in the highest traditions of free men fighting for a cause they believe just.

And, with the conclusion of the war, when the combatants fraternize with one another in mutual relief, and the diplomats return to the center of the stage, the Chaco dispute offers important lessons in negotiation. For in this rare instance, the state whose arms had beaten the aggressor preserved the military triumph at the peace table.

CHAPTER ONE

DIPLOMATIC ANTECEDENTS

The collapse of the Spanish Empire, a by-product of the Napoleonic demolition of the Old World system, resulted in the appearance of many new Western Hemisphere political entities. The ensuing friction incident to boundary determination occasioned sporadic, flagrant hostilities. The most serious of these conflagrations flamed only after a long period of slowly rising temperatures.

The first warning of impending tension between Bolivia and Paraguay appeared in the mid-nineteenth century. After learning that an 1852 treaty between Paraguay and Argentina recognized the Rio Paraguay as belonging to the former "from bank to bank," the Bolivian chargé d'affaires in Buenos Aires protested that his country had riparian rights on the west bank between parallels twenty and twenty-two. The following year, La Paz issued a gratuitous decree claiming the littoral of the Rio Paraguay to 26° 54' south. Nevertheless, in 1855 the Foreign Minister returned to the original claim, asserting sovereignty down to twenty-two degrees, "more or less."[1]

During the 1865–1870 War of the Triple Alliance, Bolivia remained quietly on the side lines after assurances by the Allies that her rights on the west bank of the Rio Paraguay would be protected. When Paraguay's defeat was complete, Bolivia attempted to secure Allied recognition of her Chaco claims. The victors, however, would have none of this and turned her away empty-handed. After protracted negotiations, Argentina and Paraguay divided the Chaco into three parts. The region south of the Pilcomayo was recognized as belonging to Argentina; the portion from the Rio Verde to Bahia Negra, to Paraguay. The area between the main arm of the Pilcomayo and the Verde was submitted to the arbitration of the President of the United States. In 1878 cases were duly presented at Washington. Bolivia again sought to inject her Chaco claims, but was advised that the President could not consider her case because La Paz was not a party to the treaty soliciting his decision. President Rutherford B. Hayes found Paraguay "legally and justly entitled" to the disputed region.[2]

Bolivia never fully accepted the decision, insisting that it was in no way binding upon her, a bystander. She believed that her actions and protests prior to and after the arbitration fully protected her rights. Merely by ruling as to the better claims between Argentina and Paraguay, the Hayes Award in no manner could affect a third party. Paraguayans, however, henceforth regarded the region as indisputably their own and usually rejected La Paz's disavowal. They maintained that Bolivia had tacitly recognized and accepted the award, both by silence and by deed.[3]

Thus from 1852 to 1879 the Chaco question emerged slowly and falteringly. There was no well-defined, generally accepted doctrine on either side. Each groped uncertainly with the problem, and neither had a lucid concept of the opposing position. Neither protested the explorations and colonies of the other, because each was tacitly aware that the other possessed claims in the little known region. The boundary lay where these claims met, but circumstances did not necessitate haste in its exact definition. Paraguay had taken no real interest in the upper river in many years, and certainly the impotent oral pretensions of a country almost inaccessible by land caused little concern in Asunción. In these years of slow communications, unenlightened populations, and relative calm in chancelleries, the Chaco problem could readily have been solved had Bolivia been admitted, for this purpose alone, to the diplomatic liquidation of the War of the Triple Alliance.

Striving to settle the Chaco question quickly, La Paz accredited Dr. Antonio Quijarro as Minister to Paraguay in 1879. His appearance at Asunción was opportune. Paraguay, still a pitiful, defeated province, believed facilitation of pending Bolivian activity in the river basin would stimulate her own stagnant econ-

omy. In a few days of bargaining with Foreign Minister José
S. Decoud, Quijarro yielded his initial demand of a border along
the Rio Verde and settled for the division of the Chaco by a
parallel from the mouth of the Rio Apa at 22° 5′ straight west
to the Pilcomayo. The Paraguayan congress, however, failed to
act on the treaty. On the Altiplano no action was taken until
August 1881 when the National Convention ratified with the
condition of acquiring land on the lower Pilcomayo for a port.
As Quijarro wrote, this clause "occasioned insuperable difficulties"
and caused the failure of the treaty.[4]

Late in 1885, Paraguay, casting about for a method to rehabil-
itate her desperate finances and encourage development, commenced sale of her public lands. Included was much of the Chaco,
even into the interior. Since there was no real capital in Paraguay, most of the land found its way, through speculation in
options, into the hands of Argentine carpetbaggers.[5]

In the hope of gaining either ratification or a new arrangement, La Paz sent Dr. Isaac Tamayo to Asunción as Minister
in early 1886. Paraguay was resentful toward the Altiplano for
procrastination on the previous treaty, and had re-established
a military garrison at Fuerte Olimpo, a colonial fortress on the
west bank of the Rio Paraguay. Tamayo protested that this action,
north of the line of the 1879 treaty, violated a tacit status quo
created when the pact was signed.[6]

On 15 November 1886 the Bolivian Congress, under pressure
of the Paraguayan land law, overrode the opposition to approve
the Quijarro-Decoud Treaty as originally written. Tamayo then
entered friendly discussions with Dr. Benjamín Aceval, Paraguayan Foreign Minister. In these talks, which avoided consideration of colonial titles, Aceval indicated Paraguay would
never consider rearbitration of the Hayes Zone. Consequently,
the treaty signed 16 February 1887 submitted to arbitration by
Leopold II, King of the Belgians, only the region lying between
the mouth of the Apa and one league north of Fuerte Olimpo,
and bounded on the west by 60° 39′ 46″. Bolivia was recognized
as owner north and west, and Paraguay as owner south of this
zone.[7]

On the Altiplano the cabinet split on whether the treaty accurately reflected Tamayo's instructions; at Asunción no action was taken. In January 1888, Paraguay extended her military control on the west bank up to Bahia Negra. Dr. Claudio Pinilla, left in charge of the legation by Tamayo, sharply protested this apparent violation of the recently signed agreement.[8]

Trouble then developed over the activities of Miguel Suárez Arana, a Bolivian developer. On 4 July 1885 he had solicited approval from the Paraguayan government for a port site on the Rio Paraguay from which to make preliminary explorations for a wagon road to La Paz, to be eventually followed by a railroad. He admitted that no point below Bahia Negra could be selected without approval of Asunción. The Minister of Interior immediately consented, but specifically stipulated that no port could be established without prior consent of the Paraguayan Congress. Suárez agreed, but selected a spot 10 kilometers south of Bahia Negra, naming his camp Puerto Pacheco. When the Bolivian flag was observed flying over the tents, Paraguayan officials grew alarmed and reacted by decreeing military control up to Bahia Negra. In September 1888 matters reached a climax when a citizen had recourse to Paraguayan law, charging the camp's administrator with crimes, including murder. When a Guaraní military party from Olimpo arrived, the offender fled. Pinilla protested the seizure of the "port" and any land sales which had been made in the Chaco. He asserted that the 1887 treaty had created "a status quo in the possession, and had regularized the jurisdiction, of both States within their respective assigned zones." He then asked for his passports.[9]

In November, Bolivia's Congress belatedly ratified the 1887 treaty, albeit with suggestions which amounted to rewriting the agreement. Although Paraguayan Foreign Minister Centurión had reasserted his country's full and legitimate rights in the Chaco, Pinilla (in Buenos Aires) worked for a confidential arrangement to pave the way for an exchange of ratifications. Since apparently the disputed Puerto Pacheco would then be returned to Bolivia, La Paz ordered Pinilla to return to his post. In Asunción, however, he found the belief prevalent that the treaty had lapsed owing to expiration of the time limit specified for ratification. Consequently, after a final declaration asserting

Bolivian rights to the entire region down to the confluence of the Pilcomayo and the Paraguay, Pinilla once more took leave of his legation.[10]

Each country now having asserted full claims to the entire Chaco, it was logical to set about finding evidence to support the contentions of the chancelleries. At Asunción, Congress entrusted Dr. Alejandro Audibert with the preparation of the first extensive case, *Los límites de la antigua provincia del Paraguay,* published in 1892. The next, unsuccessful, Bolivian envoy to Asunción, Dr. Mariano Baptista, devoted much of his time to preparing a memorandum which embodied his country's first title presentation. In this document he revealed the existence of a division in Altiplano ruling circles: some favored search for legal titles; others advocated an agreement favorable to economic development. Baptista, an adherent of the second school, stressed Bolivia's need for a port on the Plata system and found basis for her rights in the *uti possidetis* of 1810, in Laws of the Indies, and in *cédulas reales.*[11]

Baptista's successor, Dr. Telmo Ichaso, was instructed to reopen "debate and negotiations of boundaries," founding his position in the *uti possidetis* of 1810, and aim for the entire Chaco north of the Hayes Award. He might seek arbitration, but not above the twenty-first parallel, which pertained to the "original and never disputed Upper Peruvian jurisdiction of Chiquitos." After several months devoted to consideration of the respective cases and titles, Ichaso and Foreign Minister Gregorio Benites of Paraguay signed the third boundary treaty on 23 November 1894. This drew a diagonal line across the Chaco from three leagues above Olimpo to 61° 28' west on the Pilcomayo.[12]

The treaty attracted negligible support in both countries. In Asunción, Audibert conducted a vigorous campaign of opposition in the press. The Andean Congress took no action, and in May 1896 the Paraguayan Senate passed a law authorizing a "scientific commission" to make further study and explore the question in accordance with historic titles. Consequently, relations lapsed for a time, with neither government displaying any interest in settlement.[13]

Asunción accredited her first Minister to Bolivia, César Gondra, on 17 December 1898. Since the studies of the commission of 1896 were now complete, Paraguay was ready to reconsider the 1894 treaty. Gondra was to establish bases for mutual ratification, but unfortunately he was unable to present his credentials on the Altiplano due to a revolution then in progress. The only government he found was a *de facto* Junta located at Oruro and made inaccessible by a general uprising of fearsome rural Indians. After an exchange of wires and consultation at La Paz with Tamayo and other prominent statesmen, he left the country in May 1899.[14]

Following an unsuccessful mission to Asunción by Antonio Quijarro, Paraguayan Foreign Minister Flecha laid down Paraguay's position for the twentieth century. He arbitrarily denied the validity of the Andean case based on descendency from the colonial Audiencia of Charcas, asserting that Guaraní titles were firm up to the borders of the colonial dependencies of Upper Peru, particularly Chiquitos and the Intendancy of Cochabama. These borders, stretching in the west to the Rio Parapetí, could be defined only by title study in negotiations, and Paraguay was ready at any moment to proceed in this manner. Accordingly, she planned to maintain diplomatic representation at La Paz.[15]

In reply, Federico Diez de Medina lucidly defined the Bolivian position. Basing her rights on her succession territorially to the Audiencia of Charcas, protected by her actions of the past century, La Paz insisted that her claims were intact to the entire west bank of the Rio Paraguay down to the Pilcomayo. Diez de Medina thus implicitly asserted that the dispute was now a territorial question as opposed to the Guaraní contention that merely boundaries were involved.[16]

With this exchange of notes, the dispute between Bolivia and Paraguay actually passed into the new century. Previously, efforts at settlement were characterized by compromise for the convenient settlement of the issue and advancement of commercial prosperity and economic growth. Now each had arrived at a crystalline position based on the documentary evidence which archivists were beginning to produce in La Paz, Asunción, Buenos Aires, London, and Spain. Paraguay, gradually incorporating much of the Chaco into her government and administrative system, would be less willing to part with any portion of it; Bolivia, on the outside looking in, would become more determined as years passed to secure what she believed her sister had usurped from her birthright.[17]

The dilemma which caused all efforts at settlement through title study to flounder was the overlapping of Bolivia's rights to the limits of the *audiencia* and Paraguay's rights to the limits of the original *provincia*. This was due to their distinct characteristics, and made any genuine comparison impossible—unlike entities cannot be compared. Each litigant sought to confine the extent of the other's claim in terms of her own jurisdictional antecedents; a manifest impossibility, this was responsible for the great ill-feeling engendered and was the nucleus of the title controversy.

In November 1903, Brazil obtained Acre from Bolivia by the Treaty of Petropolis and as a sop to the Andean pride ceded a small strip north of Bahia Negra on the west bank of the Rio Paraguay, held by her as heir to the colonial Portuguese regime, which had arrogated it from Spain. This aroused Guaraní protests, since in the 1858 López-Paranhos Protocol, Brazil had recognized Bahia Negra as her border with Paraguay.[18]

Early in 1906, new informal talks opened at Asunción between Doctors Emeterio Cano, the Bolivian Minister, and Manuel Domínguez, Paraguayan Minister *ad hoc*. Hardly had the talks begun when Asunción grew concerned over reports that Bolivia had founded two military posts, Guachalla and Ballivián, well down the Pilcomayo. Pinilla, then Foreign Minister, stated on 20 April that these garrisons were intended to bring civilization, and not to threaten Paraguay. In a letter to Cano, however, he spoke more candidly of an

> aggressive and bellicose plan on our part, a plan that has always been in the minds of all Bolivian statesmen, but whose execution required elements of communications and resources to make it effective; meanwhile we are separated from the Paraguay coast by the immense deserts that today impede us, checking our advance.[19]

In negotiations, Domínguez persistently sought an examination of titles, while Cano preferred arbitration or an arrangement of mutal convenience. Cano insisted that no conclusive titles were known, but Domínguez, apparently flush with the results of Paraguayan studies made in accordance with the law of 1896, thrust two bulky volumes upon him. Domínguez also offered an ingenious proposal: let Bolivia extend far enough south between the twentieth parallel and Olimpo to satisfy her port needs. Paraguay would advance up the 62nd meridian in the west for an equal distance. The diagonal line thus drawn would meet the needs of each—Bolivia would have a river bank; Paraguay, territory. As an alternative, he offered Bolivia a free port on the upper Paraguay.

Cano's final proposal was a border along the twenty-first parallel to the 63rd meridian west of Paris [sic], thence south to the Pilcomayo. When it became clear that each had candidly made his maximum authorized concession, the talks came to a halt.[20]

Since the conversations appeared doomed, Argentine Foreign Minister Dr. Estanislao S. Zeballos stepped forward, offering mediation for confidential conversations among negotiators with limited powers. Pinilla and former Paraguayan Foreign Minister Soler were brought together at Buenos Aires where they signed a protocol on 12 January 1907.

This act provided for submission of the Chaco dispute to the arbitral decision of the President of Argentina. Article II stated that

> the zone submitted to said arbitration is that included between parallel 20° 30′ and the line which Paraguay may maintain on the north in her allegations, in the interior of the territory between meridians 61° 30′ and 62° west of Greenwich.

Article VII then provided:

> The High Contracting Parties obligate themselves from this moment, pending the fulfillment of this agreement, not to change or advance the possessions existing on this date. . . . The status quo shall be faithfully observed under the guarantee of the Argentine Government.[21]

In 1906, Bolivian activities along the Pilcomayo had first excited Paraguayan concern. Apparently, Paraguay at this time sought the status quo provisions to forestall such moves. In 1886 Tamayo had first attempted to assert a status quo doctrine, and in 1888 Pinilla alleged that the 1887 treaty created "a status quo . . . and regularized the jurisdiction of both States within their respective zones." Paraguay henceforth took recourse to this Bolivian-created doctrine, seeking to halt Andean advances.

The arbitration zone was essentially bounded on the west by the final lines proposed by Cano and Domínguez, while in the north 20° 30' was an exact splitting of the difference. However, the protocol had a grievous flaw in that it failed to confirm this compromise northern line, indeed making it the minimum attainable by Paraguay while leaving open to her unlimited pretensions lands above this parallel. Later, Paraguayans maintained that Soler had sought 19° 30' as the exterior northern limit of the arbitration zone, but Pinilla had preferred the more ambiguous wording.

In Paraguay the pact was greeted with great rejoicing, her hopes for territory realized at last. Bolivian opinion, however, found little to appreciate. Allegedly, Pinilla had acted without consultation with his government. Certainly his actions were not in harmony with his previous record. On the Altiplano, the Senate opposition led by Dr. Daniel Salamanca vigorously assailed the agreement as a grave error; in a booklet, Dr. Bautista Saavedra viciously attacked Pinilla's "giveaway" and urged strong measures against Paraguay. In explanation of Pinilla's actions, the United States Minister reported greater concessions had been made than ever before in the interests of commerce. Brazilian discrimination had ruined Puerto Suárez (a shallow "port" on the Cáceres lagoon), and La Paz therefore elected to set aside other considerations to gain an anchorage near 20° 30'.[22]

The agreement quickly failed, however. Cano and Domínguez, who were to implement the protocol with a formal arbitration treaty, were unable to reach agreement, in large measure due to the Bolivian's attempt to convert the Paraguayan region of the Chaco into the arbitration zone. When Cano died inopportunely the project collapsed.[23]

The Chaco question hung suspended until a 1912 exchange of

notes between Paraguayan Foreign Minister Dr. Eusebio Ayala
and Bolivian Minister Dr. Ricardo Mujía. After argument of
the status quo of 1907—Ayala maintaining that the provision was
an immediate obligation, Mujía that it had lapsed with the death
of Cano and the renunciation of his task by the designated arbitrator, the President of Argentina—a new protocol was signed at
Asunción on 5 April 1913. In exchange for Paraguayan willingness to declare all previous treaties and pacts nullified, Bolivia
accepted retention of the status quo provision. The High Con-
tracting Parties agreed to negotiate within two years of ratification
"a definite treaty of boundaries." Direct negotiations were specified, but if they failed, resort would be had to arbitration. Article IV asserted that until final settlement or arbitration, "the
status quo stipulated in the agreement of 12 January 1907 shall
remain in force, both parties declaring that they have not changed
their respective positions since that date."[24]

Ratifications were exchanged in July 1913. Both sides now
viewed full discussion as desirable, including consideration of
titles. By 1911 the Guaraní technical commission, then composed
of Domínguez and the equally eminent Dr. Fulgencio Ricardo
Moreno, had compiled a major work of over 2,000 documents.
Bolivian agents and scholars had been active abroad, and Mujía
now set himself the task of organizing the Andean titles for the
forthcoming talks.[25]

After some delay, Mujía and Paraguayan plenipotentiary designate Moreno, both of whom had been absent from Asunción,
opened their negotiations 26 March 1915. Mujía wished an arrangement of convenience in order to secure for Bolivia a fluvial
outlet through the Plata. Moreno sought titles comparison as a
method for arriving at a mutually acceptable boundary, but endeavored to localize talks to the north where Bolivia wished a
port. The resulting exchange of papers provided an opening for
Mujía to inject his *Bolivia-Paraguay*, a massive study consisting
of three volumes of narrative, five large volumes of documents,
and one supporting folio of maps. Embracing the entire Bolivian
case, this work served to thrust negotiations beyond a limited
sector of the Chaco into the realm of an intensely doctrinaire
discussion which actually did not cease until after the Chaco

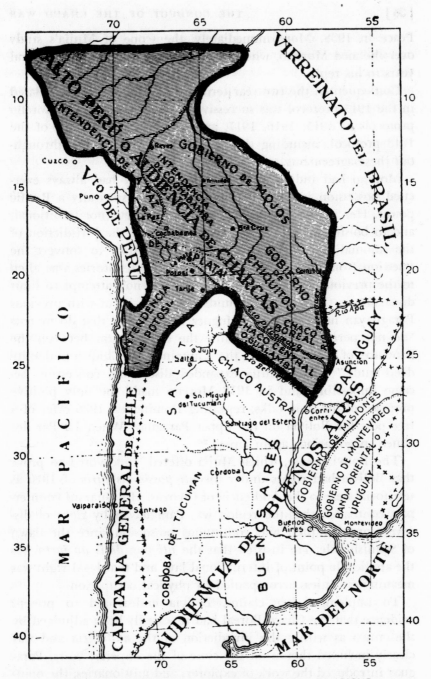

BOLIVIAN VERSION OF COLONIAL POLITICAL DIVISIONS

Peace in 1938. More immediately, the scope of Mujía's study overwhelmed Moreno, who found it neccessary to devote several years to his reply.

Consequently, the two-year term for final settlement stipulated in the 1913 protocol was successively extended in Mujía-Moreno protocols of 1915, 1916, 1917, and 1918. The provisions of the 1913 protocol, including the status quo, were retained throughout these agreements.

Moreno had indicated that while Paraguay had always exercised possession in the Chaco, Bolivia was historically a Pacific power. Her interest in the Plata Basin was new, not traditional, and to bolster it she invoked an extension of the jurisdiction of the colonial province of Chiquitos. This effort to convert the question from one of boundaries to one of territories was alien to the previous course of the dispute. Moreno's attempt to limit discussion to the northern boundary was consistent with previous Paraguayan negotiators. Domínguez had written that documents "do not permit us to determine the demarcation between the Province of Paraguay and the Captaincy of Chiquitos despite deep study." When Mujía expanded discussion, concession became impossible, and in 1918 Moreno made the only positive proposal of the long talks, repeating Domínguez' 1906 offer of a free port for Bolivia on the upper Paraguay. When La Paz declined, negotiations again lapsed.[26]

The Bolivian case, which Mujía offered, endeavored to prove that Bolivia had rights under the *uti possidetis juris* of 1810 as territorial heir to the Audiencia of Charcas. His Guaraní counterpart contended that the region was Paraguayan by right of discovery and conquest and continuous possession since the dawn of Spanish rule. He insisted that the *uti possidetis de facto* was the applicable point of international law, and that legal right was meaningless unless accompanied by physical occupation.

To implement her claims, Bolivia endeavored to present evidence that the Chaco Boreal had repeatedly been adjudged by the crown as within the jurisdiction of the *audiencia* and was clearly included therein at the close of the imperial years. Paraguay introduced the work of explorers and missionaries, the opinions of colonial personages, and the history of the Bishopric of

Asunción to substantiate continuous possession confirmed by the final will of the Spanish monarchy, the Ordinance of Intendants.

Each of the disputants then produced replies to the main thesis of the other; these led to counterpropositions *ad infinitum*. Researchers minutely probed the colonial histories of the contenders ignoring no significant fact. The resultant literature is a vast quicksand bog from which the unwary investigator must extricate himself lest he squander years in an unrewarding pursuit of a definitive title.[27]

Bolivia believed that the Mujía-Moreno talks had failed. The chauvinistic Dr. Bautista Saavedra and his Republican party, once in power through revolution, intensified activity in the Chaco. Saavedra, who believed Paraguay too poor to resist gradual penetration down the Pilcomayo, directed construction of Fortines[28] Nuevos Magariños, Muñoz, and later Saavedra. Hostile elements hindered and harassed this work; floods alternated with drought. In 1923 high waters drove the Andeans out of their low positions and forced them up to higher ground, where they built Saavedra, a favorite target for savages. Early in 1924 this new *fortín* touched off significant alarm in the Paraguayan press.[29]

In 1921, Paraguay herself had begun military colonies around her Chaco outposts, thus giving them a dual role as forerunners of civilization. The chief of the Pilcomayo *fortines* completed a plan for extensive military developments, which motivated wide travels by Captain Juan B. Ayala along the untamed and primeval *límites* of the 1907 Paraguayan zone. Unfortunately, domestic upheaval in 1922–1923 halted this project, along with normal diplomatic intercourse.[30]

Paraguay, with a view to strengthening her grip on the western interior, in 1924 accepted 1,765 Canadian Mennonites as colonists. These pacifistic folk, asking only to live according to the dictates of their faith without interference from the world, unwittingly became tools in the Chaco dispute. Paraguay answered Bolivia's consequent protest, maintaining that since the community had been contracted through the Argentine house of Casado, the largest owner of the 1885 Chaco lands, it was merely a private affair situated within the 1907 status quo lines.[31]

Bolivian *fortines* and Paraguayan colonization led to a mutual desire for the resumption of negotiations. Various tentative proposals, including unofficial invitations to the United States to intervene, came to nought. Then, in November 1924, Argentina came forward with her good offices for a preliminary accord at her capital. Although Paraguay immediately accepted, Bolivia viewed this offer as an alternative to further direct negotiations.[32]

In both countries a prolific outpouring of polemical writings began to fill the press and the bookshops. No level of society was overlooked by the propagandists. From schoolchildren to intellectuals, there was suitable material available written by the contentious scholars of both States. "El Chaco es Paraguayo," the Guaraní cried with conviction, goaded on by the opposition Colorado party. In the La Paz Foreign Office, a propaganda section was charged with publicizing abroad Bolivia's rights. The Center of Propaganda and National Defense was formed to direct such a domestic propaganda campaign that the Aymara and Quechua soon knew full well that the ancient enemy of the plains must be expelled from the Chaco. The result was an emotional fervor which made compromise difficult.

Notes

1. *British and Foreign State Papers*, XLII, 1256-58; César Gondra, *La diplomácia de los tratados* (Buenos Aires, 1906), 104-110; República Argentina, Ministerio de Relaciones Exteriores, *La Politica Argentina en la Guerra del Chaco* (Buenos Aires, 1937), I, xxi-xxii; Leon M. Loza, *El laudo Hayes* (La Paz, 1936), 14-15; David Alvéstegui, *Bolivia y el Paraguay* (La Paz, 1926), 192; Appendix 6, Reply of Bolivia, in *Proceedings of the Commission of Inquiry and Conciliation* (Washington, 1929), 1008-1010; Antonio Quijarro, *Bolivia, Politica Internacional* (Buenos Aires, 1887), 88.

2. Loza, 30-36, 64-77, 188; Alvéstegui, 187-193, 200-204; *Politica Argentina*, I, xxi; Benjamín Aceval, *Chaco Paraguayo. Memoria presentada al Arbitro* (Asunción, 1896), 79, 83, 104, 157-163; *Chaco Paraguayo. Appendix and Documents Annexed to the Memoir Filed by the Minister of Paraguay* (New York, 1878); Eduardo Amarilla Fretes, *El Chaco en el primer cincuentenario del Fallo Arbitral del Presidente Hayes* (Asunción, 1932), 45-52; *British and Foreign State Papers*, LXVIII, 97-100; Appendix 11, Reply of Bolivia, in *Proceedings*, 1140;

República de Bolivia, *Ministerio de Relaciones Exteriores y Culto, Notas y el Memorándum de Bolivia contra el tratado de arbitraje Argentina Paraguayo de 1876* (La Paz, 1929), 15-64; República del Paraguay, *Memoria del Ministerio de Relaciones Exteriores Presentada al Honorable Congreso, 1878,* 19-55. (Cited hereafter as *Memoria,* with year.) For an excellent summary see John Bassett Moore, *History and Digest of the International Arbitrations to which the United States Has Been a Party* (Washington, 1898), II, 1925–1943.

3. Loza, 187-191; Reply of Bolivia, in *Proceedings,* 955; Manuel Domínguez, *Bolivia atropelló el statu-quo y sus reconocimientas del laudo Hayes* (Asunción, 1935), 3-24.

4. For negotiations see Miguel Mercado Moreira, *El Chaco Boreal* (La Paz, 1920), 143-146. Also consult Alvéstegui, 246-256; Gondra, 14, 20; República del Paraguay, *Paraguay-Bolivia. Tratados y Protocolos* (Asunción, 1927), 3-4; Telmo Ichaso, *Antecedentes del tratado de límites celebrado con la República del Paraguay* (Sucre, 1894); Ricardo Mujía, *Bolivia-Paraguay. Exposición de los títulos que consagran el derecho territorial de Bolivia sobre la zona comprendida entre los Ríos Pilcomayo y Paraguay* (La Paz, 1914), III, 791-798; *Annexes,* V, 7-13; Manuel Domínguez, *Nuestros Pactos con Bolivia* (Asunción, 1928), 3-5; Quijarro, *Bolivia Política,* 59-60, 74-76. (Altiplano and Andean are hereafter used interchangeably with Bolivian for purposes of variety, while Guaraní is used for Paraguayan.)

5. Alvéstegui, 411; Appendix 3, Memorial of Paraguay, in *Proceedings,* 648-649, 713.

6. Mujía, *Bolivia-Paraguay,* III, 798-805; Alvéstegui, 225; Mercado Moreira, 159; Appendix 3, Memorial of Paraguay, in *Proceedings,* 654; República de Bolivia, *Mensaje del Presidente Constitutional de la República al Congreso Ordinario de 1885,* 13. (Cited hereafter as *Mensaje,* with year.)

7. Mujía *Annexes* V, 14-15, 19-31; Alvéstegui, 271-274; Ichaso, 4-8; Paraguay, *Tratados y Protocolos,* 5-8.

8. Mujía, *Bolivia-Paraguay,* III, 819; Alvéstegui, 277; Bolivia, *Mensaje 1887,* 3; Paraguay, *Memoria 1887,* 7; Appendix 4, Memorial of Paraguay, in *Proceedings,* 717-719.

9. Appendix 10, Memorial of Paraguay, in *Proceedings,* 891-894; Gondra, 170, Alvéstegui, 289, 399-400; Mujía, *Bolivia-Paraguay,* II, 824; Isidro Ramírez, *Alrededor de la cuestión Paraguayo-Boliviano* (Lima, 1930), 129-134; Alejandro Audibert, *Cuestión de límites entre El Paraguay y Bolivia* (Asunción, 1901), 111-116.

10. Mujía, *Bolivia-Paraguay,* II, 826-840; *Annexes,* V, 35-39; Ramírez, 137-144; Ichaso, 7-8; Audibert, *Cuestión de límites,* 117-135; Paraguay, *Memoria 1890,* 6, 71-72; Bolivia, *Mensaje 1890,* 2.

11. Paraguay, *Memoria 1890,* 7; República del Paraguay, *Cámara de Senadores de la República del período legislativo del año 1896*

(Asunción, 1896), 229; Mariano Baptista, *Obras Completas,* IV, *Asuntos Internacionales* (La Paz , 1932), 169-198; Ichaso, 272-286; Mujía *Annexes,* V, 41-68; Alvéstegui, 301-306.

12. Bolivia, *Memoria 1895,* 86-89; *Mensaje 1895,* 90-91; Ichaso, 13, 16, 289-328; Mujía, *Bolivia-Paraguay,* III, 860-861; *Annexes,* V, 83-134; Gregorio Benites, *Exposición de los derechos del Paraguay en la cuestión de límites con Bolivia* (Asunción, 1895), 190-229.

13. Bolivia, *Memoria 1895,* 105; *1896,* 42; *1897,* 27-30; Mujía, *Bolivia-Paraguay,* III, 874-877; *Annexes,* V, 141; Alvéstegui, 315; Francisco Iraízos, *El sudeste de Bolivia* (La Paz, 1901), 65; Appendix 3, Memorial of Paraguay, in *Proceedings,* 667, 733; *Cámara de Senadores . . . año 1896,* 84-89.

14. Paraguay, *Memoria 1900,* 21-42; Mujía, *Bolivia-Paraguay,* III, 883; *Annexes,* V, 182; Bolivia, *Memoria 1900,* 46; Antonio Quijarro, *La cuestión de límites entre Bolivia y el Paraguay* (Buenos Aires, 1901) .

15. Mujía *Annexes,* V, 275-287; Alvéstegui, 329; Bolivia, *Memoria 1902,* 326-334; Paraguay, *Memoria 1902,* 86-91.

16. Paraguay, *Memoria 1903,* 51-62; Bolivia, *Memoria 1902,* 334-349; Mujía *Annexes,* V, 288-311.

17. Eduardo Diez de Medina, *De un Siglo al Otro, Memorias de un hombre público* (La Paz, 1955), 192; Paraguay, *Memoria 1900,* 8; *1901,* 14; Iraízos, 28. Note also, Bolivia, *Memoria 1903,* 77.

18. Mujía *Annexes,* V, 312-333.

19. Mujía, *Bolivia-Paraguay,* III, 904; *Annexes,* V, 374-444; Gondra, 175; Alvéstegui, 375; Bolivia, *Memoria 1906,* 29; quotation from Paraguay, Ministerio de Relaciones Exteriores, *Libro Blanco. Documentos relativos a la conferencia de Washington para el estudio de un pacto de no agresión con Bolivia . . .* (Asunción, 1933), 102-103. For corroboration, see Eduardo Arze Quiroga, ed., *Documentos para una historia de la Guerra del Chaco* (La Paz, 1951), I, 43; Iraízos, 10.

20. Mujía *Annexes,* V, Part II, 3-36; Domínguez, *Nuestros Pactos,* 11-16. See also Bolivia, *Memoria 1903,* 72. Bolivia occasionally measured longitude from Paris.

21. Appendix 8, Memorial of Paraguay, in *Proceedings,* 851-852; Mujía *Annexes,* V, Part II, 39-41; Paraguay, *Tratados y Protocolos,* 11-12; *Paraguay-Bolivia, Protocolos y Notas cambiadas* (Asunción, 1927), 3.

22. Paraguay, *Paraguay-Bolivia. Cuestión de Límites* (Asunción, 1924) , 5; Domínguez, *Nuestros Pactos,* 17; Alvéstegui, 355-357; Cecilio Báez, *Historia diplomática del Paraguay* (Asunción, 1932), II, 291. United States Department of State, *Papers Relating to the Foreign Relations of the United States* (Washington, 1907), 87-89. (Cited hereafter as *Foreign Relations.*)

23. Domínguez, *Nuestros Pactos,* 17; Alvéstegui, 359. See also Bautista Saavedra, *La cuestión fronteriza con el Paraguay* (La Paz,

1908). República del Paraguay, Ministerio de Relaciones Exteriores, *Informe del Plenipotenciario Dr. Domínguez acerca de las negociaciones Domínguez-Cano posteriores al adjuste Soler-Pinilla de 1907* (Asunción, 1929), 5-61.

24. Mujía, *Bolivia-Paraguay*, III, 921-944; *Annexes*, V, Part II, 45-106; Bolivia, *Mensaje 1910*, 8; *Memoria 1910*, 52-55; Appendix 8, Memorial of Paraguay, in *Proceedings*, 836, 853-857; Paraguay, *Protocolos y Notas*, 5-12; *Mensaje 1913*, 15-16; *1914*, 19.

25. Bolivia, *Mensaje 1913*, 12; *Memoria 1914*, 25; Mujía, *Bolivia-Paraguay*, I, iv, x, xiii, xvi; III, 945; *Proceedings*, 787; *Política Argentina*, I, 5.

26. República del Paraguay, Ministerio de Relaciones Exteriores, *Cuestión de límites con Bolivia. Negociaciones diplomáticos 1915-1917* (Asunción, 1928-29), 2d ed., I, 7-9; Bolivia, *Memoria 1916*, 322-340; *1917*, 99-146; *1918*, 25; *1919*, 47; quotation, Domínguez, *Nuestros Pactos* 17; Ricardo Mujía, *Anotaciones a la "réplica" del Excelentísimo Sr. Ministro Plenipotenciario Especial del Paraguay Don Fulgencio R. Moreno* (La Paz, 1916); Paraguay, *Mensaje 1917*, 18; *1919*, 17; *1920*, 22; *Tratados y Protocolos*, 14-20; *Protocolos y Notas*, 13-16; Appendix 8, Memorial of Paraguay, in *Proceedings*, 858-859; Mercado Moreira, 226.

27. For a concise, yet more complete, summary of the respective cases, see David H. Zook, Jr., *The Evolution of the Chaco Dispute* (Ann Arbor, 1959), 91-120.

28. *Fortines* were more akin to camps than to forts, since they were collections of rude huts rather than fortifications. The word, untranslatable, will be used hereafter.

29. Colonel Miguel Aliaza, *Los derechos de Bolivia sobre el oriente y el Chaco Boreal* (La Paz, 1928), 34-36; Cornelio Rios, *Los derechos de Bolivia sobre el Chaco Boreal y sus límites con el Paraguay* (Buenos Aires, 1925), 90-91; Bolivia, *Memoria 1921*, 54. For a lucid statement of his attitude see Bautista Saavedra's *La cuestión fronteriza*. Note also Colonel Oscar Moscoso Gutiérrez *Recuerdos de la Guerra del Chaco* (Sucre, 1939), 25.

30. Paraguay, *Paraguay-Bolivia. Cuestión de límites* (1924), 18.

31. Paraguay, *Mensaje 1925*, 18; Bolivia, *Mensaje 1924*, 2; *Memoria 1923*, 42. Also consult República del Paraguay, Ministerio de Económica, *Las colonias Mennonites en el Chaco Paraguayo* (Asunción, 1934), 5. For true origins of the Mennonite migration see Joseph Winfield Fretz, *Pilgrims in Paraguay* (Scottdale, Pa., 1953), 12-23, 229-233, or Eduardo Amarilla Fretes, *El Paraguay en el primer cincuentenario*, 171-174.

32. Bolivia, *Mensaje 1922*, 64; *1923*, 5; *1925*, 6; *1927*, 79. *Memoria 1924*, 73; *1925*, 72-74; *1927*, 9; Paraguay, *Paraguay-Bolivia, Cuestión de límites* (1924), 15-16; *Mensaje 1925*, 19-20; Diez de Medina, *De un*

Siglo, 242-247; U. S., *Foreign Relations,* 1924, 282-286; *Política Argentina,* I, 14-15; Paraguay, Ministerio de Relaciones Exteriores, *Libro Blanco, Documentos relativos a las conferencias de Buenos Aires sobre la cuestión de límites Paraguayo-Boliviana y algunos antecedentes, 1927-1928* (Asunción, 1928), 4, 37-38.

CHAPTER TWO

INTERNATIONAL CONFERENCES

The Buenos Aires Conference

Following lengthy talks at La Paz in 1926, Bolivia formally accepted the Argentine offer of good offices as a method for further negotiation. In February 1927, Paraguayan Foreign Minister Enrique Bordenave, in a note to his Andean counterpart, reiterated his country's understanding of the territorial status quo. From President Bautista Saavedra's reference in his 1925 *mensaje* to *fortines* to "guard the line of the status quo," he inferred Bolivian acceptance of the Guaraní understanding of this point. However, in Dr. David Alvéstegui's new book, *Bolivia y el Paraguay,* he found a map which graphically illustrated (probably for the first time) the location of Bolivia's line of Pilcomayo positions. He was alarmed to find that the new *fortines* were past the lines of the 1907 status quo in "territory unquestionably Paraguayan."[1]

At 1500 hours, 25 February, at the Bolivian Fortín Sorpresa situated near the Pilcomayo, a Paraguayan officer, three enlisted men, and an Indian guide appeared. Second Lieutenant Rojas Silva and his scouting party, exploring waterways, inadvertently wandered into the Andean outpost and were immediately taken into custody. Due to the carelessness of the captain in charge, Rojas Silva was placed in a small hut and guarded by a single conscript to await interrogation. Following accepted practice, the lieutenant attempted to escape and in the resulting struggle was killed by the guard. First blood had been let in the Chaco Boreal, a few drops which would swell eventually into a torrent!

Immediately, La Paz notified Asunción of the incident, saying that it had taken place in the former's territory in violation of her sovereignty. Bordenave replied that his government knew nothing of the matter, but its agents were under strict orders not to go beyond 61° 30′ west which marked "the beginning of the zone of the status quo pacted in 1907 and maintained without interruption until the moment." Bolivia promptly released the prisoners and expressed regret for this isolated event without international significance.[2]

Opinion in the fluvial nation was greatly aroused by the affair. Eusebio Ayala traveled to Buenos Aires in late March and conferred confidentially with Bolivian Foreign Minister Gutiérrez, apparently reaching an understanding and securing verbal agreement for the desired conference. Bolivia responded to the indignation by yielding diplomatically to Guaraní desires. Consequently, on 22 April 1927, Gutiérrez and Lisandro Díaz Leon, Paraguayan Minister to La Paz, signed a preliminary implementation of their reiterated acceptance of Argentine good offices. Article IV provided that if agreement proved impossible, the plenipotentiaries would state the reasons for disagreement and "fix the exact zone which will form the subject of the decision of an arbitral court to be appointed by mutual agreement."[3]

Responding to sharp attacks for omitting mention of the 1907 status quo from the protocol, Bordenave informed Gutiérrez that Asunción did not regard this latest protocol as modifying in any manner the status of the border question as defined in existing agreements. When Bolivia agreed, the way was open to the Buenos Aires conference.[4]

About this time, the Paraguayan Minister at Santiago (Vicente Rivarola) began to feed Chilean reports on Bolivia back to Asunción. Having lost his coast in the War of the Pacific, these documents asserted, the Bolivian condor sat on his mountain perch, contemplating his wounds. Bautista Saavedra's Republican party, revindicationalists all, never gave up hope of reopening the question of the Pacific. The opposition Liberals joined them in a united bipartisan policy of retaking the lost Puerto Pacheco on the Rio Paraguay. Although to some this seemed as likely as a Bolivian port on the moon, the Altiplano schools and press engraved the "port sentiment" on the Bolivian spirit, enhancing the emotional aspect of the Chaco dispute.[5]

By coded wire, Rivarola informed Asunción on 13 April 1927 that his sources advised him that La Paz had contracted over

£2,000,000 of arms in England. This made a settlement at Buenos Aires unlikely, since Bolivia would probably procrastinate until the arrival of these weapons enabled her to bargain from a strong position.[6]

The Rojas Silva incident had revealed to the world that the Chaco was a potential powder keg. Knowledge that Bolivia had purchased arms, the 1927 report of her War Minister on improved roads and establishment of an advance supply depot at Fortín Ballivián, and President Siles's *mensaje* statement that "routes of penetration" were being studied—all these tended to substantiate the alarmist cries in the Asunción press and bring deep concern to the neighboring countries. What was not known—for it was the most closely guarded secret of the Chaco dispute—was that in 1925 President Eligio Ayala launched a program of arms acquisition for Paraguay designed to equip a modern army of 24,000 with the latest equipment. Contracts were let in many countries on a cash basis and paid for from current revenues. To counteract a 1926 Altiplano effort at creation of a fleet of merchant craft on the upper river, a secret decree 21 March 1927 even authorized the purchase of two modern gunboats. Diplomats and scholars had sought a settlement for nearly half a century. Now it was indeed time that the neighbors stepped in![7]

The Buenos Aires Conference opened 29 September 1927. Quickly it became apparent that Paraguay wished the linear status quo of 1907, as preserved in succeeding pacts, to be the first topic of consideration. She was concerned with Bolivian violations of this agreement, and apparently wished to secure Andean retirement behind 62° west as a condition to consideration of a final settlement. The Bolivian delegation sought to avoid discussion of the status quo, but finally yielded. The result was an exchange of papers and a debate which continued until mid-December when it became clear no agreement was possible. Bolivia refused to retire her *fortines,* maintaining that to do so would be to expose all of the Chaco to Paraguayan encroachment. She viewed the 1907 status quo as one of actual positions of the moment and in no way related to the lines created for arbitration by Pinilla and Soler. She also alleged that once Asunción had secured the linear status quo, she would lose all interest in final settlement because that would involve giving up a portion of her *de facto* holdings. This added to Paraguay's apprehension, and stimulated her desire to obtain security in the Chaco.[8]

To save the Conference, Dr. Isidoro Ruíz Moreno, the Argentine observer who had attended meetings on behalf of the host government, came forward with a three-point suggestion for activating the mired talks:

1. Paraguay to agree to proceed directly to arbitration of the fundamental question.
2. Both countries to demilitarize *fortines,* or to withdraw by fifty kilometers each those facing each other, this to be confirmed by a neutral military commission.
3. A declaration that advances of each served to create a *de facto* situation, conferring on them no rights, and that such advance could not be alleged as a basis for claims before an arbitrator.[9]

On this basis talks resumed 7 May 1928. The Bolivians attempted to follow the "method" of the Argentine suggestion, which to them meant the order of points. An immediate break was then averted only by considering a *modus vivendi* and an arbitration agreement in alternate meetings. In the subsequent discussions, Paraguay again sought dismantlement of the Bolivian *fortines,* and Bolivia argued for a very limited arbitration zone encompassing only the Paraguayan Chaco heartland south of the mouth of the Rio Apa and east of 59°. This, of course, degenerated with great ill feeling into a title debate. Ruíz Moreno attempted unsuccessfully to gain support for international policing of a neutral zone between the respective *fortín* lines. A new impasse having been reached, the conference was adjourned in July.[10]

The Buenos Aires Conference of 1927–1928 marked a complete departure from previous diplomacy. Bolivia now denied Paraguay any part of the Chaco. She viewed it as her exclusive sovereign territory, a belief predicated upon the complete rejection of all possessory actions of Paraguay since 1536. She talked much of juris arbitration as her policy, but this was not conciliatory, since she was willing to arbitrate only her neighbor's section, and not even the whole of that. In order to prevent consideration by the arbitrator of Paraguay's full claims, Bolivia insisted that the zone in contention be first defined by direct agreement. She rejected any status quo or *modus vivendi* except possibly that of the moment. Although she believed Paraguay was seeking to create a *de facto* situation which, with the passage of time, would become permanent, she was most disturbed by the unfavorable lines of such a status quo. She would not withdraw an inch from her *fortines*, the sole evidence of Altiplano rights in the Chaco, even to permit neutral policing of a buffer zone. She would consider only some theoretical disarmament.

Paraguay, fearful of war and resentful of Bolivian advances, particularly in the zone of the Hayes Award, sought to have Bolivia pushed back or controlled as a guarantee that her own possession would go unmolested. She attempted to gain this by clinging to her transitory victory of 1907 through a now unilateral interpretation of the linear status quo, by a new *modus vivendi*, by a withdrawal or dismantling of the *fortines* of *both* countries, or by the creation of a nonaggression pact. She was willing to arbitrate either the status quo question or the basic issue, but only if her full claims were considered. These extended to the Rio Juarú on the north, although in earlier diplomacy Bahia Negra had always constituted their implicit limit. She did not seek, however, to confine the extent of the claims Bolivia might submit to impartial decision, although tacitly she would exclude the Hayes Zone.

The pressure of the man in the street, mouthing the doctrinaire assertions of polemicists, scholars, and chauvinistic publicists, was a force neither government dared ignore. The result was the impossibility of direct agreement, definition of the arbitration zone, or creation of a *modus vivendi*—in short, of any relaxation of the existing grave situation. There were now only two alternatives: someone must yield fundamentally; or, diplomacy being bankrupt, military solutions would be tried.

Vanguardia

After the close of the Buenos Aires Conference, Rivarola supplied his government with an extensive and detailed report on the Bolivian arms contracted in England with Vickers at a price of £2,190,000. Included with four bombers, four fighters, and seven training aircraft, were 65 batteries of artillery, 50,000 rifles, 10,000 carbines, 300 machine guns, 760 automatic rifles, and an abundance of ammunition. In Paraguay, Chief of the General Staff Lieutenant Colonel José Félix Estigarribia had been beefing up Chaco defenses with new roads, telegraph lines, and construction of *fortines* where the Andean threat was believed greatest.[11]

Bolivia, which actually had only 2,700 men in the Chaco, responded to the intensified Paraguayan activity by reconnaissance and careful study of her own situation. In the *Oriente*, the task was entrusted to Colonel Victorino Gutiérrez, commander of the 5th Division at Puerto Suárez. On 22 August at 2200 hours, Gutiérrez, two lieutenant colonels, Lieutenant Filiberto Lozada, a sergeant, and an Indian were in their hammocks in a palm grove located in the swamps along the Rio Negro (Otuquis), when they were surprised and taken into custody by Paraguayan cavalry. After an exchange of notes between Foreign Offices over respective rights in the region, the officers were released. Following through with the original purpose of the party, a captain, two lieutenants (Lozada and Tomás Manchego), and a company from the 13th "Quijarro" Infantry arrived on 5 September 1928 at a point on the Otuquis midway between Paraguayan Fortín Galpón and Bolivian Fortín Vitriones, which "from this day took the name of Fortín Vanguardia."[12]

In October the Chilean Military Attaché in London quoted the Bolivians negotiating the Vickers deal as saying that "in a few more months Bolivia would make war on Paraguay." Bolivia, however, unsuccessfully sought United States intervention against Paraguay's new *fortines*, Boquerón and Toledo. Early in November, Bolivian patrols penetrated to Cacique Ramón, a Guaraní *fortín* near the Mennonite colonies, and alarmed some of the settlers. Bailón Mercado, Minister to Paraguay, advised La Paz that he feared the government might undertake some heroic enterprise as a sop to public opinion. The General Staff had gone to Concepción; cavalry, troops, and trucks were entering the Chaco. On 3 December, the Bolivian 5th Division was

ordered to take precautions in all positions, but word did not
reach isolated Varguardia, which had been under surveillance of
Guaraní cavalry. The previous day soldiers catching crows for
meat had seen "República Paraguaya" inscribed on nearby
trees.[13]

On the morning of 5 December a few of the *conscriptos* were
preparing coffee in the *fortín,* when they thought they saw a
flock of ostriches in the thick brush. When they advanced, horsemen materialized in the morning haze. One galloped forward
under a white flag. He was a Paraguayan trooper! The type-
written message he gave to Lieutenant Lozada, the commander,
read:

> The Paraguayans knowing that you have occupied our ter-
> ritory, we allow you ten minutes to stack arms and be ready for
> us, one hundred meters south of the barracks. Otherwise we shall
> open fire.

From all sides Guaraní infantry was advancing. Manchego dis-
tributed the single case of ammunition, 15 to 20 rounds per
man, and fired a warning shot into the air, though there was
no real battle. In ten minutes Paraguay occupied the *fortín,*
sacked it, captured two officers and nineteen men, killed five,
and pursued the rest of the 43-man garrison toward Vitriones.
By evening the prisoners, less one who escaped and one who
was shot when he fell exhausted in the road, were interned at
Fortín Galpón.[14]

Here indeed were shots heard round the world. What had been
a little-known, and less understood, seemingly minor Latin Amer-
can dispute suddenly made the headlines throughout the world.
On 5 December the initial Paraguayan dispatches originating
with Major Rafael Franco, commander of the 5th Infantry at
Bahia Negra, who had perpetrated and executed the entire adventure without the knowledge of Asunción, accused the Bolivians of aggression, firing on Paraguayans, and causing violence.
From La Paz, President Siles sent a circular to all legations de-
nouncing Paraguayan aggression against a small Andean *fortín.*[15]

The Bolivian General Staff immediately ordered the 5th
Division, "Proceed energetically—take Galpón." At the moment
the entire division had but 540 men in the 9th "Warnes" and

13th "Quijarro" Infantry at Roboré, Puerto Suárez, and Vitriones. By 8 December this feeble force arrived at Vanguardia, occupied the place, and advanced 100 men through tall swamp grass and muck that barred the route to Galpón. Rain intervened, raising the water level, and forcing abandonment of any counterattack in this sector.[16]

La Paz severed relations with Paraguay on 8 December, giving chargé d'affairs Captain Elías Ayala an hour to close his affairs and board a train. Paraguay reciprocated that evening by packing Mercado off to Formosa by motorboat. Although Asunción was quiet, La Paz was filled for days with war demonstrations and war sentiment. General Hans Kundt was recalled from abroad. Boy Scouts asked to be mobilized. Students demonstrated. Siles suspended the constitution, and crowds screamed, "We want War!" Youths massed outside the offices of the General Staff screaming "Viva Bolivia! Muera el Paraguay." Newspapers fanned the belligerent crowd and urged it on. Yet few really knew where the Chaco was, and even fewer understood what a war there would mean on the individual, human level.[17]

Then, on 14 December, after troop build-ups on the 4th Division's western Chaco front, three platoons from the 6th "Campos" Infantry attacked Guaraní Fortín Boquerón, taking the place after some fighting. At the same time elements of the 8th "Ayacucho" Infantry at Cuatro Vientos overran Fortín Mariscal López, routed the garrison, and killed fourteen men, four Indians, and the lieutenant in command. In the afternoon the Bolivians pulled back, but left the 6th Infantry in occupation of Boquerón. Bolivian reserves were called up, and on the following day an Andean bomber dropped four duds on Bahia Negra.[18]

While in La Paz bands played and 40,000 persons cheered the capture of Boquerón, Paraguay was provoked to the same fever pitch which had earlier characterized La Paz and led to mobilization of the Reserves. At this untimely moment, a shipload of the Vickers arms docked at Rosario. Asunción was filled with war preparations, and in this critical hour even the opposition came to the support of the government. Reinforcements were shipped north to halt what was believed to be an impending full-scale Andean assault. In Buenos Aires, however, it was believed that Boquerón would open the way for conciliation, since the Altiplano would feel itself avenged.[19]

On 17 December, General Patricio A. Escobar issued orders for general mobilization of the Guaraní. The tiny 3,000-man army formed a cadre for 10,000 reserves who appeared for service; they were awkwardly organized, and defensively deployed along the west bank of the river with a thin screen of cavalry. Paraguay was unready for war; her new weapons were ordered but still not received, her General Staff had formulated no mobilization plans, and she would easily have been annihilated. Fortunately for her, Bolivia's partial mobilization also proved a failure for like reasons. Due to the manifest military incapacity of the contenders, war did not develop at this time.[20]

Meanwhile, following unsuccessful efforts of Paraguay to treat the incident within the scope of the Gondra Pact of 1923, the International Conference of American States on Conciliation and Arbitration, coincidently meeting at Washington, stepped forward with good offices. A commission composed of Cuba, Colombia, Mexico, the United States, and Uruguay, was accepted by the disputants and empowered with authority to effect conciliation. Under a protocol of 3 January this group labored from 13 March to 13 September 1929. Prisoner exchange and a bare conciliation agreement were effected, but efforts to settle the basic issue were without success. The disputants agreed to mutual forgiveness, re-establishment of the "state of things" prior to 5 December 1928, and renewal of diplomatic relations. Paraguay was to restore the buildings at Vanguardia; Bolivia to evacuate Boquerón, leaving it as found, without the presence of Asunción authorities. The Paraguayans accepted this act, albeit at the last minute and under pressure.[21]

While Paraguay was unhappy that the act of conciliation implied she was an aggressor, Bolivia painted the verdict as a vindication. Although the £1,000,000 indemnity which Foreign Minister Tomás Elio had promised the country was not achieved, nevertheless, Bolivia was very fortunate. Her use of violence at Boquerón could well have exposed her to an unfavorable decision, just as her bellicose attitude immediately thereafter invited general censure. At Asunción martial law was necessary to control popular disapproval of the act. Uruguay, entrusted with effecting the conciliation formula, struck a typical snag when Bolivia insisted Vanguardia must be rebuilt as a condition for the return of Boquerón, since the wording regarding Vanguardia in the 12 September act preceded that concerning Boquerón. Facing the crowds, the Paraguayan government could not accede to this demand.[22]

To add to the tension, Bolivia, believing Paraguay had aggressive designs, prepared an offensive for January 1930. On the sixteenth, fighting broke out between patrols at Huijay (Carayá), a small outpost occupied by Paraguay near Boquerón. Military activity stepped up all along the front, and on 20 January Paraguay (having obtained the Bolivian code by espionage) intercepted a wire in which General Hans Kundt, German-born chief of the Bolivian General Staff, ordered the 4th Division at Fortín Muñoz to attack Fortines Ayala (Nanawa), Rojas Silva, and Cacique Ramón on 26 January; at the same time the 5th Division was to clean up the Vanguardia sector. A squadron of aircraft was leaving La Paz on the twenty-second. Bolivia, caught redhanded when Asunción released the orders to the press, protested her innocence and quietly cancelled the orders. She asserted that the incident had been planned by Paraguay to avoid compliance with the act of conciliation and to bring new international intervention. The United States legation at La Paz reported the clash had been provoked by Siles for domestic political purposes.[23]

Finally, on 4 April, Asunción secured a protocol entrusting Uruguay with execution of the conciliation formula, without stating details. This avoided direct acceptance of the Andean terms, although the method followed was essentially that demanded by La Paz. Before any new disturbance could occur, Bolivia underwent a constitutional crisis in which Siles, attempting to illegally remain in power after the expiration of his term, was expelled by a revolt led by General Blanco Galindo, a delegate to the Buenos Aires Conference. Well occupied at home, Bolivia's *de facto* government ignored the Chaco issue. Restoration of diplomatic relations and the exchange of the *fortines* on 23 July 1930 closed a phase of the Chaco dispute.[24]

The difficulty of negotiations, however, was now critical. No Paraguayan government dared make a direct agreement which could satisfy Bolivia's desires. La Paz asserted that the zone above Olimpo was not contentious, and on that basis might have allowed reservation of the Hayes Zone to Paraguay. Thus the region she considered in dispute was almost double the arbitration zone of the 1887 Tamayo-Aceval Treaty. The great sacrifice to the river republic that such a concession would involve made direct talks impossible, as La Paz well knew. Paraguay's stress, meanwhile, of the linear status quo of 1907 was consistent with her responsibility to defend title to the lands she had sold in 1885. The Argentine holders, from their strong position in the Guaraní economy, bound Asunción to a firm position which in essence appealed to the Anglo-Saxon principle of possession as legally admissible title.

The Nonaggression Pact Conference

From the Buenos Aires Conference onward, Bolivia's titles explanations fell on a world increasingly sympathetic to her small antagonist. Almost incessant, exaggerated reports of her military moves and aggressive intentions came from Chile and Argentina. In the United States it was difficult to find support for a nebulous, involved plea of colonial documents against Paraguay's physical, visible occupation, and exploitation of the Chaco. Indeed, from the Andean position, this factor rendered North America suspect while doubtlessly stimulating the intense desire of Asunción for an American settlement.[25]

Having lost out in the north when Paraguay occupied Puerto Pacheco and made palpably clear that she would retain her hold, Bolivia attempted to flank her opponent, driving down the Pilcomayo below the Paraguayan holdings and posing a threat to nuclear Paraguay. When the front door of Arica slammed in her face with settlement of the Pacific question in 1929, Bolivia turned full force toward her back door to the sea, the Rio Paraguay. Faced with being permanently encloistered in his mountains, the Bolivian condor began to go mad with thirst for salt water.[26]

Leading statesmen and the man in the Asunción street alike found intolerable Bolivia's military occupation of the western extremity of the Hayes Zone. Eusebio Ayala admitted that La Paz had a perfect right to contest his country's title, but he denied her right to invade what had been adjudged to Paraguay in international arbitration. Getting the Bolivian army out and securing a reciprocal security pact were the prime aims of Paraguayan diplomacy, as well as conditions to final settlement.[27] No Altiplano government, however, dared withdraw a *fortín,* just as no Paraguayan would even consider vacating Bahia Negra in La Paz's favor. The political impasse was complete—only temporary measures to gain time and avert a military solution were diplomatically practicable.

After Siles's ouster, the Junta of General Carlos Blanco Galindo presided only until 4 March 1931 when Dr. Daniel Salamanca, the compromise presidential candidate, was inaugurated. A man universally regarded as honest, Salamanca had spent his entire long public career on the benches of the opposition. Politically identified with the *genuinista* faction of the revindicationalist Republican party, his inauguration was not an omen of peace in troubled times. He was a gaunt, uncompromising ascetic widely known as a chauvinistic advocate of extreme measures against Paraguay. As Enrique Finot wrote:

> Well known as were the opinions of the new President on the energetic policy that must be followed in the Chaco dispute, they patronized the fear that he would adopt measures which would oblige the country to go to war.[28]

With Bolivia's return to constitutional government, Dr. Gerónimo Zubizarreta, Paraguayan Foreign Minister, addressed the five-nation Commission of Neutrals at Washington on 20 April 1931 repeating acceptance of their good offices. These had first been offered shortly after the closing of the Washington Conference of 1929, but Bolivia had declined, alluding to an eventual opportune moment. Zubizarreta affirmed the gravity of Andean advances into the Hayes Zone and asserted the time had arrived to ascertain if good offices could be carried out.[29]

Before the Neutrals had time to arrange anything positive, an incident occurred in Washington between Bolivian Minister Eduardo Diez de Medina and Paraguayan chargé d'affaires Pablo

Max Ynsfran. The Andean legation issued a statement on 18 June based on alarm over Paraguay's new Fortín Corrales which was farther west than some of Bolivia's *fortines,* the Argentine military mission contracted by Asunción, and the appearance on the upper Paraguay of two new 1,000-ton gunboats. (Purchased in Italy, these vessels were among the finest in the world.) Tension was increasing, Diez de Medina emphasized, at the very moment when La Paz was reducing military spending. Ynsfran immediately retorted through the press that Bolivian economies were not due to peaceful intent but to financial difficulties, resulting from vast arms expenditures. Paraguay's gunboats were no secret and, as in all countries, they were instruments of surveillance, not ornaments! The result of this exchange was the severance of relations between Bolivia and Paraguay, a sharp blow to the cause of peace.[30]

After patient negotitions, the Neutrals secured agreement of the disputants to the study of a nonaggression pact. Bolivia declined any troop withdrawals, honestly explaining that they served as the only barrier to Guaraní expansionism and posed a visible evidence of Bolivian sovereignty. Orders, however, had been issued to the army against any innovations. Because of difficulty in arranging a date, and last minute fears that Bolivia would not appear, all the American Republics joined on 19 October in supporting the proposed 11 November 1931 conference.[31]

Meanwhile, an armed clash occurred in September which nearly crippled the latest diplomatic efforts. The Paraguayan garrison of Masamaklay, an outpost of Fortín Nanawa, had been removed for lack of water, it being the dry season. Although covered by daily patrols, the position was seized on 6 September by a Bolivian patrol and ironically renamed Fortín Agua Rica. An effort at recapture ordered by Lieutenant Colonel José F. Estigarribia, commanding in the Chaco, failed completely on the twenty-fifth.[32]

Fanned by the opportunistic, rabble-rousing *Liga Nacional Independente,* which bleated national prostration before the cordilleran invader, students and radicals attempted a month later to overthrow the government of Paraguayan President José P. Guggiari. The cooperation of troops under Major Rafael Franco, the ambitious author of the Vanguardia incident, was prevented by

Estigarribia's timely shifting of forces. When the students were repelled with loss of life, the Colorado party left the legislature and forced a crisis. The President resigned and the Vice-President took over. On the *fortín* line, young officers desperately planned to seize Bolivia's Fortín Yucra to draw popular attention to the Chaco. The Nonaggression Pact Conference thus acquired a backdrop of extreme uncertainty in which compromise by Paraguay was politically infeasible.[33]

In the ensuing conference, the Bolivian delegation offered a draft treaty 9 December which provided simple, short-term reciprocal security on positions of the moment. On 18 January the Guaraní offered a counterproposal predicated upon the thesis that a nonaggression pact could not be founded on recognition of prior aggression, that is, of violations of the linear 1907 status quo. A pact should also have an indefinite semi-permanent term until the final settlement of the Chaco question.[34]

Incipient in both proposals was a desire to regularize a status quo: for Bolivia, that of the moment; for Paraguay, that of 1907. From the standpoint of preventing hostilities that of La Paz was perhaps the most practical, as it required no change in the existing situation and was on the order of a truce. Thus the Nonaggression Pact Conference was experiencing little success in calming the excited disputants.

Rumors of impending war were rampant. Rivarola, Asunción's Minister at Buenos Aires, forwarded Argentine military intelligence reports indicating aggressive Bolivian intentions. "The war of Bolivia on Paraguay is an inevitable fact," he wrote, "and that will be my final and definitive opinion." Bolivia was completing her Chaco road net and building up supply centers.[35]

A fresh exchange of papers (25 February and 15 April 1932) deteriorated into a bitter title controversy from which Assistant Secretary of State Francis White, the presiding officer, endeavored to extricate the conference. Reports of pending war had reached an unprecedented volume in the press. On 18 April, Rivarola wrote President-elect Eusebio Ayala that he had confidentially learned Paraguay would have "the decided help" of Argentina in case of war, albeit *"debajo del poncho."* In conversations with the delegations, therefore, Mr. White filled the unenviable role of middleman, hammering out a draft, and seeking to allay passions.[36]

The White draft of the Nonaggression Pact, 6 May 1932, provided peaceful settlement of differences, resumption of relations, and direct negotiations within six months. If unsuccessful within two years, an arbitration agreement on all points outstanding would be concluded. Machinery for investigating incidents was provided. No troop advances, mobilizations, or concentrations were to occur in the Chaco, and patrols meeting were to withdraw immediately for five kilometers toward their respective bases. The respective rights and titles were to be unaffected by the treaty. Article V provided that neither litigant would advance his existing extreme positions (which were to be ubicated and named in the final copy;) these, however, being mentioned only in the interests of peace and constituting no recognition of rights in favor of either.[37]

Paraguayan Foreign Minister Higinio Arbo replied on 2 June that his government was disposed to sign a treaty which included effective security guarantees, such as mandatory troop reductions. If a separate treaty of double arbitration (that is, arbitration first of the extent of the disputed zone, followed by arbitration of the zone itself) were signed at the same time, Asunción could even accept the White draft virtually as it stood. Bolivia, however he observed, barred arbitration, hoping to gain the bulk of the Chaco through prior agreement, leaving only a small Paraguayan-held zone to the tribunal. As for Article V, this actually jeopardized the peace in that

> Bolivia will endeavor, with a mere announcement of agreement on this point, to advance her positions following her policy of desiring to seize by military occupation the territory which is in dispute.[38]

The clear foresight of Dr. Arbo was borne out by the fact that within two weeks the Chaco War was commenced by Bolivia through exactly the method he foretold. Even as he wrote, Bolivian troops were already marching to a rendevous with Mars.

On the Altiplano, Dr. Daniel Salamanca convened his cabinet to prepare amendments to the draft which would provide prior definition of the arbitration zone, abolish the five-kilometer withdrawal, and assure complete freedom of action within the advanced position lines.[39] Actually, Salamanca was procrastinating in order to gain time for the military move already under way, which would start the long impending war. His desire for complete liberty behind the lines of advanced positions was in effect the creation of a new linear status quo, but in this case one to Bolivia's liking.

Time was running out on the efforts of neighboring states to prevent war. The Neutrals had proceeded at a leisurely pace, feeling that the disputants could not be hurried and that only extreme patience could bring them to agreement. The history of the Chaco dispute supports this belief. But while Bolivia was seeking time to complete a military program, Paraguay wished to keep the conference in session as long as possible in the hope that it would act as a restraining influence and prevent hostilities by compelling the perpetrator of any new incidents to come to terms. The impotence later revealed by the Neutrals, however, shattered these hopes and was a major factor in the consummation of all-out war.

Paraguay was primarily concerned with *security,* which to her meant the absolute, definitive removal of Bolivian armed forces from their existing line of *fortines* and from the Hayes Zone as defined by Asunción. Bolivia sincerely desired a simple truce from clashes. The conference had been most desired by Paraguay, whereas Bolivia required the goading of international pressure even to appear. Her grave economic problems caused by a drop in tin prices might have made her bellicose elements amenable to temporary relaxation in tension; however, the need to distract from such cares, establish the *genuinista* Republicans in power, and implement Bolivia's claims, impelled President Salamanca to a forceful program in the Chaco. The result was war.

Notes

1. *Política Argentina,* I, 17-18; Bolivia, *Memoria 1927,* 43; *1928,* 90; *Mensaje 1928,* 9; Appendix 8, Memorial of Paraguay, in *Proceedings,* 862-867; Paraguay, *Protocolos y Notas,* 19-25; *Libro Blanco 1927–1928,* 25-31.
2. *Libro Blanco 1927–1928,* 26-32; Appendix 8, Memorial of Para-

guay, in *Proceedings*, 867-871; Paraguay, *Protocolos y Notas*, 26-33; Bolivia, *Memoria 1927*, 45-46.

3. *Proceedings*, 267-270; República de Bolivia, Ministerio de Relaciones Exteriores, *Actas y documentos de las conferencias de plenipotenciarios Bolivianos y Paraguayos* (La Paz, 1929), 1-4; *Política Argentina*, I, 20; Paraguay, *Protocolos y Notas*, 36; *Libro Blanco 1927–1928*, 34.

4. *Proceedings*, 876-888; Paraguay, *Protocolos y Notas*, 37-40; *Libro Blanco 1927–1928*, 32-33, 36-38; *Política Argentina*, I, 21.

5. Bolivia, *Memoria 1925*, 3; Vicente Rivarola, *Memorias diplomáticas* (Buenos Aires, 1952), I, 50-59, 61, 75, 79; Bolivia, Ministerio de Relaciones Exteriores y Culto, *La reintegración marítima de Bolivia* (La Paz, 1929), 6.

6. Rivarola, I, 64, 77, 80, 86-89, 95; *New York Times*, 16 August 1927, 34.

7. Bolivia, *Mensaje 1927*, 78; *Memoria de Ministerio de Guerra y Colonización 1927*, 12, 115. Not with any great hope of solution, however. Officials were generally pessimistic. U. S., *Foreign Relations*, 1927, 319; Major Angel F. Rios, *La defensa del Chaco* (Buenos Aires, 1950), 42, 129, 369-396, 424-426, 439-448.

8. Bolivia, *Actas*, 7-80; *Proceedings*, 273-328; *Libro Blanco 1927–1928*, 43-111; *Política Argentina*, I, 22-59; Rivarola, I, 119, 193; Amarilla Fretes, *El Paraguay en el primer cincuentenario*, 60-61; Eusebio Ayala, *Ante el País* (Asunción, 1932), 71-82. For a more detailed discussion of the arguments and subtle factors, see Zook, *The Evolution of the Chaco Dispute*, 130-141.

9. *Actas*, 85; *Proceedings*, 333; *Política Argentina*, I, 59.

10. *Actas*, 82, 86-205; *Proceedings*, 329-426; *Libro Blanco 1927–1928*, 94, 118-219; *Política Argentina*, I, 62-136; Rivarola, I, 153-155; U. S., *Foreign Relations*, 1928, 674. See also, Zook, *The Evolution of the Chaco Dispute*, 144-152.

11. Rivarola, I, 156-158, 180; Rios, 157; Pablo Max Ynsfran, editor, *The Epic of the Chaco: Marshal Estigarribia's Memoirs of the Chaco War 1932–1935* (Austin, 1950), 6 (cited hereafter as Estigarribia). Colonel Carlos José Fernández, *La Guerra del Chaco* (Buenos Aires, 1956), I, 45.

12. Actas, 203; Rivarola, I, 218; Proceedings, 425, 487-510, 797-809, 824-827; Colonel Julio Díaz Arguedas, *Historia del Ejército de Bolivia, 1825–1932* (La Paz, 1940), 611; Tomás Manchego, "El Asalto Paraguayo," *Revista Militar* (La Paz), Nos. 100-101 (1930), 274-275; Bolivia, Ministerio de Relaciones Exteriores y Culto, *Documentos relativos a la agresión del Paraguay contra el Fortín boliviano Vanguardia* (La Paz, 1929), 89-127. The League of Nations *Armaments Yearbook*, 1928, reported that Paraguay had 2,969 in her army (p. 644), Bolivia 8,000 (p. 62).

13. Rivarola, I, 197-199, 290-292; U. S., *Foreign Relations,* 1928, 678-679, 684; Manchego, 277-278; *Proceedings,* 830-836; Alberto Virreira Paccieri, *Bolivia-Paraguay, 5 de Diciembre de 1928* (La Paz, 1932), 7-9.

14. Manchego, 279; *Proceedings,* 153-172, 1070-1073.

15. Rivarola, I, 202; Fernández, I, 45; Rios, 158; Bolivia, *Documentos relativos,* 1; *Proceedings,* 442, 837-838; Major Antonio E. González, *La Guerra del Chaco* (Sao Paulo, 1941), 31; General Juan Bautista Ayala, *La Guerra del Chaco hasta Campo Via* (Buenos Aires, 1958), 39.

16. Díaz Arguedas, *Historia del Ejército,* 573, 610-613.

17. *Documentos relativos,* 2-13; *Proceedings,* 443-448; Rivarola, I, 219-221, 226; *Times* (London), 11 December, 15; 13 December, 14; *New York Times,* 9 December, 20; 10 December, 1, 2; 15 December, 5.

18. Díaz Arguedas, *Historia del Ejército,* 517, 556-558; Rivarola, I, 238-239; *Proceedings,* 133-147, 838-843, 1067.

19. Rivarola, I, 242-243; Virreira Paccieri, 144-148.

20. Fernández, I, 35-37, 45-46; Rios, 139-140; Díaz Arguedas, *Historia del Ejército,* 29; J. B. Ayala, 40-42; Colonel Rogelio Ayala Moreira, *Por qué no ganamos la Guerra del Chaco* (La Paz, 1959), 57-59, 68.

21. The basic sources for the Washington conference are the *Proceedings (op. cit.);* Enrique Finot, *Nuevos aspectos de la cuestión del Chaco* (La Paz, 1931); and Fernando González Roa, *Comisión de Investigación y Conciliación* (México, 1930). For a detailed summary, see Zook, *The Evolution of the Chaco Dispute,* 155-189.

22. Finot, 127-129, 144-151, 159-160; República de Bolivia, *Boletín del Ministerio de Relaciones Exteriores,* March-April 1929, p. 45; U.S., *Foreign Relations,* 1929, I, 861-863; 1930, I, 309-310.

23. Rivarola, II, 35; U.S., *Foreign Relations,* 1930, I, 330-331; Arze Quiroga, I, 59-63; League of Nations Publications, 1930, VII, *Political,* 1-6.

24. *Política Argentina,* I, 202-203; Rivarola, II, 38; U. S., *Foreign Relations,* 1930, I, 311-328, 343; Bolivia, *Boletín,* April-December 1930, 1-3, 21-27.

25. Daniel Antokoletz, *La cuestión del Chaco Boreal* (Montevideo, 1934), 30.

26. This is not to convey that the Tacna-Arica settlement was the chief cause in bringing the Chaco issue to a crisis. Rather, it was a single, relatively minor factor, which has been greatly exaggerated by journalists and others seeking simple explanations for complex political phenomena.

27. Ayala, *Ante el País,* 86; Amarilla Fretes, *El Paraguay en el primer cincuentenario,* 56-57. Ayala held that the Hayes Award tacitly extended from the headwaters of the Rio Verde due west (Bolivia as-

serted due south) to the Pilcomayo. Andean troops were centered in this doubly disputed triangle.

28. Enrique Finot, *Nueva Historia de Bolivia* (Buenos Aires, 1946), 372. See also U. S., *Foreign Relations*, 1930, I, 425.

29. U. S., *Foreign Relations*, 1931, I, 715-716; *Política Argentina*, I, 215-216; Paraguay, Ministerio de Relaciones Exteriores, *Libro Blanco. Documentos relativos a la conferencia de Washington para el estudio de un pacto de no agresión con Bolivia a la actuación de la comisión neutrales y trato de prisoneros* (Asunción, 1933), 3-5. Cited hereafter as *Libro Blanco. No Agresión.*

30. *Política Argentina*, I, 211-214, 225-228; Rivarola, II, 61-66; Diez de Medina, *De un Siglo*, 329; U. S., *Foreign Relations*, 1931, I, 724, 731, 733-745; Bolivia, *Memoria 1934*, 5-13; *Boletín*, June-September 1931, 58-69; Jayme DeBarros, *A Política Exterior do Brasil* (Rio de Janeiro, 1941), 110. Armament of the gunboats was each three 74 mm. antiaircraft guns, and four 120 mm. and two 40 mm. guns; Rios, 90.

31. U. S., *Foreign Relations*, 1931, I, 756-761, 764, 768-770; 1932, V, 225; Bolivia, *Memoria 1934*, 23-26.

32. U. S., *Foreign Relations*, 1931, I, 756, 764-765; Rivarola, II, 76-77; Bolivia, *Memoria 1934*, 27-28; Arze Quiroga, I, 66-67; Estigarribia, 9; González, 32; *Boletín*, June-September 1931, 69-70.

33. Harris G. Warren, "Political Aspects of the Paraguayan Revolution, 1936–1940," *Hispanic American Historical Review*, XXX (February, 1950), 4-7; Colonel Heriberto Florentín, *Lo que he visto en Boquerón* (Buenos Aires, 1957), 111-112, 124; *New York Times*, 24 October 1931, 8; 25 October, 9; 27 October, 1. Guggiari returned to the presidency 28 January 1932 to finish out his term; *ibid.*, 29 January 1932, 8; *Times* (London), 24 October 1931, 9.

34. *Libro Blanco. No Agresión*, 18-37; *Política Argentina*, I, 236-246; Bolivia, *Memoria 1934*, 38-41; Diez de Medina, *De un Siglo*, 330-333.

35. *Política Argentina*, I, 246; Rivarola, II, 80-82.

36. *Libro Blanco. No Agresión*, 38-159; Bolivia, *Memoria 1934*, 42-53; *Política Argentina*, I, 247-352; Rivarola, II, 88-100; U. S. *Foreign Relations*, 1932, V, 41-44, 53-55, 136, 139.

37. U. S., *Foreign Relations*, 1932, V, 8-13; Bolivia, *Memoria 1934*, 55-58; *Libro Blanco. No Agresión*, 160-165.

38. U. S., *Foreign Relations*, 1932, V, 13-17.

39. *Ibid.*, 18; *New York Times*, 1 June 1932, 5.

CHAPTER THREE

THE ISSUE MATURES

Military Preparations

On the eve of conflict, standing forces and war potential appeared to favor Bolivia. Her modern army, dating from the first presidency of Montes, rested on obligatory military service and an officer corps trained largely at home by foreign military missions. In 1905 a French mission began modernization of the army, but was succeeded in 1911 by a German mission headed by Colonel Hans Kundt, a man destined for a large role in Bolivian history. Serving as Chief of the General Staff from 1911-1914, 1921-1926, and 1929-1930, Kundt brought German regulations to the Altiplano and created an awesome force feared in many quarters as a threat to peace in the hemisphere. When Mr. Francis White heard Enrique Finot expounding Bolivia's military prowess, he remarked ironically, "I tremble for the safety of the United States!"[1]

The Bolivian army, as an instrument in support of the State's policy, pushed down the Pilcomayo, as has been shown, building *fortines*. In 1922-1923, during the civil war in Paraguay, activity was extensive along the *esteros*. When in 1927 the line of Paraguayan *fortines* based on Nanawa, a former Anglican mission, was encountered by exploratory patrols, the Bolivians turned northward. Lack of water had previously held them close to the river, but now with rugged determination they moved north through the strange waterless jungle forest, following a few unexcelled trail blazers. In 1929 Arce was founded, a main hub from which outposts were fanned eastward and ever northward, probing Paraguayan positions and leading to numerous minor clashes. The whole network stemmed from Muñoz, headquarters of the 4th Division, a *fortin* with crude communications through Ballivián to Villa Montes at the western extremity of the Chaco, but supplied from Argentina.[2]

It could not have been expected that Paraguay, lacking the relatively vast economic base of her antagonist, and with less than a million people, would be able to match Bolivia in the field. That, in her poverty, she could pay $4,730,733 for arms from 1926 to 1932 is a standing tribute to one of her greatest statesmen, Dr. Eligio Ayala, President from 1924-1928, thence Finance Minister until his death in 1931.[3] As chief executive, Eligio Ayala encouraged explorations of the unknown Chaco by General Belaieff, a Czarist officer who had served with Wrangel. Lieutenant Colonel José Félix Estigarribia, Ayala's friend and close associate, also participated in this work. He set himself apart from his colleagues by firsthand knowledge of the Chaco, generally an enigma to all except the few *conscriptos* and lieutenants who garrisoned the scattered outposts.

The thin line of troops, never more than a few hundred, was intended to protect Paraguay's Chaco industry and development.[4] True, as Bolivia charged, most Paraguayan enterprise was in the hands of firms with Argentine, United States, and British capital exploiting quebracho or raising cattle. But impoverished Paraguay could not develop her own lands, and cooperation with such companies was decidedly in her interest. A third of her revenues and most of her foreign exchange came from the Chaco. Such significant holdings required military protection, especially when the pressure of Bolivia became strong. Against Guaraní protection of civil establishments, Bolivia advanced militarily, her civil activity being mainly in support of the army charged with civilizing and incorporating the Chaco.

Dr. Daniel Salamanca, new President of Bolivia, had many times pondered his country's adverse geography—her nucleus on the Altiplano, dependent upon a mineral-based economy, while the lowlands stagnated for lack of markets. Bolivia's neighbors reached her lowlands ahead of her and appropriated them, dismembering her from the Pacific and the Atlantic. All that now remained were rights in the Chaco to an outlet through the Plata. Here, too, Bolivia's diplomatic efforts to achieve possession of what was her own were resisted by geographically-favored Paraguay, who moved with impunity since La Paz was far away, isolated in the clouds. Feeble Andean efforts to establish communications failed dismally.[5]

Salamanca resolved in March 1931 to accord the Chaco the full devotion which its importance to the *oriental* merited. There "existed in the Government no desire to provoke war" when it proposed "to extend and consolidate the Bolivian possession to all the territory not yet occupied by Paraguay." Although after the Rojas Silvas incident Salamanca had called for expenditures of $14,000,000 borrowed in the United States on Chaco penetrations, he was less *guerrerista* in power than out; the new project was financed by funds from Simón Patiño, the tin king, and based upon the ancient need for roads.[6]

On 13 April 1931, a month after Salamanca's inauguration, the General Staff sought approval for the link-up of the Pilcomayo *fortines* with the *Oriente;* that is, Puerto Suárez-Roboré, where the 3rd and 5th Divisions, each with a pitiful handful of men, were quartered. A solid barrier would be forged across the Chaco against Paraguay, whose cries of righteous indignation kept Bolivia on the diplomatic defensive and cloaked Guaraní expansion. On 2 May the General Staff revealed its plan for Chaco penetration, which was predicated on the belief that the importance of the Pilcomayo sector had been exaggerated. Bolivia's numerical superiority there was contained by a screening of heavy Paraguayan patrols. These diverted attention from the Toledo sector, where the Guaraní pushed westward from the Mennonite colonies, hoping to flank the Bolivian first line terminating at Castillo, a dependency of Fortín Arce. Penetration should drive east from Ballivián to Arce, then north as watering places for men, cattle, and cavalry horses were found available. From Carandaití and the Parapetí, roads should be directed toward the same objective. To cut off Corrales—the new, most westerly Paraguayan *fortín* (northwest of Arce) —a road must be built across its rear.[7]

In July an expedition under Lieutenant Colonel Angel Ayoroa and Lieutenant Germán Busch set out from Roboré to explore southward. The general objective was reincorporation of the Zamucos region, following the same route which the Jesuits had used two centuries before. All during the dry season of 1931 the

Bolivians toiled—exploring, building *fortines* and roads, and glorying in the arduous, exciting task which was theirs. On the site of ancient San Ignacio de Zamucos at 20°S. they erected Fortín Ingavi.[8]

In a secret resolution 17 October 1931 the Bolivian Chamber called upon the executive to "avoid if possible signing a pact of nonaggression with Paraguay." If this was not possible, "the pact that is signed," the Deputies resolved, "must make no zone, line or prescription of immobilization of our armed frontiers in the Chaco." Consequently, the only object of entering the conference at Washington was "to gain time to complete the preparation" on which the army had been engaged. In effect, Congress had endorsed the program of the General Staff and the President, joining them in full responsibility for the ultimate results.[9]

General Filiberto Osorio Téllez, Chief of the General Staff, reported to Salamanca 29 October 1931 on the progress of the pacific penetration. After outlining the numerous, unpublicized clashes which had occurred since 1930, he cited the grave danger in the Central and Northern Chaco where "the limits of our rights . . . are more doubtful and undefined than in the Southeast." (Having been Foreign Minister during the rule of the Junta, Osorio fully understood the titles and diplomacy of his country.) In those less known sectors Paraguay must be confined, he continued, mentioning the expedition of Belaieff as proof that Paraguay planned advances in the North Central region.[10] Possibly she even suspected Bolivia's latest moves in the Zamucos area farther north.[11]

With the knowledge gained from the activity of the dry season, the General Staff prepared its "General Plan for Penetration of the Chaco" (dated 15 January 1932). This document proposed, by *de facto* occupation of the Chaco Boreal, (1) to strengthen Bolivia's juridical position, (2) contain Paraguayan advances, and (3) gain positions favorable for future arbitral or military solutions. Once theoretical rights were thus guaranteed, Bolivia's political and defensive positions would be strong. Occupation would open the way for development and civilian enterprise, giving the army something at its back besides empty desert.

The penetration would remedy existing severe limitations on

military possibilities by expanding the theatre of operations; the 4th Division moving up through Fortín Camacho to meet the 3rd and 5th would create a new central sector. When strategic transport could be rapid and certain, and the three divisions linked, a precise "plan of operations for a war against Paraguay" could be prepared. The new road network would create behind the center a base where strategic and tactical reserves could be concentrated for shifts to either side. This would attract the center of gravity, gaining the strategic initiative. (In reality, since the Paraguayans had already made a like shift, centering on Isla Poí, the latter objective was already improbable of attainment.)

Concealing activity from the enemy was imperative, since a thrust by him while the army was devoted to this work would be ruinous, especially in the center. Link-up would be prevented and Paraguay would bring superior forces to bear. Therefore, "imprudent provocations, premature aggressions or advance suspicions" had to be avoided. In case of a Paraguayan reaction, the 4th Division would hold itself ready for a drive against the Paraguayan salient of Boquerón—Huijay (Carayá) —Toledo—Corrales. "If diplomacy directs a *premature* [italics supplied] arbitration of law," it would find Bolivia in *de facto* possession of "the major terrain in controversy" and in an excellent juridical position. Such possession would counterbalance that of Paraguay, a "factor of insuperable moral force," and greatly limit the arbitral zone. "Our inferiority, in this sense, presently is very manifest," the plan admitted. Once completed, the penetration would favor Puerto Pacheco or Olimpo as the next objectives, either by envelopment or concentrated pressure. The plan symbolized the fervor of "our visionary Captain General [Salamanca]. Stand firm in the Chaco!"[12]

While Bolivia had made well-publicized arms contracts in England, supposedly maintained numerous and powerful forces in the Chaco, and now had a comprehensive plan for incorporating most of the disputed territory, Paraguay's activities were little known and assumed to be negligible. This was in fact a skillfully fostered illusion. The Liberal governments of Eligio Ayala and José P. Guggiari actually devoted 60 per cent of their revenue to preparation for the reckoning with Bolivia. This included arms purchases, domestic military expenditures, service on the small but ruinous foreign debt contracted after the War of the Triple Alliance, and the creation of a small hard currency and gold reserve. Few Paraguayans knew of the secret preparations, for it was feared that either Bolivia would pounce before Asunción was ready, or that the pacifistic influences in the world would release adverse propaganda against her. Consequently, troops in the Chaco were kept inferior to the enemy in men and matériel and, at the expense of their morale, had strict orders to avoid incidents which might provoke war prematurely. This policy motivated charges that the government neglected defense, and led to Franco's critical blunder in assaulting Vanguardia. But the Guaraní strategy worked, for Bolivians read the Asunción press and accepted its charges that Paraguay was weak and unprepared.[13]

In July 1924 secret plans were prepared for a new 4,000-man standing army as cadre for a contemplated mobilized force of 24,000-30,000. In 1925 a proposal for four combat groups of 5,820 men each, with integral artillery, aircraft, and cavalry, was outlined by General Manlio Schenoni Lugo and accepted by Eligio Ayala. Arms for this establishment were ordered in Europe by Eusebio Ayala, then Minister to the United States, and by General Schenoni himself. The Rojas Silva incident caused frantic pleas to hasten delivery of over 10,000 Mauser rifles and carbines.[14]

Arms contracts let in 1926-1927 in Europe exceeded $2,000,000 and included rifles, pistols, sabres, ammunition, 24 Schneider 75 mm. guns, shells, aircraft engines, 7 Wibault pursuit planes, 7 Potez "25's," saddles, blankets, uniform equipment, mule harness, tents, and the like. The two gunboats were contracted in Genoa in July 1928 at a cost of £300,000. In 1929, 7,000 Belgian Mausers, 200 Madsen automatic rifles, and more ammunition were purchased. In addition, Guggiari overrode army opposition and ordered 24 Stokes-Brandt mortars costing $67,581.[15]

After Vanguardia, Paraguay lived "in a climate of war." A flight of gold to Argentina began and commerce declined because, ignorant of preparations, businessmen were sure that Bolivia would overrun their country. The opposition, whether well-meaning or opportunistic, continually made governing difficult for those working to prepare the country. Paraguay, unlike Bolivia, had no credit abroad because of (1) the oppressive 1870 loans which Ayala was now trying to pay off at $5,000 per month, (2) the debt from the War of the Triple Alliance still held over her by Argentina and Brazil, and (3) internal anarchy which made her a poor risk. In addition, there was no prospect of a domestic loan in this paupers' land.[16]

Select Paraguayan officers nevertheless studied in the best war colleges of Europe. From 1926 to 1930 a French mission instructed the infantry, revised military regulations, developed the Paraguayan artillery, opened schools of military and naval aviation, and provided training in fortifications and defensive tactics as developed at Verdun. It was followed in early 1931 by an Argentine mission to create a war college. Although complete unity of doctrine was lacking, French concepts predominated in the Guaraní army.[17]

In January 1931, Lieutenant Colonel Juan B. Ayala, graduate of the French War College and new Chief of the General Staff, was instructed by War Minister Schenoni to inaugurate a program of Chaco exploration and consolidation. "Our activity in the sense of penetration has been maintained until now in complete paralysis and it is necessary to abandon this attitude to initiate a period of activity that must not end." An organized effort at consolidation was required; *fortines* should be connected by roads and telephone lines; two-way radios were needed. Although not specifically seeking expansion, Paraguay thus sought to retain the initiative from the enemy.[18]

Ayala enthusiastically implemented Schenoni's ideas. He recognized the factor of water in the desert and directed the digging of wells and cisterns, and the creation of depots along the roads. Since existing troop dispositions did not correspond to tactical or strategic requirements, Ayala sought to reconcentrate the Chaco forces as cadres for future mobilization. He emphasized build-up in the Casado-Isa Poí sector to meet the most probable enemy line of advance. Thin screens of cavalry were left to cover the northern and southern sectors. By January 1932 when Osorio responded, stressing the center, his attempt to there obtain the strategic initiative was already belated and improbable of achievement.[19]

Pitiantuta

In December 1930 an Indian cacique reported that ten raiders had come to Laguna Pitiantuta, a fabled lake known only to the savages, and had returned in the direction of the Bolivian *fortines*. On 24 December, Estigarribia requested authority from the War Ministry to occupy the lake, which he believed to be of capital military importance. A few days later General Belaieff, an incomparable naturalized White Russian, set out from Puerto Casado with a small exploration party. In the afternoon of 13 March 1931, Belaieff became the first white man to reach Pitiantuta, a unique five-by-two kilometer body of water in a desert region, covered with aquatic vegetation and host to flocks of waterfowl. In July a platoon founded Fortín Carlos Antonio López on the east shore. By October 1931, as mentioned earlier, Osorio knew of the Belaieff expedition, but apparently was not aware that a *fortín* had been built.[20]

In January 1932, Bolivia began employing aircraft to support the penetration program. From the north, Lieutenant Colonel Felipe Rivera reported a new Paraguayan *fortín* (Bogado) in the Zamucos region. Therefore, the General Staff warned the 4th Division on 25 February against premature work on the road north from Camacho, last of the new *fortines*, for fear of discovery. However, on 24 April, Majors Oscar Moscoso and Jorge Jordán flew over Laguna Chuquisaca (Pitiantuta), observing buildings on the northeast shore which appeared to be deserted.[21]

On 3 May 1932 the General Staff directed the 4th Division to entrust Moscoso with occupation of the lake. His instructions were not clear, but there were standing orders to avoid any friction which might jeopardize the successs of the great penetration in progress. Salamanca personally endorsed Moscoso's mission to clear up the enigma of the buildings. He did not wish war, but foolishly believed that the road network could be completed with Paraguay limiting herself to diplomatic protest. A large wall map in the Cartographic Office of the General Staff portrayed in red lines the daily advance of the penetration routes—crawling vipers with the venom of war in their heads.

War became inevitable when on 21 May, in direct response to the incentive of Article V of the White draft, General Osorio wired the 4th Division that the Neutrals were pressing for prompt and precise designations of the most advanced positions. Consequently, occupation of Laguna Chuquisaca, the golden spike in the link-up of the 3rd and 4th Divisions, was diplomatically urgent and must be accomplished "before the end of the month."[22]

Moscoso, already well on his way, received this order on 3 June and immediately accelerated the advance of his eighteen men. Late in the afternoon of 14 June 1932 they reached the lake and, after many days spent in crossing waterless wastes, its sight was undoubtedly a thrilling stimulation to patriotism. Carefully skirting the shore, Moscoso was able to watch from a treetop the Paraguayan soldiers swimming along the eastern edge. His orders were "occupy," not merely observe or explore; Moscoso had been left with full initiative and disproportionate responsibility before history. He resolved to capture the Guaraní post by surprise just before dawn. Unfortunately for his country, at 0530 hours 15 June the six Paraguayan soldiers were awake preparing breakfast, and at the first sign of danger fled into the brush and escaped! The Bolivian aggression was not long secret. On 18 June five of the men reached their parent 2nd Cavalry and their report was immediately on its way to the headquarters of Estigarribia's 1st Division.[23]

Moscoso reported (16 June) on his actions and requested reinforcements to prevent Paraguayan recapture of the very valuable prize. Since diplomatic protests would surely result, he suggested saying that a Bolivian *fortín* situated in Laguna Chuquisaca (Pitiantuta), abandoned because of the seasonal floods, had been occupied by Paraguayans. On 17 June, Salamanca, who had recognized that the Paraguayan *fortín* should not be disturbed, ordered Moscoso to depart Fortín Carlos Antonio López. Osorio and Colonel Enrique Peñaranda Castillo, acting 4th Division commander, insisted that Bolivia could not afford to evacuate the lake (the only water within 75 kilometers) but should build a new *fortín* on the west shore. Osorio ordered Moscoso to that side. Peñaranda possibly had received a wire stating that "in view of necessity to retain Gran Lago [Pitiantuta] and order of abandonment by President republic urgently request you represent officer corps and your command." Consequently, although he actually did not relay the order until after *29 June,* he reiterated that Moscoso was now on the west bank, and by 25 June reported the position reinforced.[24]

In early July, Osorio asserted that historical, economic, and vital necessities required an outlet on the Rio Paraguay. Retention of Laguna Chuquisaca was of immense strategic importance since it signified the possibility of reaching the river. The lake's waters suggested an agricultural colony to consolidate Bolivian dominion. It was the last link in the chain that would seal off Guaraní expansion. To "prepare for an immediate solution to this problem which had consumed the energies of the nation for a half-century," Osorio asked 10,000,000 *bolivianos* in cash.

Salamanca replied that in the over-all Chaco problem, military considerations were important, but other factors must not be forgotten. Holding the lake could be disastrous for the Bolivian cause abroad. It could interrupt the Nonaggression Conference and bring on war or disadvantageous international pressure. "For my part, as you know, Sr. General," he wrote, "I have inclined to the solution counseled by prudence," avoiding an international complication which would "compromise the fruit of our toil and bring us to a solution imposed by force, with the consequent humiliation of our dignity." Further, Bolivia could not limit her goal to mere acquisition of a port. This restricting of objective, the result of fifty years of impotence, had convinced the world that Bolivia simply needed an anchorage whereas Paraguay required territory. This belief made it extremely difficult to pose the question in the form of reincorporating all, or as much as possible, of the Chaco to Altiplano dominion. Haste could not accomplish the latter; much time would be required.[25]

The hour for advising prudence had nearly passed, however. Bolivia had set in motion events which would cost her far more of the Chaco than she had ever dreamed, drain her treasure, destroy her political system, and bring her to the most humiliating experience of her entire unhappy life. Pitiantuta, Colonel

Días Arguedas wrote, was "the Bolivian Sarajevo, initiating the march of the apocalyptic horsemen who commenced thereafter to gallop in the far horizons of the Chaco."[26]

Diplomatic solutions had failed for half a century—failed not because of bad faith, but because of an inability to achieve a workable compromise. The reasons for this failure are complex. The influence of domestic politics and the belief on each side that procrastination would lead at some future time to a more favorable settlement; the willingness of important political segments to contemplate military solutions to achieve fulfillment of claims and internal spiritual rejuvenation; and the determination of each side to possess and defend the Chaco—these were principal causes of the bankruptcy of diplomacy.

Far too much has been written ascribing the war to irrational economic causes. Most of these charges first appeared in the cheap paper works of Communists and gained acceptance among many who should have known better.[27] The only significant economic factors were the vital position of the Chaco in Paraguay's economy, making its loss unbearable, and the desire of Bolivia to complement the economy of her *oriental* with a fluvial outlet. Oil was specifically insignificant in the origins of the Chaco War.[28] The coincidence of the war and the world depression was a happenstance. The dispute was near ignition before late 1929. Pauperish Paraguay was not closely enough enmeshed in world economic intercourse for many of her citizens to feel the depression directly, although government revenues were affected. Salamanca was following a conservative fiscal policy to cope with the severe loss of revenue occasioned by the collapse of tin prices, and the prospect of war expenses was alien to his financial program.

Succinctly, the Chaco War occurred when failure of diplomacy to achieve proud national objectives led to a willingness of each disputant to entrust the issue to military solution.

The Crisis

When news of Bolivia's seizure of Fortín Carlos Antonio López reached the Paraguayan 1st Division, Estigarribia issued orders for a reconnaissance in force. Four officers and ninety-four men set out on 22 June. An initial probing attack on 29 June revealed Moscoso in the Paraguayan *fortín* with superior strength. A prisoner divulged the Andean penetration plan and Pitiantuta's importance to Bolivia. The Paraguayan commander thereupon pulled back 20 kilometers and sent his report to Estigarribia, who directed him to maintain his position, and ordered the Palacios battalion of the 2nd "Itororo" Infantry, equipped with a Stokes-Brandt mortar, to recoup Pitiantuta at whatever sacrifice.[29]

Moscoso's immediate report of the attack reached La Paz on 2 July. The following day he finally received the instructions to go to the west side but, after burning the Paraguayan *fortín,* moved instead to the extreme northeast, where he constructed Fortín Mariscal Santa Cruz in an island of trees[30] which afforded a good field of fire. The west bank was far removed from water in the dry season; from it the east shore was beyond the range of Bolivian rifles; Moscoso decided against such a disadvantageous position. After Salamanca directed Moscoso's withdrawal unless he was strong enough to hold the lake, the General Staff (5 July) ordered him reinforced.[31]

On the sixth, Paraguay informed the Neutrals that on 15 June, without provocation, Fortín Carlos Antonio López had fallen to Andean aggression. Guggiari confided to Wheeler, United States Minister at Asunción, that news of the incident had been suppressed until verified on 29 June. Domestic opinion would tolerate no further talks with the aggressor and, therefore, the Paraguayan delegation was being ordered out of the Nonaggression Pact Conference. Secretary of State Stimson, who subscribed to the erroneous Bolivian asseveration that Paraguay had created the incident to avoid signing the Nonaggression Pact, began diligent efforts to keep her in attendance. After a lengthy meeting on 11 July, the Neutrals wired Asunción requesting data for an investigation and pleading for the delegation's return so that the incident could be settled.[32]

Foreign Minister Arbo's reply (15 July) reiterated his government's intentions to depart. He knew La Paz's report alleged that a party in search of water had found a deserted Guaraní post on the east shore of the lake, whereupon they withdrew to the west side, and were there attacked on 29 June by Paraguayan troops. This prevarication suggested that Bolivia was up to new adventures, and made talks with her undignified.[33]

On 15 July, Captain Abdón Palacios attacked Moscoso with 388 men, but getting to the well-prepared enemy defenses, manned by 170 Andeans, required hacking through thick woods, delaying the Paraguayan advance. The next day, however, the attack was pressed home. The Bolivians, many of whom were green troops, were demoralized by the mortar, a weapon alien to them, which they mistook for long-range artillery due to the trajectory of the descending shells. Assuming, therefore, that the main Paraguayan army was near, they panicked. Moscoso attempted to surrender himself, thought better of it, and abandoned his *fortin* when flight of the troops made its retention impossible.[34]

The Neutrals reminded Paraguay on 18 July that her withdrawal would prevent investigation of Pitiantuta just when the Bolivian delegation expected new data. The next day, however, La Paz released a circular accusing Paraguay of new aggression and asserting that in the absence of an agreement to the contrary, Andean forces had a perfect right at Pitiantuta. Meanwhile, war fever rose in both Asunción and La Paz; but Wheeler reported to Stimson (19 July) that Guggiari assured him the recapture of Pitiantuta satisfied Paraguay, and she would take no further action unless Bolivia launched fresh aggressions. Her delegates would now remain in Washington. The Neutrals promptly solicited suspension of all military activity on both sides.[35]

On 18 July the Bolivian 4th Division, which included only 1,457 men, had reported to La Paz the loss of Fortín Mariscal Santa Cruz. To Daniel Salamanca, flight in the face of the enemy compromised Bolivia and required vindication of her honor—reprisals must be taken immediately. General Carlos Quintanilla Quiroga was called from Oruro, and conferred with Osorio and Colonel Francisco Peña, able commander of the 4th Division, who was convalescing in La Paz from an appendectomy. The officers opposed immediate reprisals, "as very dangerous for the small army of the SE [*sic*] given its few effectives," transport, and reinforcements. Salamanca harshly overruled them, for the national dignity demanded capture of Corrales and Toledo. Advance should continue until seriously opposed. The 1st through 5th Divisions were declared "in campaign" 20 July by secret decree; the 4th was ordered to take precautions for possible Paraguayan counterattack, and also to prepare to seize Nanawa; the 3rd with its mere 700 men was placed on the defensive, link-up with the 4th being impossible with Paraguay in possession of Pitiantuta.[36]

Paraguay began preparing for any exigency. Her army stood at only 4,100, the planned cadre strength. Estigarribia, who believed that Bolivian mobilization would require three months, called for immediate reinforcement and rapid general mobilization in hopes of gaining an advantage by initiating operations before Bolivian columns could converge. The government responded realistically, calling up reserves and "putting the people in arms." The General Staff worked around the clock to concentrate men and means "in the probable theatre of operations." All medical personnel in Paraguay were mobilized. Exiles were invited to return, and opposition leaders to confer with Guggiari. To acquire urgently needed supplies, Rivarola was authorized to approach the Argentine Government. The Foreign Minister, Dr. Carlos Saavedra Lamas, strongly opposed this compromise of Argentine neutrality. Rivarola, however, went behind his back to President Justo, who referred him to Captain Casal and Colonel Rodríguez, the Navy and War Ministers, for the desired equipment.[37]

On 22 July, Guggiari appointed General Manuel Rojas Commander in Chief. Rojas was ignorant of the Chaco, in poor health, and dedicated to the school which held that the war should be fought defensively along the west bank of the Rio Paraguay, abandoning the Chaco to the enemy and hoping to defeat him when he had overextended his supply lines. Estigarribia, together with Chief of the General Staff Lieutenant Colonel Juan B. Ayala, familiars of the Chaco, held that "the defense should go to the encounter at the greatest possible distance from the river," and thus thwart the enemy offensive far inland before it could

fully develop. Nonetheless, Rojas ordered Palacios out of Pitiantuta 24 July, leaving only an outpost instructed to retire in the
face of superior forces.[38]

To the Neutrals, La Paz stated on 24 July that she could no
longer remain in the Nonaggression Conference "without di-
minishing the dignity of our country," for Paraguay had withdrawn to wage undeclared war. The Neutrals begged her to
reconsider because Asunción had now made available her data
for the investigation. They strongly, but futilely, urged both
countries to refrain from new military moves.[39]

Meanwhile, on 21 July, Colonel Peña flew into Fortín Muñoz
and issued orders three days later for the desired Bolivian reprisals. Detachments were formed under Peñaranda and Lieutenant Colonel Manuel Marzana. The former overran Corrales
and Toledo, small Guaraní garrisons screening the Mennonite
colonies, on 27 and 28 July. Boquerón was occupied three days
later, but a clever Guaraní ambush inflicted serious casualties.
General Quintanilla, since 25 July Commanding General of the
First Army Corps (I Corps) organized at Muñoz with the 4th
and newly created 7th Divisions, wished also to take Nanawa on
3 August as a complementary maneuver to divert Guaraní attention and balance the advance. For political reasons, Salamanca
vetoed the proposal, strategically dislocating the small forces
which Bolivia had in the Chaco. Having achieved his "fortines
for a fortín," Salamanca then suspended operations, a grave military error.[40]

On 1 August, in an especially arrogant note reflecting profound contempt for what Salamanca once called "the most miserable of the small republics of South America," Bolivian Foreign
Minister Gutiérrez informed the Neutrals:

> We are not interested in investigations that do not define the
> fundamental question. Bolivia desires the final solution of the
> controversy. She does not wish to be perennially on guard in the
> Chaco to contain the advances of Paraguay. It is for this reason
> that the country has reacted with all her forces, resolved to liq-
> uidate, even by arms the plea in which we defend a territory
> that we consider historically ours. We have a right to the littoral
> on the Rio Paraguay.

The Neutrals, who saw no connection between the new clashes and the fundamental question, entreated Bolivia to suspend hostilities on the basis of possessions of 1 June 1932 and enter negotiations for an arbitrated settlement.[41]

All the countries of the hemisphere joined on 3 August in a declaration calling for pacific settlement of disputes in the Americas. Aimed directly at Bolivia, and predicated upon the belief that she would easily pulverize little Paraguay, the key lines read:

> The nations of America also declare that they will not recognize any territorial arrangement of this controversy that is not obtained by pacific means, nor the validity of territorial acquisitions that are obtained through occupation or conquest by force of arms.[42]

Gutiérrez replied to the Neutrals on 4 August that suspension of hostilities would be acceptable if based on the situation of the moment. He also explained to the United States Minister that domestic considerations would not permit evacuation of the reprisal *fortines*. The Bolivian reply was "exalted and redundant"; the Paraguayan, measured and precise. Both belligerents adhered to the Continental Declaration on 5 August. Asunción accepted the Neutral proposal for a truce based on 1 June positions, and repeated her willingness to have a full investigation of events since 15 June 1932. The Neutrals then vainly redoubled their efforts to get the Salamanca government to accept. On 8 August (the same day that Huijay, a Paraguayan outpost northeast of Boquerón, was added to her prizes) Bolivia repeated that only a cessation based on positions of the moment would be acceptable. If a truce were to be made retroactive, why not go back to 1 September 1888 and begin by restoring Puerto Pacheco to its founder? A *suspension* of hostilities had, however, already been ordered.[43]

Bolivia had taken the Paraguayan *fortines* in reprisal for expulsion of Moscoso from his position at Pitiantuta when the President, acting without adequate contemplation of probable results, found no other means to dominate the situation. After meditation, Salamanca (2 August) ordered a halt to offensive operations and troop movements into the Chaco. This was a supreme military error because the Chaco divisions then totaled only 3,655 men. Bolivia had had her revenge and was ready for a truce of positions. Although Salamanca felt that the 3 August declaration created a grave international situation, he hoped diplomatic measures would prevent war and eventually leave Bolivia in permanent possession of her prizes. The Neutrals, however, initially sought a truce based on 1 June and attempted to pressure La Paz into acceptance.[44]

They next asked if she would propose cessation of hostilities based on existing positions, without prejudice to the juridical status of either disputant as of 1 June, go immediately to arbitration, abandon by 1 June 1933 the reprisal *fortines,* maintain only minimal garrisons, and permit a neutral investigating commission to enter the Chaco. In reply Gutiérrez denied that there was a juridical status in the Chaco on 1 June, asserted the right to maintain garrisons as Bolivia chose, and reiterated the refusal to abandon the Paraguayan *fortines;* La Paz would only consent to a cessation based on the positions of the moment and then arbitrate a predetermined zone. Undismayed, the Neutrals continued working unsuccessfully throughout August to secure Andean acceptance of their original proposal.[45]

On 15 August a new President was inaugurated at Asunción. An eminent diplomat intimately acquainted with the Chaco dispute, former Minister to the United States, widely traveled and cosmopolitan, financier and economist, Dr. Eusebio Ayala was the outstanding statesman of the war period, towering above the lesser figures of the hemisphere. On 13 August, in a letter to Rivarola, he confided that Paraguay would soon be militarily ready for action and possess a momentary advantage which dare not be wasted. It was said that giving up the three *fortines* would be difficult for Salamanca; if they were not surrendered, there would be greater difficulties in Asunción. If the eager army was unleashed, victories would enhance its appetite, and make peace harder. He wrote that mediation had to be complete in another week because prolonged negotiations always favored Bolivia, the sister State whose "people are not culpable for the absurd obsessions of some exhumed doctors of Charcas." Ayala himself favored an immediate reciprocal security pact, negotiation of an arbitral compromise, and the Neutral formula for ending hostilities.[46]

Argentina's Saavedra Lamas, who tacitly supported the Neutrals, meanwhile had made confidential explorations on behalf of a proposal which followed the Bolivian line: a truce based on existing positions. This made Salamanca unamenable to the Neutral proposal and angered Ayala, who had been working with United States Minister Wheeler on a plan for a demilitarized zone to include the reprisal *fortines* and Bolivia's Arce-Alihuatá zone. The Bolivian occupation of Carayá (Huijay), an outpost between Boquerón and the Mennonite colonies, ruined this plan, making clear that La Paz intended to hold the captured *fortines* as a strategic threat to the colonies and the militarily vital Casado Railroad—an intolerable threat to Paraguayan security and supply lines. Saavedra Lamas and the world, unfortunately, seemed disposed toward a solution sacrificial to Paraguay for her own protection. To avert this and alter the belief that Paraguay was impotent, a supreme military effort could not be long withheld. "If I opposed the army further," Ayala told Wheeler, "I should have no army."[47]

In La Paz sentiment was violent against diplomatic pressure to evacuate the *fortines* and accept the Neutral plan; in Paraguay, the demand was equally virulent for their return. The Neutrals floundered like an aircraft in a thunderstorm, unable to maintain a steady course. At the crucial moment they committed the supreme blunder; they vacillated, and then yielded a position of pure right to the stubbornness of the austere Altiplano. On 29 August they appealed for a simple 60-day truce, which Paraguay could not accept because it left the Bolivian army pointing like a dagger from the three *fortines*. Gutiérrez replied that Bolivia would accept a 30-day truce, but Justo P. Benítez, the new Paraguayan Foreign Minister, vetoed this, sagaciously observing that it was merely the time Bolivia deemed necessary to complete her mobilization. The Neutrals then requested a halt in mobilization, which La Paz rejected, and all the neighbors then sorrowfully witnessed the outbreak of full-scale war.[48]

Notes

1. Díaz Arguedas, *Historia del Ejército*, 37, 59, 65-66, 759-765; Bolivia, *Memoria del Ministerio de Guerra, 1912*, 3-4, 22; Fernández, II, 11; Ayala Moreira, 21-82, is the best account of Kundt's activities through 1930.
2. Moscoso, 29; Arze Quiroga, II, 41; Fernández, II, 56; Florentín, *Boquerón*, 14-18.
3. Rios, 129; Estigarribia, 6; Justo Pastor Benítez, *Bajo el signo de Marte* (Montevideo, 1934), 17, 118.
4. Rivarola, II, 111.
5. Arze Quiroga, I, 39-41; Finot, *Nueva Historia*, 372.
6. Arze Quiroga, I, 44; Rios, 156. Siles had also been interested in Chaco penetration and colonization, it will be recalled; Bolivia, *Memoria del Ministerio de Guerra, 1930*, 25.
7. Moscoso, 35; Arze Quiroga, I, 81, 83-99.
8. Arze Quiroga, I, 25-26n, 101-103, 109-133.
9. Ovidio Urioste, *La Encrucijada* (Cochabamba, 1941), 19, 172-173.
10. See below, 69.
11. Arze Quiroga, I, 71-72.
12. *Ibid.*, 135-173. See also Florentín, *Boquerón*, 30.
13. Rios, 8, 12-14, 70, 134; Paraguay, *Mensaje 1931*, 7; Benítez, *Bajo el signo*, 19; Policarpo Artaza, *Ayala, Estigarribia y el Partido Liberal* (Buenos Aires, 1946), 13; Florentín, *Boquerón*, 25-28, 32-33; Ayala Moreira, 83-84.
14. Arze Quiroga, II, 19-46, 55-65; Rios, 31, 54, 361-396; Ayala Moreira, 84-89.
15. Rios, 63-68, 85-86, 98, 397-402, 405-408, 433-438; Arze Quiroga, II, 47-50, 75-82; Fernández, I, 39-40; Ayala Moreira, 90.
16. Rios, 105, 140-145, 220; Artaza, 30.
17. Rios, 105; Fernández, I, 34; Florentín, *Boquerón*, 39; Paraguay, *Mensaje 1931*, 123-124; Arze Quiroga, II, 150-151; Major Leandro Aponte B., *Cincuenta años de aeronautica en el Paraguay* (Asunción, 1957), 72-75, 90-92.
18. J. B. Ayala, 44.
19. *Ibid.*, 45-54.
20. Fernández, I, 68-71; Florentín, *Boquerón*, 35; Moscoso, 57; Colonel Julio Díaz Arguedas, *Los Elegidos de Gloria* (La Paz, 1937), 19.
21. Arze Quiroga, I, 175-211, 217-220, 242; Moscoso, 44; Ayala Moreira, 111-112.
22. Arze Quiroga, I, 236, 243; Moscoso, 49; General Angel Rodrí-

guez, *Autopsia de una Guerra* (Santiago, 1940), 20-21; Ayala Moreira, 113.

23. Fernández, I, 74-77; Arze Quiroga, I, 45, 281; Moscoso, 53-60; Ayala Moreira, 114-116; Colonel Aquiles Vergara Vicuña, *Historia de la Guerra del Chaco.* 7 vols. (La Paz, 1941–1945), I, 7.

24. Arze Quiroga, I, 46, 257-259, 279-281, 311-317; Vergara Vicuña, I, 22; Ayala Moreira, 117-123, quotation, 121. General David Toro informed Ayala Moreira that he saw a copy of this document, unsigned, in the General Staff Offices at the time. The validity of the assertion is uncertain.

25. Arze Quiroga, I, 321-324; Díaz Arguedas, *Los Elegidos,* 14, 19. "Tell your friends, the Paraguayans," Salamanca was once quoted as saying, "that the moment would be profitable to arrange the question, that today we ask more than before and that later, we will ask more than today"; Rivarola, II, 158.

26. Díaz Arguedas, *Los Elegidos,* 21; *Como fue derrocado el hombre símbolo.* (La Paz, 1957), ii. (Cited hereafter as *El hombre símbolo.)*

27. Typical of these works are: Elio M. A. Colle, *El drama del Paraguay* (Buenos Aires, 1935) ; Roberto Hinojosa, *El Cóndor Encadenado* (Monterey, 1941); Tristan Marof, *La tragedia del Altiplano* (Buenos Aires, 1934). The best summary of legitimate economic factors is Ronald Stuart Kain, "Behind the Chaco War," *Current History,* XLII, 468-474.

28. See Justo Pastor Benítez, *Estigarribia, El soldado del Chaco.* 2d edition (Buenos Aires, 1958), 47, 56; and Ayala Moreira, 93, 96.

29. Fernández, I, 77-82; Natalicio Olmedo, *Pitiantuta* (Asunción, 1933), 12-25; Estigarribia, 17. The Paraguayan 1st Division was created in 1931 at Puerto Casado.

30. A clump of trees surrounded by open terrain was called an "island." The term appears hereafter.

31. Arze Quiroga, I, 246, 262, 283-286, 289-291, 346; II, 234.

32. U.S., *Foreign Relations,* 1932, V, 19-28; *Libro Blanco. No Agresión,* 167-173; Bolivia, *Memoria 1934,* 60.

33. *Libro Blanco. No Agresión,* 175-177; U.S., *Foreign Relations,* 1932, V, 29-31; Rivarola, II, 120-121. Actually the Bolivian falsehood was unwitting and based on Peñaranda's falsely informing La Paz that Moscoso was on the west shore. Salamanca held the army fully responsible for misinforming him and provoking war; Arze Quiroga, I, 346.

34. Arze Quiroga, I, 293-309; Fernández, I, 83-86; Olmedo, 28-50; Moscoso, 61-71; Vergara Vicuña, I, 22-29; Ayala Moreira, 127-132.

35. *Libro Blanco. No Agresión,* 179-182; U. S. *Foreign Relations,* 1932, V, 32-36; Bolivia, *Memoria 1934,* 65-67; *New York Times,* 20 July 1932, 9; 21 July, 4; 23 July, 5.

36. Arze Quiroga, I, 236, 271-274, 346-348; II, 89-91, 219-237, 261-262;

Vergara Vicuña, I, 56-57, 139; II, 58-59n; Rodríguez, 58-59; Ayala Moreira, 143-145.

37. Rivarola, II, 160-167; Fernández, I, 38; Estigarribia, 19; Benítez, *Bajo el signo*, 70; Lieutenant Colonel Cándido A. Vasconsellos, *Guerra Paraguay-Bolivia. Mis memorias de la sanidad en campaña* (Asunción, 1942), 18-19; República del Paraguay, Ejército, *Guerra del Chaco. Los partes del conductor* (Asunción, 1950), 5 (cited hereafter as *Partes del conductor*); *New York Times*, 2 August 1932, 1; 3 August, 4; 4 August, 9; J. B. Ayala, quotation, 73.

38. Estigarribia, 20-22; González, 39, 42; J. B. Ayala, 97.

39. U. S., *Foreign Relations*, 1932, V, 37-40, 46-48; *Libro Blanco. No Agresión*, 183-200; Bolivia, *Memoria 1934*, 68-73; *Política Argentina*, I, 375.

40. Vergara Vicuña, I, 59-60, 68, 70-76, 89-90, 96; II, 60-70; Fernández, I, 54, 89-90; Moscoso, 74; Díaz Arguedas, *Los Elegidos*, 30-32, 38; Rios, 247-248; Florentín, *Boquerón*, 21-22. Typical of Bolivian tactics at this time was the advance of a mass along roads or open terrain, with no security or attempt to gain surprise. As commander at Boquerón, Florentín had prepared to admit the enemy to the *fortín* with an ostentatious retreat toward Isla Poí. Once the Bolivians entered Boquerón, concealed automatic rifles decimated their ranks. Then the 112-man garrison retired; Florentín, *Boquerón*, 51, 127-129, 135-139; Ayala Moreira, 145-148.

41. *Libro Blanco. No Agresión*, 206, 210; Bolivia, *Memoria 1934*, 75-76; U. S., *Foreign Relations*, 1932, V, 49-51; *Política Argentina*, I, 384; Rivarola, II, 157.

42. U. S., *Foreign Relations*, 1932, V, 159-160; *Libro Blanco. No Agresión*, 211-212; Bolivia, *Memoria 1934*, 93-94; *Política Argentina*, I, 386-387. The exact origins of this declaration merit an intensive investigation. The incentive may have been Mexican.

43. U. S., *Foreign Relations*, 1932, V, 57-62; *Libro Blanco. No Agresión*, 213-225; Bolivia, *Memoria 1934*, 96, 100-105; *Política Argentina*, I, 385, 389-391. At the moment, the Americas believed Bolivia to be extraordinarily militant, very powerful, and ready to crush Paraguay. This attitude typified the Neutrals, provoking Bolivia, who considered herself eternally the victim of injustice and thought the Neutrals were trying to intimidate her. Alberto Ostria Gutiérrez, *La doctrina del no-reconocimiento de la conquista en America* (Rio de Janeiro, 1938), 24-31.

44. Bolivia, *Memoria 1934*, 99-100; Vergara Vicuña, I, 146-147; Arze Quiroga, II, 94, 96; Díaz Arguedas, *El hombre símbolo*, 15; *Los Elegidos*, 53; Ovidio Urioste, *La Encrucijada*, 23.

45. *Libro Blanco. No Agresión*, 227-241; Bolivia, *Memoria 1934*, 106-115; U. S., *Foreign Relations*, 1932, V, 64-71, 77-78; *Política Argentina*, I, 394-396, 399-401, 403-405.

46. Rivarola, II, 148-149; Estigarribia, 30-31; Efraím Cardozo, *Tres heroes del Paraguay* (Buenos Aires, 1952), unnumbered pages. Fear was prevalent that Salamanca would fall and be succeeded by an intransigent military government if Bolivia were required to evacuate the *fortines*; U.S., *Foreign Relations*, 1932, V, 164, 170, 227. In fact, the army was far more tractable toward Chaco settlement than the President.

47. Rivarola, II, 150-154, 167-170, 180-181; U. S., *Foreign Relations*, 1932, V, 67, 71-75, 157, 180; *Politica Argentina*, I, 373, 376, 384, 397; Bolivia, *Memoria 1934*, 180-182.

48. U. S., *Foreign Relations*, 1932, V, 77-86, 190-191, 194-197; Rivarola, II, 155; *Libro Blanco. No Agresión*, 242-253; Bolivia, *Memoria 1934*, 115-119. The Benítez observation was well founded. In July the Altiplano General Staff considered 60 days necessary for mobilization; 30 had now passed.

CHAPTER FOUR

BOQUERÓN—THE FIRST PARAGUAYAN OFFENSIVE

Paraguayan Military Strategy

Lieutenant Colonel José F. Estigarribia, Paraguayan commander in the Chaco, from the first had been convinced that a *de facto* state of war existed with Bolivia. On 30 July he called for commitment in the Isla Poí sector within twenty days of "all the available population of the country" to vanquish the enemy and save the Paraguayan Republic. To meet this need, the General Staff had planned, and now conducted, an exceptionally smooth, rapid mobilization. Estigarribia, graduate of the French War College and one of the outstanding *militares* of South American history, falsely believed that Bolivia had an elaborate war plan laid by General Hans Kundt. Guaraní intelligence exaggerated draft operations plans and the penetration program, a mistake which accelerated the coming of war by convincing Paraguayans that Bolivia was contemplating full-scale conflict.[1]

The General Staff had based its planning upon the ideas of Lieutenant Colonel Juan B. Ayala, its chief since January 1931. Ayala feared that Bolivia would employ 12,000 to 15,000 men in the Isla Poí-Casado sector within 60 days. His contemplated response was a strategic defense and tactical offense using cavalry to cover Boquerón-Toledo-Corrales. Unfortunately, Colonel Ayala was a myopic devotee of railroad strategy and was incapable of appreciating the revolution in logistics occasioned by the motor truck. Consequently, he failed to recognize the opportunity for flexibility and movement in the Chaco. Ayala could envision offensive operations only with light forces, holding the mass to the Casado Railroad. Essentially, he bound the

General Staff to defensive concepts, permitting the enemy to advance slowly in order to expose his weak commmunications to guerrilla and cavalry raids.[2]

General Rojas, Paraguayan Supreme Commander with Headquarters at Asunción, advised Estigarribia (31 July) that reinforcements were being dispatched. Following the General Staff's concept, he urged concentration for defense of the Mennonite colonies, intending to take a stand along the primary supply line, the Casado Railroad. The 1st Division, with only 2,200 men, should not seek a decision against forces known to be superior. A slow retreat could lure the enemy toward the river where later he would be defeated.

Estigarribia recognized the fallacy of conceding the Bolivians their basic objectives in the hope of defeating them later. He surmised that the main Andean drive would not be through Toledo and the colonies, but through Boquerón to Isla Poí. At the latter, renamed Villa Militar, he resolved to concentrate, regardless of Rojas' wishes. When La Paz unwisely failed to continue the advance in August, a period of tacit truce set in which favored Paraguayan initiative. Estigarribia believed the principle of reciprocal attraction of forces would enable him to draw the bulk of the Andean army to the sector of his choice and there annihilate it. He realized that communications and the scarcity of water would be the major tactical factors in the Chaco. The nearest place beyond Villa Militar where water was available in quantity was Arce, the Bolivian *fortín* at the headwaters of the Rio Verde, limit of the Hayes Award. Consequently, Estigarribia resolved to strike the enemy, not at his weakest, but at his strongest point: Boquerón-Arce. This rejected an advance through Toledo to Ballivián, the axis favored by Rojas. However, by September the program advocated by Estigarribia came to coincide with that of the General Staff and Supreme Commander, who had remained cautious until great strength had been accumulated.[3]

Estigarribia revealed his intentions on 8 August, calling for simultaneous secondary attacks from Nanawa toward Agua Rica-Murguía-Saavedra and, if possible, in the north on Toledo-Corrales. Unaware of the new road from Camacho to Carandaití, he asserted that once Arce was captured, Platanillos should be taken to secure the Guaraní right by isolating Bolivian troops farther north. Action beyond Platanillos would be dependent upon transport. (Paraguay was critically short of trucks, starting the war with only twenty.) The rainy season was the limiting factor in time. Therefore, Estigarribia requested 200 trucks and all available men, planning to attack no later than 20 August. On the seventeenth, with initial mobilization completed, he again urged action on Rojas. Superior Guaraní forces must be brought to bear, he stressed, before the enemy build-ups were complete. Above all else, Bolivia must be denied the time to compensate her disadvantage in space.[4]

When Rojas maintained silence toward these proposals, apparently content to seek a war of attrition near the Rio Paraguay, Estigarribia chose to assume consent and pressed preparations for a war of annihilation deep in the Chaco. He arrogated to himself complete authority over all forces west of the Rio Paraguay, and they obeyed. The First Army Corps (I Corps) was created (24 August) with the 1st and 2nd Divisions and the 1st Cavalry. On 1 September when strength had reached 7,499, Major Manuel Garay, new Chief of Staff of I Corps, arrived at Isla Poí with the word for which Estigarribia had waited so impatiently. From Asunción came an unsigned note supposedly written by the President authorizing the recapture of Boquerón "to demonstrate to the Neutrals and other countries of America that Paraguay possesses military capacity," and "to give satisfaction to public opinion and to the army." For international reasons, hostilities should appear the outgrowth of patrol clashes, with Paraguay seemingly innocent of aggression. Further, "it is important," Ayala slyly advised, "that the operation should appear as the result of an initiative on the part of the command." Reposing confidence in diplomatic solution and moral force, the President intended operations to terminate at Boquerón without pursuit. If the Bolivians resisted, he unrealistically assumed that his army would return to Villa Militar.[5]

The clear-sighted commander was critical of the presidential caution, believing that Ayala failed to recognize (1) that the war had already begun; (2) that if Boquerón were taken as a limited

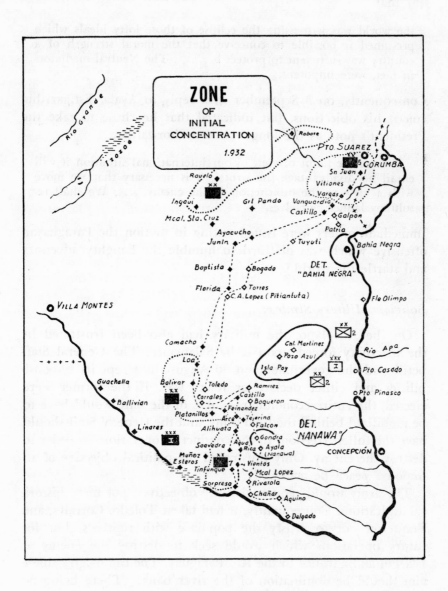

ZONE
OF
INITIAL
CONCENTRATION
1.932

objective, Bolivia would react by taking more reprisals: and
(3) that

> the world was witnessing the eclipse of those lofty ideals which
> presumed it possible to conceive that the moral strength of a
> country was sufficient to protect her. . . . The Neutral mediators
> in fact, were impotent.

Consequently, on 3 September in a reply to Ayala, Estigarribia
voiced his objections, but indicated that he chose to take the
President's note as the long-desired authorization.

> If from the point of view of our international situation it will
> entail no disadvantage [he wrote], it is necessary that we move
> with a view to the destruction of the enemy. . . . We shall re-
> solutely launch ourselves.[6]

Immediate orders were issued setting in motion the Paraguayan
offensive which was destined to humble the haughty adversary
and startle the world.[7]

Bolivian Military Strategy

On the Altiplano, the military had also been frustrated by
the inactivity forced upon it by Salamanca. The General Staff
petitioned the government on 30 August to accept its responsibilities and either declare or reject war. If the former were
elected, the entire economic resources of the state would have to
be mobilized behind the field army, and the General Staff should
have the fullest freedom in the conduct of operations in order to
destroy the enemy. Only thus could the political objective of an
imposed peace be achieved.

The army would require definite objectives, not mere historical aspirations. Consequently, it had taken Toledo, Corrales, and
Boquerón not to satisfy the populace with reprisals, but for
future operations which would seek to destroy the enemy at
Isla Poí and advance to the Rio Paraguay. The campaign's single
aim should be domination of the river bank. (There being no
war plan, the General Staff was obviously following the penetration plan.) The historical hypothesis of Salamanca, which
aimed at total reintegration, would require a nation in arms to

sustain military occupation of the entire Chaco and dictate peace at Asunción. The military hypothesis envisioned gaining the river above Puerto Casado through a secondary attack on Bahía Negra by the 5th Division, while the 3rd Division (3,000 men) took Olimpo, and the 4th and 7th Divisions engaged the main Guaraní army in the Southeast. Thus Paraguay, her right enveloped strategically, could be forced to make peace.[8]

Operations Plan # 3, allegedly prepared in April 1932 by G-3 (Lieutenant Colonel Angel Rodríguez), had been rushed to Quintanilla by air on 17 August. First outlining diplomatic considerations, the plan indicated that apparently the government contemplated total Chaco reintegration as its political objective. The military objective of the command, however, remained Olimpo and the river above. The plan contained the variant that since the vital link-up had not been completed, the *Oriente* and Southeast theatres would remain separate, becoming joint only when the 3rd Division started its march for Olimpo and the 4th Division took Isla Poí and Coronel Martínez. The 7th Division would support the right flank by cleaning up the Pilcomayo sector, while on the left the 5th Division would attack Bahía Negra. Everything possible should be done to assure the 3rd Division's rapid build-up for its important role.[9]

Fully elaborated, Plan # 3 was a Schlieffen-like conception, contemplating 10,000 men each at Boquerón and Ingavi. Paraguay, upon attacking Boquerón, would be permitted to press the Bolivian right westward as far as Ballivián, whereupon the 3rd Division would break through from Ingavi to the river effecting a strategic envelopment. A fair peace—a line from 10 kilometers above Olimpo to Ballivián—could then be drawn. Obviously, such a settlement would have given Daniel Salamanca apoplexy, although it was more realistic than his own proposals. In reality, however, Bolivia lacked the transport to implement either plan.[10]

On 21 September, Salamanca replied to the General Staff's affirmations of 30 August, bluntly stating that their purpose had been to protect the army from responsibility in case of defeat in the war. Tacitly they assumed that the government, not the army, had provoked hostilities. It had been necessary to force the Generals to take the reprisals the people justly demanded;

now the General Staff not only arrogantly asserted that the *fortines* were taken solely for their value to future operations, but also desired to rise above the government to impose its own criteria. Salamanca scorned the General Staff's limited objective, Olimpo. He asserted that a war with Paraguay must feature concentration in the southeast to take Asunción and impose peace —a worthy, but entirely unrealistic, objective.[11]

Bolivia's underestimation of her opponent was astonishing. The General Staff theorized that Paraguay could mobilize and equip only small forces and that she lacked war plans and intelligence. In December 1931 a twenty-six page Operations Plan # 1, prepared by G-3, argued that since war of maneuver would be impossible in the Chaco, five reinforced battalions of 812 men each, with integral batteries of mountain guns, would be adequate for a war with Paraguay. This document, which was the basis for current Bolivian plans, accurately reflected a decade of staff thought. In 1924, General Kundt had established a postulate when he dogmatically proclaimed that, Paraguayans being poor soldiers, Asunción could be taken by 3,000 men. Although both the Military Attaché to Argentina and General Gumusio (who had lived in Paraguay incognito) accurately reported Guaraní war preparations, La Paz disregarded their documented intelligence estimates.[12]

In the field, while Estigarribia chafed for action, the Bolivian command shared his frustration. On 8 August, Carayá (Huijay) was occupied and a firm defense ordered. Quintanilla then appealed to La Paz for reinforcements against an anticipated Paraguayan offensive (5,481 men had been detained en route to the Chaco) and again sought approval for the seizure of Nanawa. Salamanca refused and on 10 August ordered that there be no new advances without his personal authorization as constitutional Captain General. A week later Paraguayans recaptured Carayá, thereby removing the threat to Villa Militar, and downed a Bolivian aircraft for good measure. Salamanca thereupon ordered preparations for the defense of Boquerón to the death and released to Quintanilla the troops detained at Tarija. On the twenty-ninth, Osorio advised Quintanilla that Bolivia had taken the diplomatic position she would never give up the reprisal *fortines,* a stand which should further orient I Corps. Faced with the prospect of static defense, Quintanilla persisted in his desire for Nanawa, a militarily reasonable proposition which would have further disrupted the Guaraní first line of *fortines* and secured the Andean right. In answer to query whether he was capable of seizing Rojas Silva, he expressed confidence and a great desire for operations. This move, splitting Nanawa from Villa Militar, was finally authorized and announced on 8 September as a "reprisal" for Huijay.[13]

Boquerón

The response of Paraguay had been slow and deliberate, awaiting mobilization of the "organic, logistic and combative capacity of an army worthy of the name." Diplomatic pressure of the Neutrals tacitly helped her by gaining a halt to the hasty, emotional responses of the Salamanca government. Had Bolivia conducted general mobilization during August and struck promptly, she would likely have attained the river and won the war. Instead she remained passive, mobilizing in dribbles; this enabled Paraguay to bring to bear her decisive advantage in space, and to achieve earlier concentration of numerically superior forces. Their timely employment by Estigarribia was destined to prevent Bolivian concentration and gain a supreme moral triumph.[14]

By 7 September 1932 Paraguay had massed her rapidly mobilized green army at Villa Militar, with smaller nuclei at Bahia Negra and Nanawa. Ready for the offensive was the 1st Division (2nd and 4th Infantry, 2nd Artillery, 2nd Cavalry, and 1st Engineer Battalion) with a strength of 3,831; and the 2nd Division (1st and 3rd Infantry and 1st Artillery) totaling 3,668. At Nanawa a small detachment was formed around the 4th Cavalry, while at Bahia Negra the 3rd Division in formation (5th Infantry, marine and cavalry detachments, and the 3rd and 5th Artillery) numbered about 2,000. Each infantry regiment totaled 1,300 to 1,600 men, and cavalry regiments were 800 to 900. This represented only levels for the initial phase of mobilization, but the full strength of 2,517 and 967 men respectively was never to be attained. These forces were equipped with 21,363 rifles and carbines, 408 machine guns and automatic rifles, 59 pieces of artillery, and 24 mortars; the bulk of the arms were relatively new, and additional stocks had been ordered in July.[15]

Bolivian forces consisted of the small 3rd and 5th Divisions at Roboré and Puerto Suárez, the 4th Division spreading from Camacho down to Alihuatá, and the newly created 7th Division stretching along the Pilcomayo below Saavedra and facing Nanawa. The exact strength is impossible to determine because concentration had not been completed, and after Salamanca permitted resumption of troop movements, new contingents arrived almost daily. Nonetheless, I Corps had approximately 3,900 men in early September. The regiments were really battalions of only 300 men each in three companies. The entire army had available over 100,000 Mausers, 1,200 machine guns and automatic rifles, and a fairly numerous but often obsolete artillery. Bolivia's new Vickers arms had not yet arrived in quantity. She had no mortars, but possessed a Tank Group and an excellently equipped Air Force which, although poorly employed, controlled the skies throughout the war.[16]

Logistically Paraguay, with her shorter lines of supply and communication, was superior to Bolivia, an advantage which largely negated the greater size and wealth of the Altiplano-centered republic. Paraguay used the American-owned Puerto Pinasco Railroad, but relied mostly on the Casado line, which ran 160 kilometers into the Chaco. Her river vessels complemented this facility at Puerto Casado, thus forming a cohesive transportation system of relative quality. From Kilometer 145 of the railroad, Asunción's municipal buses, 60 requisitioned trucks, and some ox carts had to suffice, and here lay the weakest feature of the system.

Bolivia had no rail lines into the Chaco, but a fleet of barges and small craft was organized on the Pilcomayo to transport supplies from Villa Montes to Ballivián. Salamanca, saying that the country could not afford them, had refused to purchase 600 trucks which Osorio requested on 25 April 1932. He compounded his error by launching the July reprisals without resolving the fundamental problem of transport. The trucks acquired by requisitioning were unequal to the burden of distance relative to desired utilization. Poorly supplied Bolivian troops walked to the Chaco and often deserted en route, crossing the Pilcomayo. Bolivia had always relied on local purchase across that stream in Argentina to supply the Army of the Southeast, and purchases in Corumbá, Brazil, to sustain the Army of the *Oriente*. Significantly, Paraguayan products were commonly sold by stores at Muñoz, including "Alfonso XIII" cigarettes with the words "contribute to the National Defense" stamped on each.[17]

On 7 September the Paraguayan I Corps began the march from Isla Poí, optimistic from commander to lowest recruit that the invader would abandon Boquerón with little resistance. The next day Major Carlos Fernández' 1st Division, reinforced with the 3rd Infantry, advanced from Pozo Valencia, pushed back the enemy outposts, and came up to within 3 kilometers of Boquerón. Although Bolivian pilots reported the advance, they saw only the few trucks and assumed that small forces were involved. In the afternoon Estigarribia issued a general directive envisioning turning Boquerón on the left and pressing the enemy until local security was obtained. Fernández thereupon ordered an energetic pursuit toward Arce and assigned the 2nd Cavalry to cut the road to Yucra (Yujra or Jujra) to trap part of the fleeing garrison. Completely lacking maps, the army relied upon the recollections of Lieutenant Heriberto Florentín, the former commander of Boquerón. A gross error of the Paraguayan officers was failure to reconnoiter to locate the enemy positions. Fernández and the regimental commanders simply rode forward and scanned the terrain from treetops.[18]

Unknown to the attackers, Bolivia had carefully prepared the defenses of Boquerón. Since mid-August the garrison had diligently constructed field fortifications under direction of Major Germán Jordán, a student of French defensive doctrine. Perhaps thrown psychologically off balance by the ambush of 31 July, the garrison was eager to adopt a defensive approach. Trenches, protected by quebracho, lay hidden along the edge of woods. Concealed machine gun nests rested on platforms in trees. A vital well of water had been dug. Lieutenant Colonel Marzana, one of Bolivia's finest *jefes*,[19] commanded 28 officers and 683 men equipped with 13 machine guns, 27 automatic rifles, 3 pieces of

aged artillery, and 2 new antiaircraft guns. The men were veterans
of nearly two years in the Chaco, and the officers were mostly
professionals. The night of 8 September they gathered around
fires, chewed coca leaves, and discussed the great masses of Guaraní troops whose arrival had been heralded by their chatter and
the rumble of trucks. The tropically fragrant night was pierced
by the hungry howls of Chaco foxes.[20]

On 9 September the enthusiastic, inexperienced young Paraguayan army disturbed the silence of dawn with "¡Viva el Paraguay!" The 2nd Cavalry, starting off toward the Yucra road,
skirted the woods, met the deadly spew of Bolivian machine guns,
and was forced to cut through the brush. At 0530 the artillery began firing, relying for orientation solely on Florentín's memory.
The 2nd and 4th Infantry then advanced frontally without exact
knowledge of the enemy's location, and were detained. Fernández
rode fearlessly along the lines, encouraging his men, but the hasty
creation of the army quickly revealed itself. While it possessed
the material means to pulverize Boquerón, it lacked the essential
experienced leadership. The 2nd and 3rd Infantry virtually collapsed after initial repulses—the officers inexperienced and weak,
the men demoralized and devoid of discipline in the use of their
scarce water rations. The 2nd Cavalry, when it finally reached
the Yucra road, acted indecisively and returned for water for man
and beast. The 4th Infantry suffered heavy losses as it hurled
itself against the strong defenses. By nightfall the *fortín* remained
solidly defiant, the attackers chastised and beaten. As darkness
fell the Bolivians smoked Paraguayan cigars, drank maté, and ate
biscuits taken from the dead.[21]

The lessons of the day were explicit and foretold the character
of the entire war. *Water* was a vital factor. For the attacker, there
was none west of Isla Poí whence requirements had to be hauled
by truck or cart. If the undisciplined troops were thirsty, they
abandoned the front lines and went in search of refreshment,
attacking the tank trucks to sate their longings. It was obvious
that lack of water could of itself destroy an army in the Chaco. As
in the World War, *defense,* when field fortifications contained
the fire power of numerous automatic weapons, was vastly superi-
or to frontal assault. Small, well situated forces could contain

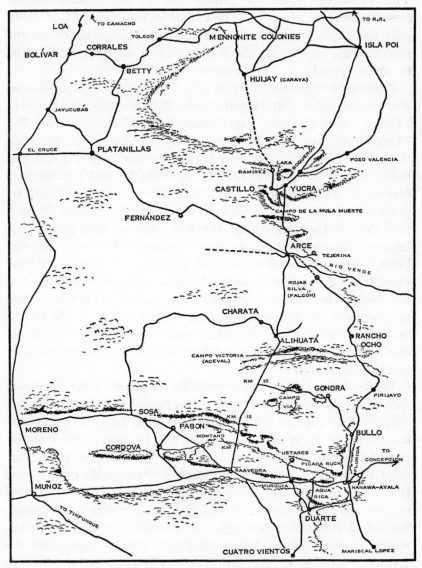

MAIN THEATRE OF OPERATIONS, 1932-1933

attacking armies. *Terrain* had to be intimately known beforehand. This knowledge could be gained only by heavy patrolling or close aerial reconnaissance. The extent to which motorized *transport* was available would be the limiting logistic factor on the size of forces which could be maintained in the field, and on the flexibility possible in their employment.[22]

Prisoners interrogated on that first day confirmed the erroneous Paraguayan belief that Marzana had 1,200 men, and the Bolivian I Corps a total of 5,000. Regrouping, Fernández ordered the 2nd "Toledo" Cavalry to occupy Yucra. On 10 September, however, the unit advised that its horses lacked water and it could not move. Fernández asserted that water could be had 7 kilometers forward at Yucra if only it would fulfill the mission. These reports were relayed to Estigarribia, who made the painful decision that the cavalry horses must die from lack of feed and water, because transport was not adequate to provide for both man and beast. Later reports falsely alleged Yucra taken; other data indicated the enemy was evacuating. Unfortunately, this got onto the telegraph system, which not only connected *fortines* but also went to Asunción. As a result, the Press Office reported the fall of Boquerón, although by nightfall attacks had to be called off due to the continuing disorganization in the 2nd and 3rd Infantry and the 2nd Cavalry.[23]

While the attacking Paraguayan 1st Division, with the exception of the 4th Infantry, continued to flounder before the hearty defense of Boquerón, the Bolivian command failed to appreciate the size or strength of the assailants. On 10 September, Peña reported from his 4th Division command post (CP) at Yucra that the Guaraní were disastrously defeated. Quintanilla embellished this report with the allegation that Estigarribia was a suicide, and ordered energetic pursuit to Isla Poí. Largely due to underestimation of Paraguayan strength, the Bolivian command then impatiently employed its forces piecemeal. On 10 September the Lairana battalion of the 14th Infantry left Yucra by truck to clear the road, and was annihilated, but Captain Tomás Manchego of Vanguardia fame entered Boquerón with a company. On 11 September the Montalvo battalion and the legendary Captain Víctor Ustares[24] were sent into the *fortin*. The next day Ustares came out on patrol supporting Peñaranda's detachment, and was killed. The latter unit was employed in three small columns, two of which moved from Ramírez and Lara, while Moscoso advanced from Yucra with 100 men. Although involving 2,700 men and tank support, all these scattered endeavors failed owing to lack of coordination and vigor. Peña advised Quintanilla on 16 September that the *fortín* had no food or ammunition and recommended retreat to defensive positions at Arce with screening forces on a line from Castillo to Yucra. A diplomatic effort should be made to "save the Marzana detachment and to complete our preparation."[25]

Having withstood the weak relief efforts, the Guaraní command resolved to launch a fresh frontal attack on Boquerón. The 2nd Division under Major Gaudioso Núñez had taken over the western portion of the perimeter, and the 6th "Boquerón" Infantry had also come up. The latter, reinforced to 1,800 men, was staffed by cadets and faculty of the Escuela Militar and led by Major Arturo Bray, a scholarly and brilliant officer with exceptional command ability, who had fought with the British in the World War. Total forces of 7,565 were available with artillery, the decisive Stokes-Brandt mortars, and the Air Group (pursuit squadron and reconnaissance bomber squadron) under Lieutenant Colonel Almonacid, an Argentine air veteran of the war in France.[26]

Inside the *fortín*, a message was received by air on 11 September from Salamanca proclaiming "on Boquerón depends the destiny of our Chaco." Unfortunately, Peña had not brought Boquerón's stores up to the 30-day level commonly maintained in Bolivian *fortines*. The besieged—Indians from all parts of Bolivia—were good, sober soldiers, but long sleepless nights had undermined their stamina. Marzana toured the positions daily, encouraging his officers and men to comply with their "destiny" of staying inside the *fortín*. On 16 September he issued a stirring proclamation appealing to their patriotism.[27]

While the battle raged, the Neutrals continued efforts to curtail the expanding hostilities. On 10 September they called for immediate cease fire and definitive arbitration. Both belligerents replied favorably, Paraguay, however, indicating that she would require security guarantees. Consequently, motivated by intense desire to halt military action immediately, the Neutrals proposed a 10 kilometer withdrawal from existing positions, virtually a complete reversal of their original stand for restoration of 1 June 1932 positions. Paraguay accepted (16 September), although she pointed out that a 10 kilometer withdrawal was geographically impracticable (due to water, as has been seen), and suggested instead 60 kilometers on each side of the 60th meridian for a period of two weeks. Thereafter, Bolivia should retire west of the 62nd meridian; Paraguay, to her river. This proposal obviously was consistent with Asunción's policy of getting Bolivia back to her 1907 status quo line.[28]

On the same day, Quintanilla transmitted Peña's request for a cease fire within 24 hours to enable evacuation of Boquerón. Salamanca had pressed General Quintanilla to sustain the *fortín* energetically and attack Isla Poí; now he authorized withdrawal if Boquerón was untenable, and informed the Neutrals that La Paz would accept immediate simple cease fire. When Paraguay refused, authority to abandon the *fortín* was restricted to a threatened disaster. Unfortunately, General Carlos Quintanilla lacked the courage to make a realistic decision, and instead supplied La Paz with falsely optimistic reports to protect a misconceived "honor" of the army. On 16 September he was still abed at noon, unable to decide whether to evacuate or to sustain the *fortín*. Fearing that the government would later hold him culpable, he resolved anew to break into Boquerón, lift the siege, and thus meet both tactical and political demands.[29]

On 17 September the planned Paraguayan attack jumped off and progressed slowly through the woods, closing in on Boquerón. Then, late in the day when the troops were tired, the Bolivian attack ordered by Quintanilla hit the rear of the 6th Infantry on the Lara road, folded up two battalions, and succeeded in reaching Marzana with eight cases of ammunition, food, and two machine guns. Estigarribia ordered the perimeter tightened on the following day, repelled new attacks by Peñaranda, and loosely sealed Marzana to his destiny; however, the troops which had entered 17 September fought their way out four days later;[30] After the failure of the 17 September attack the Guaraní also settled into a war of positions. Artillery and mortars, responsible for the bulk of Bolivian casualties, pounded the fatigued garrison. The infantry slowly dug its way by night toward the inner Bolivian lines, where the Andean Indians were subsisting on mules and scanty air-dropped food. When all the mules were gone, the bones were scraped and eaten, the hides soaked and chewed.[31]

Bolivia had replied to the Neutrals on 16 September willing to grant an immediate cease fire. This might have permitted her to retain Boquerón and to supply and strengthen it, but was intended to evacuate the garrison. Paraguay replied that her own terms were reasonable and the only ones which could avert war. The next day the Neutrals again proposed a cease fire, to be policed by them. Bolivia accepted; Paraguay reiterated her position and asked security guarantees. The Neutrals agreed that her stand and proposal were meritorious, but did not meet the need for immediate truce, for which they then appealed. Asunción, however, remained firm, obliging the Neutrals to communicate her proposal to Bolivia and recommend approval.[32]

Peña informed Quintanilla on the nineteenth that Paraguay was now waging a war of attrition which Bolivia, with only limited troops available, could not afford. With promised reinforcements marching from Villa Montes, I Corps wavered until 22 September; then, recognizing the facts, it advised La Paz that the *fortín* could not be held much longer. Salamanca had now become wholly dominant; Osorio, through an exaggerated sense of subordination to the constitutional civilian authority, had become an errand boy too timid to advise the President. Consequently, La Paz ordered continued defense, air resupply (which had already proved to be a dismal failure) , and preparations for attack on the Paraguayan right by the 3rd Division. Lacking trucks, this was impossible. Quintanilla thereupon ordered a new attempt to relieve the siege and, should it fail, authorized Peña to evacuate the garrison. A better move, had he been capable of the decision, would have been to employ his air force in an interdiction campaign. Thus inferiority on the ground could have been offset by air superiority. Paraguay's logistics could not have withstood intensive air attack. Quintanilla had no understanding of air power, however, and clung to two-dimensional strategy. On 25 September a desperate Bolivian attack from the west encountered the Paraguayan 3rd Cavalry, a fresh regiment which was just entering the lines, and failed completely. The fate of Marzana's detachment was now sealed, for the men lacked ammunition and were too exhausted to fight their way out. Further, Marzana had 150 wounded, untended for lack of medical supplies (their wounds larvae-infected by giant moths), and he would not leave them.[33]

Water was determining the course of the battle. The men, deprived of adequate liquids for over a week, began to dehydrate; their physical appearance changed, and they became mere skeletons; often they were more than a little mad. On 19 September most of the Paraguayan army abandoned the lines when water did not arrive at the usual hour due to a reorganization of the service, assigning each regiment its own vehicles. Inside Boquerón the main well came under fire and was soon contaminated with bodies.[34] The water level of the Paraguayan wells at Villa Militar was dropping alarmingly from the demands of the large army. If they went dry, transport would not be adequate to make the extra 50 kilometers from the Mennonite colonies without a large number of troops leaving the front. This would weaken the army enough for the Bolivians to raise the siege, relieve the garrison, and continue resistance indefinitely. Consequently, Estigarribia issued orders for a full-scale attack.[35]

On 22 September, La Paz replied to the Neutrals, rejecting Paraguay's last proposal on the usual grounds that her military withdrawal would leave Paraguay, with her civilian populations and developments, in control of the Chaco. If she gained such an arrangement, Asunción would be content and would avoid the final juridical settlement which Salamanca desired. The Neutrals replied to both countries with a new appeal for immediate, unconditional truce; this constituted a total reversal of their original August position and acceptance of the initial Andean proposal. Bolivia accepted, naturally, while Paraguay appended the condition of immediate total withdrawal of armies from the Chaco, reduction in forces, and submission to "international justice." Paraguay, Foreign Minister Benítez said, did not desire a mere truce, but unconditional arbitration. La Paz chose to regard this as a subterfuge, because it clearly meant arbitration of the full Paraguayan claim; this she had been unwilling to admit since the Buenos Aires Conference, because it included territory she considered indisputably Bolivian.[36]

Paraguay suffered 1,513 casualties at Boquerón, plus evacuated sick and missing probably totaling over 2,000. Her 1st and 2nd Divisions now had only 3,390, less than half the number who had so gaily begun the battle. Reinforcement, however, had actually increased total strength at Boquerón to 8,390 by 26 September. Following an artillery barrage (24 guns and 11 mortars) the troops charged and, to their surprise, were met by undiminished enemy fire, primarily because the artillery had not been concentrated. The noose tightened to within 50 meters, but Boquerón held out and even regained some lost positions in a night counterattack. Although Paraguayan infantry began to murmur against sterile frontal attacks, these tactics continued for two days; the gallant defenders remained unsubdued.[37]

A Council of Generals convened on 27 September at Muñoz attended by Osorio, Quintanilla, Julio Sanjinés (Commanding General of the Communication Zone), and the former Presidents, Generals Montes and Blanco Galindo. Grandly they resolved to hold Boquerón ten more days, using two Junker tri-motors for air resupply, meanwhile gaining time for a possible diplomatic solution leaving the *fortín* in Andean hands. Fresh troops called up on 24 September would be brought to break the siege. From an aircraft, Montes and Osorio dropped this decision to the besieged on 28 September, a noble but very empty gesture for the aged and respected Montes.[38]

The following morning Paraguay prepared to resume the attack, but Marzana's brave Bolivians had resolved the previous night to capitulate. White flags blossomed all around the perimeter. Guaraní soldiers leaped ferociously across no-man's land, only to extend their hands in brotherly greeting when they saw the emaciated, suffering men in the trenches. They offered their food and medical kits to the vanquished, as all alike fraternized in extreme joy that the bloody battle of Boquerón was ended. Lieutenant Colonel Manuel Marzana surrendered but 240 ablebodied men![39]

Boquerón was the first decisive battle of the Chaco War, giving Paraguay an enormous psychological advantage. The vanquishment of approximately 4,000 Bolivians by twice as many Paraguayans demonstrated that the Guaraní, through numerical and material superiority, had gained the complete domination of the campaign. Their army, poorly trained but better equipped and with thrice the firepower, had defeated the cream of Bolivia's forces, and in the experience had changed from raw country boys to veteran troops. Their Stokes-Brandt mortars were the surprise of the battle—the tactically decisive weapon—while the automatic rifle was proved for firepower in the brush. Great optimism swept over Paraguay, replacing a previous resignation to a heroic, last-ditch defense. Inversely, Bolivian morale was shattered by the realization that "the most miserable of the small Republics of South America" had won the first battle and fielded powerful, dominant forces.[40]

Until 23 September, Marzana could have escaped to fight another day, but Boquerón was held for two reasons. For the government, it was a political commitment; for the army it was the essential forward base for advance to the Rio Paraguay, the anticipated military role in support of the political policy. Political and military prestige was deeply involved. By employing a massively superior army, Estigarribia attracted "all the forces destined for the strategic maneuvers of the invasion, liquidating them successively," and obliged the Bolivians to go on a total tactical and strategic defensive.[41]

In manpower, Bolivia suffered losses of nearly 2,000, including prisoners. With her smaller field troops, these were relatively higher than the Guaraní losses and much more difficult to replace quickly. Nevertheless, at the beginning of October 1932 each country had total forces of around 20,000, the vital difference being in their deployment. In the main theatre Bolivia had about 5,500 with 2,000 more en route, while Paraguay fielded 12,000.[42]

Crisis in the Bolivian Command

The fall of Boquerón did not bring the collapse, as many had expected, of the Salamanca government, but it shook the very foundations of the civil-military relationship on the Altiplano.

Salamanca, since the beginning of the penetration plan, had exercised an increasingly personal influence on military decisions. The constitution provided the President with the archaic post of wartime Captain General, but to assume this role he was expected to entrust the government to the Vice-President and place himself at the head of the field army. Daniel Salamanca had no knowledge of military matters, and wisely rejected the latter course; yet, although abjectly ignorant of tactical considerations, he sought to direct operations.

The manifest ineptness of the Quintanilla command convinced Salamanca of his obligation to intervene, and Osorio's subordination of General Staff functions to the President provided him an unlimited field of action. With the exception of Generals Osorio and Lanza, and Colonels Peña and Ferrufino, the President had a general contempt for the military leaders, whom he regarded —rightly in many cases—as a privileged, undisciplined caste incompetent for war. He viewed their demands for war necessities with a peacetime eye to the country's immediate ability to pay, and overlooked the fact that the Bolivian Army had always been primarily a political, not a military instrument.[43]

When news of Boquerón belatedly circulated in La Paz, the populace demonstrated against the government and command, calling loudly for the return of General Hans Kundt. To the people's just discontent, Salamanca sacrificed Osorio, assigning him as Commanding General of the Second Army Corps (II Corps) created from the 3rd and 5th Divisions. General José Leonardo Lanza was summoned to La Paz as interim Chief of the General Staff, pending the arrival of Kundt, whose recall was voted 30 to 26 in a stormy secret session of Congress. When notified, Quintanilla retorted that neither Kundt nor anyone else could compensate for lack of troops, arms, munitions, transport, and general organization. Kundt's recall expressed lack of confidence in the national command, he lamented, echoing those who felt reliance on a mercenary leader indicated (correctly) that Bolivia was a people disorganized![44]

Quintanilla's Chief of Staff was Lieutenant Colonel David Toro, a leader among the "political" officers, an opportunist, and an allegedly brilliant but corrupt rogue who had been exiled (along

with Kundt) by the 1930 Junta for his support of the Siles government in which he served. Ever ready to arrogate "speaking
for the army," Toro persuaded Quintanilla, who had succumbed
to deep depression, to circulate a petition in I Corps. Although
Peña and officers on the front accorded it little support, the I
Corps command, in a startlingly insubordinate document (8 October), claimed that the entire combat army knew responsibility
for the defeat lay squarely with the government for accepting war
without preparation. Salamanca had obliged the army to initiate
hasty operations for domestic political ends. The President had
assumed direction of operations at the expense of the army, and
now offended it gravely by removing Osorio. The army, however,
would continue to recognize only Osorio, the document announced.[45]

Salamanca retorted (9 October) that Osorio had been removed
with popular approval and his own consent. The actions of the
I Corps command had the character of treason in the face of a
foreign enemy and should be contemplated. Quintanilla was
ordered to report to La Paz immediately. Frightened, he attempted
to retreat and save himself by saying (10 October) that all was
now normal and the wishes of the government would be obeyed;
the President, however, rightly insisted on his removal, entrusting
I Corps to Colonel Francisco Peña.[46]

The Paraguayan Offensive

Shortage of transport, the water problem, ignorance of terrain
due to deficient aerial reconnaissance, an exaggerated estimate
of Bolivian I Corps strength, and Paraguay's paltry resources had
dictated that Estigarribia follow a cautious policy. Paraguay, in
light of her very limited financial capacity, could have replaced
only with extreme difficulty the arms losses which would have
accompanied a defeat. Consequently, Estigarribia during and after
Boquerón avoided "agile maneuvers" and exercised "extreme
operative prudence." He lacked the trucks to haul water to forces
beyond Boquerón, and therefore had been limited to that *fortín*
until its fall made available a new water supply. Meanwhile, his
army was trained on the field of battle, acquiring the capacity to

win the entire Chaco; Colonel Estigarribia's rejection of "strategic speculations of doubtful realization" possibly saved it for its greater purpose.[47]

On 6 October, Paraguay informed the Neutrals that she applied unconditional arbitration to the boundary question, not a fixed zone. She contended that only a matter of borders, and not the Chaco Boreal, was at issue. Thus she sought to deny Bolivia the right to lay claim to the whole Chaco. Her own claimed boundary was the "natural limits"—the Jaurú-Parepetí line. Three days later Bolivia expressed concern over Neutral efforts at arbitration at the very moment Paraguay was launching a general offensive. She accused Asunción of perennially exaggerating the size of the disputed area in hopes of acquiring all the truly controversial zone in a settlement. Since the Chiquitos missions had extended south to 21° 30′, La Paz could admit no area north of the Rio Apa to contention, and considered the headwaters of the Rio Verde at 59° 50′ an appropriate western limit for the arbitration zone.[48]

On 8 October began the incredibly slow advance through the jungle toward Arce of the reorganized 9,200-man Paraguayan I Corps. Marching along with the 1st and 2nd Divisions was a new 4th Division (6th and 7th Infantry, 3rd Cavalry) under Lieutenant Colonel Nicolás Delgado, another French War College graduate. Intense thunder and lightning ruptured the night, heralding the rainy season and warning the Guaraní to hasten. The Bolivian 4th Division's defenses, however, hindered the progress of the vastly superior, but cautiously employed Paraguayans. Estigarribia still overestimated the enemy, hesitated to charge into unknown terrain, and was deeply concerned with logistic problems. On 11 October, after directing the 1st Engineers to construct an all-weather road from Boquerón, he issued orders for an envelopment to reach the enemy rear at Kilometer 11 of the Arce-Yucra road. Peñaranda (who had taken command of the 4th Division when Peña acquired I Corps) retreated by night to save his forces. Quintanilla's alleged decision, made before his removal, to resist at Yucra prevented the preparation of strong defenses at Arce such as Salamanca now suggested. Unfortunately, Peña, who had previously preferred an elastic defense, acquired Quintanilla's addiction for ground and specified that "every foot of terrain between Yucra and Arce must be strongly contested."[49]

Insubordination, which Toro and Quintanilla had set in motion among officers, spread rapidly to the fatigued Andean troops, deteriorating their faith in the *jefes*. Defeated, poorly supplied, and even lacking a mail service, the Bolivian soldiers were easily demoralized. Fresh units coming up from the rear contained defeatists. Consequently, although Peñaranda brought up artillery and believed he could defend Campo de la Mula Muerta, Paraguayan attacks easily panicked the newly arrived regiments. Late on 21 October, in the face of a threatened flanking move, the 3rd, 15th, 20th, and 35th Infantry broke and fled. Of over 3,000 men, only the veteran regiments held ("Loa," "Campero," and 16th Infantry, and 5th "Lanza" Cavalry), and they were too few. Peñaranda ordered retreat, fired Arce, and continued south to Alihuatá. On the same day, Peña issued Top Secret orders for a four-stage retreat, in case of necessity, to a line through Magariños—Ballivián and northward.[50]

In La Paz the problem of supreme direction continued. Lanza queried Salamanca (19 October) as to whether the army might initiate offensive operations on its own without presidential direction. The approaching rainy season presumably would halt activity and necessitate more and better transport. Like other *jefes*, Lanza stressed the need for general mobilization. Salamanca replied that offense or defense would depend upon military possibilities; he himself did not wish to direct operations. "The final and only objective of Bolivia in her long contention with Paraguay," he reiterated, "is the revindication of the Chaco, or of the greatest possible portion of this territory, including that of a coast on the Rio Paraguay."[51]

Realization of that objective received a severe blow on 23 October 1932 when the Paraguayan army entered flaming Arce, Estigarribia's initial goal. Apparently, the Guaraní commander had not anticipated such an easy triumph and, still troubled with transport for the rainy season, he tarried overlong at the headwaters of the Rio Verde, enabling Peñaranda to break off contact and save his command.[52]

At Alihuatá, Peñaranda courageously attempted to restore the spirit of his defeated 4th Division. He had planned to retreat his loyal forces to Fortín Fernández, but Guaraní patrols cut the road, obliging all to move southward. After ordering food prepared, he convened the officers, challenged their patriotism, and announced his determination to die rather than return in shame to the Altiplano. "Who will accompany me? One step forward! Adjutant, take note!" Eighteen volunteered; then others, seeing the aide writing names, also came, raising the total number to seventy-two. The commander thereupon formed the troops, directed the bands to play the national anthem, and gave a stirring address. Only 300 responded, making a total along with the loyal regiments of but 1,008 men willing to fight! "I wished to execute the traitors on the spot," Peñaranda later wrote, "but with a handful against 3,000 determined, armed men, it was not possible."[53]

Meanwhile (12 October) the Neutrals proposed that the belligerents sign an accord providing for separation of troops, demobilization, and reductions in force. United States Minister Feely reported from La Paz that General Montes upon his return from the Chaco had told Congress in a secret session that the country was entirely unprepared for war, and that her Chaco army was in appalling condition. From this the Minister concluded that the Altiplano would welcome a coerced peace to extricate it from difficulties, although official protests would be vehement.[54]

Saavedra Lamas, probably working to restore Argentina's international prestige in order to further the domestic position of the Justo government, grew increasingly active in his efforts to assert Buenos Aires' priority of action in the Chaco question. Submitting a sharp blow to the wallowing Neutrals, Argentina advised (18 October) that she would not support any action beyond mere good offices and moral influence. At the same time Saavedra Lamas was urging Paraguay to sever connections with the Neutrals. Success for any fresh effort by Buenos Aires was dimmed, however, by widely publicized Bolivian allegations stemming from the equipment *"debajo del poncho"* which Rivarola had obtained from the Argentine arsenals. President Ayala scornfully dismissed these charges, saying that Bolivia, unwilling to admit her despised opponent was better armed, sought to blame defeats on the "injustice" of alleged Argentine aid to Paraguay. Consequently, La Paz remained highly unamenable to mediation from Buenos Aires.[55]

Along with Paraguay, Bolivia accepted a Neutral proposal for talks in Washington between Juan José Soler and Enrique Finot. Immediately a snag was encountered (27 October) when Soler, directly reflecting Paraguay's military success, made any agreement conditional upon an indemnity and compensation for families of the Guaraní dead and maimed. To entreaties to remove the demand, Soler replied (1 November) that Paraguay wished a peace, not a truce. While the Bolivian army occupied any part of the Chaco, peace was impossible. Although victorious in the war she had not provoked, Paraguay still desired to submit the boundary question to an arbitrator's decision.[56]

The Bolivian General Staff, meanwhile, proposed a strategic retreat by stages, as planned by Lieutenant Colonel Felipe Rivera Lino, to a firm line from Camacho through Tres Pozos and Conchitas to Ballivián. An offensive would then be prepared from Camacho, northern terminus of the line. This strategy closely followed the prewar operations plans of Colonel Rodríguez aimed at luring the enemy to Ballivián by a Fabian retreat, whereupon his right would be enveloped. Salamanca nevertheless ordered a tenacious resistance at Muñoz and Platanillos, strong reinforcement of Ballivián, and preparations to retreat the 7th Division to Saavedra. He endorsed the build-up of a new 8th Division for offensive action, and assigned General Arturo Guillén (27 October) as Commander of I Corps. Two days before, the 4th Division abandoned Alihuatá when Paraguayan patrols, who roamed the Chaco forests "*como Pedro en su casa,*" threatened their escape. Now the Guaraní 2nd Division moved in, and on 30 October the 1st Division occupied Fortín Fernández.[57]

Bolivia promptly informed the Neutrals (4 November) that she was willing to withdraw to Vargas-Madrejón-Camacho-Platanillos-Muñoz-Esteros (the retreat line of the Rivera plan as modified by Salamanca) if Paraguayan troops withdrew a proportionate distance. Bolivia, however, would not reduce her armed forces; to require her to do so would be sacrificial to the national dignity and sovereignty.

The same day, Wheeler reported from Asunción that popular demand was very strong for breaking off with the Neutrals.

Ayala has been hampering military advances so far as he is able, aware that the more reverses Bolivia suffers, the more difficult it will be for her to recede from her position, but this Government has reached the point where it must either negotiate or go forward.

The Argentine Minister reported that war fever was high in Paraguay. Since everything focused on war, all enterprises except agriculture had halted. Victory had so exalted the army that no government could oppose its bellicose propositions. Feely advised from La Paz that a March offensive was being planned but, considering finances, he could not see how the present Andean army could be maintained so long.[58]

Guillén informed Salamanca that I Corps lacked "everything." Argentina had closed the Pilcomayo before adequate supplies had been obtained for the rainy season. There was a shortage of trucks, and the human element—poorly trained, demoralized, incompetently-officered reservists—was not combat-worthy. Salamanca replied that an honorable peace could not be obtained at the moment. He charged poor morale to fundamental military errors at Boquerón and Quintanilla's treason before the enemy. Guillén responded that there was no grave lack of discipline in I Corps, and reinforcements would improve the sombre situation.[59]

Estigarribia had been concerned for some time for his right. Although Toledo had been recaptured (27 September), he feared Lanza would bring the 3rd Division down from the north and pounce upon the exposed Paraguayan flank. Unaware at the time of the road between Camacho and Carandaití, he resolved to take Platanillos, secure his right, and cut off all Andean forces between Pitiantuta and Jayucubás. Although he estimated these at about 1,000, they were actually very few: the 1st "Colorado" Infantry with a mere 342 men! An additional purpose was to confuse the enemy as to the line of advance of Estigarribia's principal mass. All available trucks (44) were mustered, and on 6 November the Paraguayan 1st Division captured Platanillos. The 1st Cavalry, moving west from Toledo on a converging axis, completed the mopping up of Loa, Corrales, Bolívar, and Jayucubás on 8 November, concluding the sweep of the first Paraguayan offensive.[60]

Before he departed the Chaco, Colonel Franciso Peña, recognizing the technical limitations of Peñaranda, provided him with a divisional Chief of Staff able to compensate for his deficiencies. Lieutenant Colonel Bernardino Bilbao Rioja, the Air Force Chief and possibly the best major commander Bolivia had in the Chaco War, developed with Peña a plan for a defense line at Kilometer 7 of the Saavedra-Alihuatá road. Bilbao then began restoring morale by marching south from Alihuatá (25 October) with the remnant of the 4th Division. At Kilometer 7 he set his men to work digging in with bayonets and mess plates. The long Bolivian retreat had ended.[61]

Peñaranda at this point went on leave, placing Bilbao in command of about 900 men. With Major Jordán, creator of the defenses at Boquerón, he initiated entrenchment along the edge of the woods. From this advantageous position an excellent field of fire stretched across a grassy prairie. The usual treetop machine gun nests were erected. To the rear, adequate roads assured supply or retreat. Gradually reinforcements were received. On 2 November, Bilbao enlightened his 1,500 troops (with whom he conversed daily) on the probable nature of the enemy attack. He cautioned against treachery—ambushes in the brush, Guaraní in Bolivian uniforms, or shouting "¡Viva Bolivia!" to confuse—and against wasting ammunition. While the enemy fire was dense, it was commonly high. Paraguayan tactics usually involved flanking through the woods under cover of secondary frontal attacks. His officers, Bilbao cautioned, must indoctrinate their men on the true capability of artillery and mortars; in the past these had terrified Andean forces. With preparations such as these (and machine guns at his rear to guarantee that his men did not flee), Bilbao prepared a surprise for the Guaraní.[62]

When Peñaranda retreated south, the Paraguayan 2nd Division had been ordered to conduct an energetic pursuit. The Nanawa detachment, which until then had kept the Bolivian 7th Division occupied through incessant feints against Agua Rica and Murguía, was directed to cut the fleeing 4th Division's rear. Unable to comply en masse due to terrain and the water situation, it had pushed a cavalry patrol across Kilometer 22 of the Alihuatá-Saavedra road on 24 October, deciding Peñaranda to abandon the former. Lieutenant Colonel Luis Irrazábal, commanding at Nanawa, thereupon recommended a prompt, concerted drive on Saavedra, but Estigarribia was already committed to the Platanillos operation and therefore declined to use his strategic reserve, the 4th Division, at Arce. As a result, the slow advance of the 2nd Division gave Bilbao time to prepare his defenses.[63]

Lieutenant Colonel Fernández, the 1st Division's able commander, proposed to strike directly at Muñoz from Platanillos and destroy the Andean army by strategically enveloping the Bolivian 4th and 7th Divisions. Guillén greatly feared such a maneuver, advising La Paz that in its way stood only a few demoralized troops at Puesto Moreno. Since Muñoz was untenable, retreat would be necessary to Ballivián. Although Fernández' plan would therefore doubtless have succeeded, it was unwise in the light of available intelligence and transport, and Estigarribia refused. He ordered the 1st Division back to Arce for much needed rest and rehabilitation, having decided to reconcentrate his forces for a frontal approach to what he now considered the main Bolivian threat, Saavedra.[64]

The 3rd "Corrales" Infantry, after a cautious advance, pushed back Bilbao's outposts at Kilometer 12 on the afternoon of 6 November and, confidence high, mounted an attack the following day. Bilbao's forces withstood their test. A new effort to envelop the Bolivian right on the eighth was frustrated by Andean artillery. The following day the attackers were reinforced with the 1st Infantry. Bilbao wished to counterattack, but Guillén withheld approval until reinforcements arrived on 10 November, giving the 4th Division 3,500 men with 6 aircraft for close support. When the Andeans attempted to turn the enemy right, they encountered the newly arrived Guaraní 2nd Infantry, and were halted in bloody fighting. Bilbao captured numerous arms, but suffered 317 casualties against 139 for Paraguay. He wished to launch new attacks, but Guillén refused, giving the Guaraní time to dig in and relieve exhausted troops. Nevertheless, for Bolivia 10 November 1932 was a memorable and victorious day, because the Paraguayan threat was temporarily neutralized and the front stabilized (although as much from overextension of supply lines as from Andean resistance). Confidence in themselves coursed through the veins of the Altiplano army. "They shall not pass!" Bilbao dynamically informed his command.[65]

Estigarribia reacted by replacing the 2nd with the fresh 4th Division and ordering his crack 1st Division to prepare to march. The new 5th Division at Nanawa was directed to redouble its attacks. On 24 November, La Paz correctly advised I Corps that Paraguay's probable intentions were to strike Saavedra from the north and the south, flank Kilometer 7 to cut the Muñoz road, trap the 4th and 7th Divisions, and then converge for a grand drive on Muñoz. Salamanca therefore suggested that the 7th Division be pulled back to Saavedra. Estigarribia, after attacks failed on 16 and 19 November, was obliged for logistical reasons to re-concentrate his forces, but he prepared for all-out attack before the rainy season would halt operations.[66]

This was a perfect concession to the desires of General Lanza, whose strategy was to attract the Paraguayan army to the Saavedra sector, then launch an offensive with II Corps (3rd and 8th Divisions) against its lightly held right. Platanillos was the first objective. The II Corps would continue toward Toledo, I Corps would then flank Kilometer 7 and advance on Arce-Boquerón, while a new III Corps struck Bahia Negra-Olimpo. Unfortunately, while the tactical success of Bilbao facilitated this strategy, I Corps perverted the plan by calling for more and more reinforcements until the opposing armies were drawn into Kilometer 7 and neutralized. Quite probably, knowledge that Lanza was only an interim Chief (pending the return of Kundt) weakened his authority, especially over I Corps where Toro, his personal foe since the 1930 revolution, remained formidable as Chief of Staff.[67]

After patrols found water available toward the Muñoz road, and adequate supplies were accumulated, Estigarribia issued orders for a turning of the Bolivian left by the reinforced 1st Division. It was assumed that the road lay 12 kilometers distant, across the largely open terrain of the *cañadón*.[68] Once the Muñoz road was reached, the flanking forces would attack Saavedra in cooperation with the 5th Division (moving from the southeast) and the 4th Division, which would strike Kilometer 7 frontally.

The night of 30 November the 1st Division moved out. Unfortunately, the guides failed to arrive, some units reported late, thorny bushes impeded progress, and the van became disoriented while hacking its way through an island of trees. Decisively, Paraguayan knowledge of the terrain was deficient; the Muñoz road had been confused with that to Puesto Sosa.[69]

When dawn came, Fernández turned his 3,700 men southeast, realizing that discovery was imminent and hoping at least to take Kilometer 7 from the rear. Instead, artillery which Bilbao had sagaciously placed on the Bolivian left at Puesto Montaño ended the Paraguayan maneuver. The Andeans, having anticipated the Guaraní move for two weeks, had reinforced their flank. Fernández asked aerial reconnaissance, but the lone Paraguayan Potez was shot down by the dominant Bolivian Air Force. Fresh assaults on 7 December failed, as did a 5th Division attack on Cuatro Vientos. Peñaranda (who had reassumed command of the Andean 4th Division on 29 November) employed strong air support and the Tank Group, and contemplated a flanking movement of his own to cut off the Paraguayan I Corps from Alihuatá. Furious Guaraní attacks, lack of troops, and profuse rains conspired, however, to prevent broad Bolivian maneuvers.[70]

At Platanillos the Bolivian 8th Division (General Julio Sanjinés) moved up on 12 December and attacked the next day. Estigarribia, well informed of the enemy intentions, had garrisoned the *fortín* with his 1st Cavalry (about 700) and ordered firm defense. However, when the 2,000 Bolivians struck, the 3rd squadron deserted its positions, thus admitting the assailant to the *fortín*. Defense collapsed, although the commander reorganized on the Fernández road. As Sanjinés had in fact endeavored to surround the garrison, its flight perhaps saved it from total destruction.[71]

In view of the extreme battle fatigue and illness prevalent in his poorly fed army, the aggravation of logistic difficulties by the torrential rains, the uselessness of further frontal attacks against the now firm Bolivian 4th Division defenses, and the renewed threat to his right posed by Sanjinés' success at Platanillos, Estigarribia bowed to the inevitable and officially determined on 14 December to revert to the defensive. Major Caballero Irala's

1st Engineers were brought to Kilometer 7 to dig wells and construct the heavy fortifications which signified security at the cost of ability to attack readily.[72]

The Neutrals' Defeat

Since the outbreak of hostilities, each side had accused the other of atrocities, maltreatment of prisoners, bombing of hospitals, and similar practices. Bolivia was especially vociferous in alleging Guaraní savagery and inhumanity to prisoners, but careful study of all the sources relating to the war indicates that neither side had a monopoly on virtue. Flagrant incidents could probably be charged to individuals acting on their own against the express desires of higher echelons. Bolivia missed an excellent chance to secure written agreement on war practices when Paraguay submitted a draft treaty through the Neutrals on the care of prisoners of war. When La Paz rejected it because it would have required each state to pay the expense of its captured nationals, the usual polemic developed which, predictably enough, deteriorated into a discussion of the *uti possidetis* of 1810 and the status quo of 1907! The prisoners were left to fate.[73]

By December the Neutrals understood that Paraguay insisted, as a requisite to a cease fire, on demilitarization to guarantee that Bolivia would not again strike her. Bolivia would not demobilize unless the Chaco question was settled definitively, and she would accept only a very limited territorial arbitration; Paraguay now voiced approval solely for an equally limited boundary arbitration. Consequently, the Neutrals made a maximum effort and brought forth their final compromise proposal to halt hostilities.[74]

The Neutral plan, presented formally on 15 December, endeavored to meet the desires of both States, end hostilities, and solve the Chaco issue. It called for a convention stipulating cessation of hostilities within 48 hours; ratification "in the form in which it is written" within 30 days; and rapid withdrawal of troops within 48 hours of ratification—Paraguay to the river, Bolivia to a line from Vitriones to Ballivián. Reserve forces would then be demobilized. A neutral commission would supervise execution of the peace. One hundred Paraguayans would police the Chaco east of the Bolivian withdrawal line and 60° 15'; one hundred Bolivians would police west of 60° 15' and beyond the line. Negotiations for arbitration would begin 15 days after ratification and, if unsuccessful within 3 months, experts named by the American Geographic Society, Royal Geographic Society, and Sociedad Geográfica de Madrid would "define the area of the Chaco," which would then be submitted to arbitration.[75]

In preliminary soundings, it was palpably evident that Ayala could not accept a proposal which left half the Chaco in Andean control while his own victorious army withdrew to the Rio Paraguay. The success of Estigarribia's concept, defense inland, had forever obviated Paraguayan willingness to arbitrate more than the boundary or to withdraw an inch so long as Bolivians remained in the Chaco. The Neutral plan, Asunción felt, left Bolivia in an advantageous strategic position to reorganize for a fresh drive. From experience skeptical of Neutral ability to restrain La Paz, whose honesty and good intentions were equally suspect, Paraguay reposed her confidence in a victorious, albeit halted, army. The Neutral line was approximately the retreat line proposed by Colonel Rivera from which Bolivia planned to launch a new offensive. It did not gain what Paraguay had always and consistently desired—Bolivian withdrawal behind the 1907 status quo line—and left the policing of the western end of the Hayes Zone (as Asunción interpreted it) to Bolivia.[76]

Feely had informed Stimson that Bolivian acceptance of the line was at best "a remote possibility," but delimitation of the Chaco by experts would be wholly unacceptable, as it was incompatible with the Bolivian insistence on a previously defined arbitration zone. La Paz intimated she might be willing to go back 45 years and resurrect the Aceval-Tamayo treaty![77]

Although the Neutral proposal was wholeheartedly supported by nineteen American republics, Paraguay remained determinedly opposed. Withdrawing from Washington, Soler stated that the Neutrals had been impotent to contain Bolivian aggression. Consequently, Paraguay had been obliged to launch an offensive and expel the invader from her *fortines*, removing his threat to her civilian Chaco enterprises. She could not accept any truce which left the enemy capable of again disturbing the peace. A few days later, Foreign Minister Benítez reiterated his country's view that the proposal left Bolivia in a superior strategic position. He demanded guaranteed security for the River republic.

The Neutrals insisted that their plan had been misinterpreted and callously pointed out, ignoring military reality, that in August Paraguay would have been satisfied with restoration of the 1 June status quo. Guaraní departure from Washington could be taken only as intent "to continue the war and confide the future of your situation to the chance of arms"—a chance which at the moment had given better results in obtaining Paraguayan desires than had four years of the Neutrals![78]

Bolivia informed the Neutrals that she already accepted most of the plan and considered it a suitable basis for talks. Knowing the Paraguayan attitude, it seemed useless to examine it further.[79]

Faced with only tentative Bolivian acceptance and Paraguayan rejection, the Neutrals were forced to capitulate as the major international group working to solve the Chaco question. Their failure signaled the effective end of efforts to "prevent war" as compared to securing a peace. On 30 December 1932 the Neutrals admitted defeat and wired the ABCP powers—Argentina, Brazil, Chile, and Peru—to learn what steps they were prepared to take to end armed conflict in the Americas.[80]

Notes

1. Estigarribia, 15-16, 23; Fernández, I, 49, 63; J. B. Ayala, 66, 73-75, 105; Rios, 109, 113. Estigarribia was Paraguay's military man of destiny. Born on 21 February 1888 at Caraguatay, he was of humble rural origin and intended to be a farmer. Caught up in the revolutionary turmoil of the early twentieth century, he entered the army. A short, quiet, unassuming man, he was the antithesis of a Latin *caudillo* in his simple field uniform with the sleeves invariably too short. Disciplined and patient, his great attribute was the ability to analyze realistically all aspects of the broad situation, and then pyramid tactical decisions into strategic and political triumphs. Exercising a complete seniorial domination over his associates, he was able to maintain effective discipline of an army composed of one of the most anarchi-

cally individualistic peoples in the world. The incomparable military genius of the Chaco War, he was Paraguay's greatest soldier. See Efraím Cardozo, *Tres Héroes;* Justo Pastor Benítez, *Estigarribia. El soldado del Chaco,* 1st ed. (Buenos Aires, 1943), 11-41; 2d ed. (1958), 34-45.

2. J. B. Ayala, 54-59, 71-72.

3. Estigarribia, 23-28; Fernández, I, 111; J. B. Ayala, 97-100, 107-110; Benítez, *Estigarribia,* 1st ed., 49-50.

4. Estigarribia, 29, 32-33; Fernández, I, 41, 110; J. B. Ayala, 63; Rios, 239.

5. Estigarribia, 34-35, quotation, 36; J. B. Ayala, 76; Fernández, I, 100-101; Florentín, *Boquerón,* 151-153.

6. Estigarribia, 37-39, quotation, 37, 39.

7. *Ibid.,* 40-41.

8. Arze Quiroga, I, 333-341; Vergara Vicuña, II, 21-34; Rodríguez' text of this document (41-53) says 12,000 men for the 3rd Division. Ayala Moreira (142), who was in G-2 at the time, says Plan # 3 did *not* exist in the General Staff until August. Implicitly, therefore, it was only prepared for use against Salamanca in case of defeat.

9. Rodríguez, 68-71; Toro, 19; Vergara Vicuña, II, 47-50. Angel Rodríguez was a former professor of topography at the Colegio Militar, and military attaché to Brazil. He had been a Lieutenant Colonel since 1923, when he was 24 years of age; Díaz Arguedas, *El hombre símbolo,* 332-333.

10. Rodríguez, 80-81, 99-100; Vergara Vicuña, II, 2-7. Lack of roads rendered Salamanca's strategy ridiculous; J. B. Ayala, 70.

11. Arze Quiroga, I, 343-351; Rodríguez, 78; Vergara Vicuña, II, 39, 51, 55-56; Ovidio Urioste, *La Encrucijada,* 4-13. Salamanca's attitude was that once a place was occupied, it must never be relinquished. Loss of Pitiantuta (and later Huijay) convinced him that the command and General Staff were incompetent.

12. Ayala Moreira, 46, 138-139; Moscoso, 101; Rios, 14-16; Major Alberto Taborga T., *Boquerón* (La Paz, 1956), 23; Arze Quiroga, II, 235; *New York Times,* 8 August 1932, 9; Rodríguez, 15, 19-20; J. B. Ayala, 32; Vergara Vicuña, *Bernardino Bilbao Rioja* (La Paz, 1948), 200-201, 205; Urioste, *La Encrucijada,* 30; Lieutenant Colonel Julio C. Guerrero, *La guerra en el Chaco* (Lima, 1934), 71.

13. Arze Quiroga, II, 97-105, 137; Fernández, I, 108-119; Vergara Vicuña, I, 103-105, 115-122, 136, 150-161, 166, 168, and II, 71-78; *Política Argentina,* I, 408; *Partes del conductor,* 10-12; Díaz Arguedas, *El hombre símbolo,* 15, 24-25; *Los Elegidos,* 51-54; Urioste, *La Encrucijada,* 24; Ayala Moreira, 149-150.

14. Vergara Vicuña, I, 143-145; Guerrero, 115-116.

15. Fernández, I, 100, 115; Colonel Enrique Vidaurre, *El material de guerra en la campaña del Chaco* (La Paz, 1942), 3; González, 17,

36-37, 43-45; Rios, 127, 163, 246-247. Strength and arms figures vary. Manpower is based on Fernández, arms on Rios, since these seem to be the most accurate. Note also J. B. Ayala, 62-64, who places 1st and 2nd Division strength on 9 September at 8,720 (pp. 81, 85).

16. Rios, 159; Benítez, *Bajo el signo*, 18; Arze Quiroga, II, 9. Bolivia employed 3 medium and 2 light tanks in the Chaco, but possessed 12 machines. Vidaurre, *Material de guerra*, 291; Rivarola, II, 282.

Bolivian interest in air power began with 1913 experiments with a Bleriot aircraft. In 1916 Congress authorized a school of military aviation, but not until 1920 was the law implemented. In that year a Curtis Wasp was assembled at La Paz under the direction of Donald Hudson, a Curtis "tech rep," who was rewarded with a Lieutenant Colonelcy and the post of Chief Pilot of the nascent Air Force. The four pilots included Lieutenant Bernardino Bilbao Rioja, a 1918 graduate of the Chilean flying school. Hudson's Bolivian career was short, ending in a crash 19 May 1920. The suspicious, xenophobic Bolivians believed that under the pay of foreigners "jealous" of Bolivia, he had deliberately crashed! Other planes followed and finally in 1925 the School of Military Aviation actually got under way with Hans Haeverly of Switzerland as chief instructor and Major Bilbao Rioja as Commandant. In 1927 Jimmy Doolittle flew a Curtis into La Paz, seeking orders for the company. Flights to the Chaco began in the same year. By 1928 the Air Force possessed a Training Group and a War Group, the latter equipped with Fokker C-V and Breguet XIX recon-bombers reaching speeds of 140 MPH. Vickers "Vespa" fighters began arriving in 1929. During the war heavy reliance was placed on Curtis Hawk and Osprey aircraft. Díaz Arguedas, *Historia del Ejército*, 86-101; Vergara Vicuña, *Bilbao*, 85, 90, 110, 144-147, 164-165; C. G. Grey and Leonard Brigman, editors, *Jane's All The World's Aircraft* (London, 1928), 8 b; 1929, 3 b; 1931, 4 b.

17. Fernández, I, 93-94; Florentín, *Boquerón*, 155; Ayala Moreira, 134; J. B. Ayala, 37; Vergara Vicuña, I, 166; Guerrero, 78-91; Rios, 236, 266; Moscoso, 99; Taborga, 21; Rodríguez, 28-31, 40; *New York Times*, 28 July 1932, 9; Ovidio Urioste, *La Fragua* (n. p., n. d.), 34, 79, 106; General Nicolás Delgado, *Historia de la Guerra del Chaco* (Asunción, n.d.), I, 12; Manuel Maria Oliver, *La guerra en el Chaco Boreal* (Buenos Aires, 1935), 12, 65; Colonel Enrique Vidaurre, *El 41 de Infantry* (La Paz, 1936), 18.

18. *Partes del conductor*, 13; Estigarribia, 42; Fernández, I, 112-123, 128; Florentín, *Boquerón*, 158, 163-165, 173, 175-178; Urioste, *La Fragua*, 145; Lieutenant Colonel Basiliano Caballero Irala, *Nuestros zapadores en la Guerra del Chaco* (Montevideo, 1939), 18. The Paraguayan Press Office, following President Ayala's desire that an attack appear to be the outgrowth of Bolivian probes, reported the repulse of an enemy column moving toward Pozo Valencia.

19. The term *jefe*, used hereafter, refers to a field grade officer.

20. Arze Quiroga, II, 10; Vergara Vicuña, I, 103; Rios, 249-250; Fernández, I, 126-128; Taborga, 25, 30; Moscoso, 84.

21. Estigarribia, 43; Fernández, I, 129-143; Taborga, 31-33; Rios, 251-253; Florentín, *Boquerón*, 24, 164, 169-170, 179-186.

22. Fernández, I, 170; Florentín, *Boquerón*, 161; Rios, 267; González, 53; Delgado, I, 14.

23. Caballero Irala, 22; Fernández, I, 136, 144-149; Rios, 123; Estigarribia, 44; *Partes del conductor*, 14. Cavalry quickly proved impracticable in quantity. During Boquerón thousands of fine, irreplaceable mounts perished, and thereafter most of the cavalry on both sides fought on foot; Rios, 273-278; Florentín, *Boquerón*, 240; Captain Edmundo Nogales Ortiz, *Nuestra caballeria en la Guerra del Chaco* (La Paz, 1938), 11.

24. Ustares was Bolivia's foremost Chaco explorer, a fearless little man who roamed far and wide, becoming intimately familiar with the Chaco. He was feared by the Paraguayans, and his loss early in the war was an enormous setback for his country. Fernández, I, 173.

25. Arze Quiroga, II, 137-147, 220; Estigarribia, 45; Florentín, *Boquerón*, 188, 204; Vergara Vicuña, I, 194-198, 216-220, 231-274; II, 92-93, 95-107; Díaz Arguedas, *Los Elegidos*, 102; *Partes del conductor*, 15-16; Moscoso, 81-82, 90-93; Ayala Moreira, 159; Fernández, I, 150-184, 201-204. Manchego was killed in Boquerón and buried in the same grave with the Paraguayan officer who had captured him at Vanguardia. The latter, mortally wounded, had been recovered by Bolivians from the battlefield. On 12 September, Rivarola (II, 241) reported four camouflaged tanks had passed through Villa Montes.

26. Fernández, I, 177, 185-198; Aponte B., *Cincuenta años*, 123, 137, 214; Delgado, I, 21; Florentín, *Boquerón*, 210; Oliver, 22, 52, 90; *New York Times*, 31 July 1932, 7.

27. Taborga, 35-53; Fernández, I, 199-200; Arze Quiroga, II, 107; Moscoso, 130; Vergara Vicuña, II, 94.

28. *Libro Blanco. No Agresión*, 254-261; Bolivia, *Memoria 1934*, 120-123; *Política Argentina*, I, 411-414; U. S., *Foreign Relations*, 1932, V, 86-89. Upon the inauguration of Ayala, the intransigent Dr. Gerónimo Zubizarreta became chairman of the National Boundary Commission, which was not merely the center for title study and case preparation, but also the "drive motor of the diplomatic battle." No relaxation in Guaraní demands could be expected; Cardozo, *Tres héroes*. The Chaco question had absorbed the attention of the country's best minds for 30 years; it would continue to do so for a few more; Benítez, *Estigarribia*, 1st ed., 43; 2d ed., 26, 100.

29. Arze Quiroga, II, 6, 106, 109-112, 239, 270; Moscoso, 135; Urioste, *La Fragua*, 170; Vergara Vicuña, I, 271-276, II, 109.

30. Rios, 257-259; Vergara Vicuña, I, 265; Fernández, I, 212-218; Florentín, *Boquerón*, 213-222.

31. Taborga, 59-63, 66-68; Fernández, I, 229-252; Florentín, *Boquerón*, 229; Vergara Vicuña, II, 115. There were originally three machine gun mules. Augmented by five Guaraní animals which ran into Boquerón 16 September, the total probably was eight.

32. Rivarola, II, 197-198; *Libro Blanco. No Agresión*, 263-275; Bolivia, *Memoria 1934*, 124-132; *Política Argentina*, I, 415-420.

33. Arze Quiroga, II, 113-116; Moscoso, 141; Vergara Vicuña, I, 281, 294-306, 308-309, 321, II, 122-129; Díaz Arguedas, *Los Elegidos*, 90, 108; Fernández, I, 245, 262-264, 315; Taborga, 107; Moscoso, 85; González, 51. Bilbao Rioja, Air Force Chief, objected to the absurd use that Quintanilla was making of his air arm, urging bombing of Isla Poí, the Casado Railroad, and a psychological warfare raid on Asunción. Quintanilla angered and drew his pistol, but the Air Chief's "was already at his temple." The timely intervention of General Montes averted bloodshed, but the Air Force continued to be employed in scattered activity. A concentrated interdiction campaign such as Bilbao desired could have won the war; Vergara Vicuña, *Bilbao*, 204.

34. Thirst was so desperate *"que varios bebian orines,"* with which machine guns also were cooled.

35. Fernández, I, 219-225, 245, 267-272; Florentín, *Boquerón*, 201; Díaz Arguedas, *Los Elegidos*, 92; Estigarribia, 46; Taborga, 64-66; Caballero Irala, 25, 27; Urioste, *La Fragua*, 247.

36. *Libro Blanco. No Agresión*, 276-286; Bolivia, *Memoria 1934*, 133-138; *Política Argentina*, I, 421-424; U. S., *Foreign Relations, 1932*, V, 92-98.

37. Rios, 280; González, 58; Taborga, 78; Fernández, I, 272-304, 326; Florentín, *Boquerón*, 232-234. Total Paraguayan strength during the battle of Boquerón is not concisely known. Casualties and evacuated sick were considerable, and reinforcements steady, keeping up a constant change in personnel. The commonly accepted figure of 15,000-17,000 Paraguayan troops in the Chaco is probably high. General J. B. Ayala (p. 61) asserts that 12,000 were sent into the Casado sector during Boquerón and an additional 4,000 (p. 85) employed elsewhere. These figures seem realistic.

38. Moscoso, 139; Urioste, *La Fragua*, 223; Vergara Vicuña, I, 323-329; Fernández, I, 293, 314; Vergara Vicuña, *Bilbao*, 203; General David Toro Ruilova, *Mi actuación en la Guerra del Chaco* (La Paz, 1941), 16; *New York Times*, 25 September, 8.

39. Rios, 260; *Partes del conductor*, 21; Fernández, I, 315-317; Estigarribia, 47; Florentín, *Boquerón*, 235-236, 249; Taborga, 81-86. The total number surrendered is unclear. Contemporary accounts, including Taborga, who was inside Boquerón throughout the battle, say 619. Fernández, to whom they surrendered and who had access to

official records, says there were 24 officers and 820 men. This may refer, however, to the entire battle and not simply to Marzana's garrison.

40. Estigarribia, 48; Fernández, I, 322; Moscoso, 143; Florentín, *Boquerón*, 24; J. B. Ayala, 33-34; González, 61; Urioste, *La Fragua*, 314; *New York Times*, 30 September 1932, 1; Delgado, I, 9; Nogales Ortiz, 95; Major Hugo René Pol, *La campaña del Chaco* (La Paz, 1945), 27.

41. Fernández, I, 325-326; Rodríguez, 73; Guerrero, 121.

42. Fernández, I, 326; II, 16, 37; Vergara Vicuña, II, 458; Ayala Moreira, 169. Bolivian I Corps strength is from the latter, who was at this time Corps G-3; but with the addition of 2,000 corps reserves listed by Fernández.

43. Rodriguez, 12; Arze Quiroga, II, 272-275; Urioste, *La Encrucijada*, 104.

44. Arze Quiroga, II, 118, 246-247; Díaz Arguedas, *Los Elegidos*, 215-216; *El hombre símbolo*, 38-39. Kundt's recall was favored by Bautista Saavedra's Republican Socialist *guerristas*. The Liberals, led by General Montes, and including Vice-President Tejada Sorzano and Diez de Medina, were more pacific; Rivarola, II, 245.

45. Arze Quiroga, II, 248, 257-259; Taborga, 22; Moscoso, 144-145; Vergara Vicuña, I, 425, 443-444; Fernández, II, 18-19; Díaz Arguedas, *El hombre símbolo*, 31-33; Urioste, *La Fragua*, 129; Ayala Moreira (175-178) stresses that the I Corps protest was essentially against the recall of Kundt.

46. Arze Quiroga, II, 222, 249-255; Vergara Vicuña, I, 452-459; Díaz Arguedas, *El hombre símbolo*, 33-36. Upon reaching La Paz, Quintanilla was imprisoned for two years (p. 318). The crisis in the Bolivian command was faithfully and immediately reported to Asunción by Rivarola, whose intelligence system was excellent; Rivarola, II, 203.

47. González, 67; Estigarribia, 49; Rivarola, II, 223; Florentín, *Boquerón*, 25; Fernández, I, 323-325, II, 35-36; Vergara Vicuña, *Bilbao*, 234.

Ayala personally promoted Estigarribia 4 October. Other major commanders also were advanced; Benítez, *Estigarribia*, 1st ed., 82; Delgado, I, 16.

48. U. S., *Foreign Relations*, 1932, V, 100-102; *Libro Blanco. No Agresión*, 287. Note that the Bolivian army had located San Ignacio de Zamucos, southernmost Chiquitos mission, at only 20° south.

49. Fernández, II, 36-37, 40-46, 49-50, 55-59; Delgado, I, 23-27, 193-194; Arze Quiroga, II, 117-118; Vergara Vicuña, I, 435-436, 440; II, 174 189, 194, 204, quotation, 202; Caballero Irala, 33; Díaz Arguedas, *Los Elegidos*, 137-144.

General Manuel Rojas, the forgotten Paraguayan Supreme Commander, had planned the 4th Division as his command reserve for use against Lanza's 3rd Division at Ingavi. When Delgado reached Boquerón on 2 October, Colonel Estigarribia informed him that the 4th Division would be a part of I Corps, to which Delgado agreed, frustrating Rojas' plans; Delgado, I, 10, 13.

50. Vergara Vicuña, I, 438, 460, 484-493, 511; II, 223-224, 248, 252; Díaz Arguedas, *Los Elegidos*, 148-149; Fernández, II, 60-63; Delgado, I, 29-35, 195-196; Urioste, *La Fragua*, 121, 313. As early as 22 September, Peña had decried *jefes'* lack of will to fight. Many of them abandoned their posts and troops. Vergara Vicuña, II, 126. In November, visiting the Chaco, Lanza met *jefes* fleeing the war in government cars; Urioste, *La Encrucijada*, 70. The contemporary world belief that Bolivian officers were excellent, but troops poor, is just another of the innumerable myths of the Chaco War. Ayala Moreira, 180-187.

51. Arze Quiroga, II, 263-265, quotation, 265.

52. Fernández, II, 66; Delgado, I, 28, 36, 197; Vergara Vicuña, I, 502-506; *Partes del conductor*, 27-28.

53. Vergara Vicuña, I, 513-516, quotation, 515; II, 247, 256; Díaz Arguedas, *Los Elegidos*, 152.

54. U. S., *Foreign Relations*, 1932, V, 102-104; *Libro Blanco. No Agresión*, 288; Bolivia, *Memoria 1934*, 139; Rivarola, II, 241.

55. *Política Argentina*, I, 424-427; U. S., *Foreign Relations*, 1932, V, 205, 245; Rivarola, II, 207, 210, 216-217. Argentine citizens contributed generously to the Paraguayan Red Cross. The Argentine National Health Department made drugs available for the Guaraní army. President Justo assured Rivarola of his personal help, granting requested supplies whenever possible; Rivarola, II, 234-238, 254-256.

56. *Libro Blanco. No Agresión*, 289; Bolivia, *Memoria 1934*, 140-141; U. S., *Foreign Relations*, 1932, V, 104-105; *Política Argentina*, I, 443.

57. Vergara Vicuña, I, 508-509; II, 249, 272-273; Arze Quiroga, II, 125-127; Toro, 16-17; Díaz Arguedas, *Los Elegidos*, 149-150; *El hombre símbolo*, 37; Rivera was a former student at Columbia University, military attaché, and professor (p. 334); Urioste, *La Fragua*, 321; *La Encrucijada*, 104; Estigarribia, 45. Peña, who had been sick ever since his removal from a La Paz hospital in July to conduct the reprisals, had resented his own assignment to the I Corps command.

58. U. S., *Foreign Relations*, 1932, V, 105-110; *Política Argentina*, I, 443.

59. Arze Quiroga, II, 266-270; Vergara Vicuña, II, 342-346; Rivarola (II, 243-244) supplied Asunción with a copy of Guillén's revealing wire. Salamanca took exception to Guillén's reply, directing him to limit himself to obeying orders. This marked the beginning of poor relations between them.

60. Fernández, I, 305-306; II, 69-75, 279-280; Delgado, I, 39-41; Vergara Vicuña, I, 517; II, 265, 291-295; Estigarribia, 51-52; Benítez, *Estigarribia*, 2d ed., 62; Ayala Moreira, 197-198.

61. Vergara Vicuna, II, 262-264, 281; *Bilbao*, 210-222. Unlike the ruling clique of army officers, Bilbao Rioja had no political affiliation and possessed a proper respect for the government and civil authorities. Possibly this was due to the influence of his British wife (pp. 44-45).

62. Arze Quiroga, II, 223; Vergara Vicuña, II, 270-271, 291, 303-308; *Bilbao*, 228-244; Díaz Arguedas, *Los Elegidos*, 169; Ayala Moreira, 191-194; Toro, 23-24. Toro had a profound hatred of Bilbao, probably stemming from his 1930 exile by the Junta of which Bilbao was a member. His statements must be evaluated in this light.

63. Fernández, II, 79-80; Delgado, I, 40, 42, 198-200; Díaz Arguedas, *Los Elegidos*, 154-159, 168. Widely publicized, but unworthy of inclusion in a serious history, were the cowardly actions of a band of border rabble led by one Placido Jara who styled themselves "Macheteros de Muerte." In January 1933 some of these individuals were integrated into the 6th "Escobar" Cavalry; Fernández, II, 175. See also Ayala Moreira, 196.

64. Fernández, II, 76, 312-313; Estigarribia, 53; Benítez, *Estigarribia*, 2d ed., 62; Rios, 279; Vergara Vicuña, II, 334-335.

65. Vergara Vicuña, *Bilbao*, 249-281; Fernández, II, 80-91; Benítez, *Estigarribia*, 2d ed., 62; Delgado, I, 43-46; Díaz Arguedas, *Los Elegidos*, 171-180; González, 74; *Partes del conductor*, 32-33; Vergara Vicuña, II, 308, 317, 327, 331-332, 352-356, 362-364, 368-369, 379-383, 450; Ayala Moreira, 199-211.

66. Arze Quiroga, II, 129-133; Fernández, II, 92-93, 139, 287-288; Delgado, I, 46-53; Benítez, *Estigarribia*, 2d ed., 64.

67. Guerrero, 152-154; Vergara Vicuña, II, 409-421, 716-717. Toro and Kundt were bitter against Generals Blanco Galindo, Osorio, Lanza, and Mariaca Pando, and Lieutenant Colonels Bilbao Rioja and Emílio González Quint, who had made up the 1930 Junta which exiled them as members of the Siles Government (p. 422). Toro, as a 30-year-old Lieutenant Colonel, entered the Siles regime as Minister of Government; Díaz Arguedas, *El hombre símbolo*, 330.

Colonel Heredia, Chief of the Spanish Military Mission Bolivia had contracted, collaborated with Lanza in strategic planning; Rivarola, II, 279.

68. Cañadón—an open prairie among the trees.

69. Fernández, II, 97-107; Delgado, I, 60-63; Benítez, *Estigarribia*, 2d ed., 66; Ayala Moreira, 213-214.

70. Fernández, II, 108-125, 139-155; Delgado, I, 64-66; Díaz Arguedas, *Los Elegidos*, 213; *Partes del conductor*, 38; Estigarribia, 54;

Ayala Moreira, 212; Vergara Vicuña, II, 494-497, 510-535, 549-551, 559-561, and for Cuatro Vientos action, 575-590; Aponte B., *Cincuenta años*, 169-172.

71. Fernández, II, 176-193; Delgado, I, 67; Benítez, *Estigarribia*, 2d ed., 64; Díaz Arguedas, *Los Elegidos*, 218-224.

72. Caballero Irala, 33-50; Fernández, II, 173; González, 83; Estigarribia, 55; Delgado, I, 59, 68-71. The Paraguayan ration at this time was under 2,000 calories per day, water was inadequate and bad, and sleep far too rare.

73. *Libro Blanco. No Agresión*, 331-367; Bolivia, *Memoria 1934*, 142-143; Arze Quiroga, II, 134. Note also the pamphlet, República de Bolivia, Foreign Office, *Bolivian-Paraguayan Conflict* (La Paz, 1932). Paraguay required Bolivian prisoners to mail their letters in envelopes inscribed: *"Bolivia no tiene ningun derecho sobre la posesión del Chaco*—Antonio Quijarro." Luis Terán Goméz, *Bolivia frente a los pueblos del Plata* (La Paz, 1936), 39.

74. U. S., *Foreign Relations*, 1932, V, 112-114.

75. *Libro Blanco, No Agresión*, 291-296; Bolivia, *Memoria 1934*, 144-146; *Política Argentina*, I, 448-452; U. S., *Foreign Relations*, 1932, V, 126-129.

76. U. S., *Foreign Relations*, 1932, V, 115-118, 120-123, 125. If there were a Theodore Roosevelt on the scene, Ayala wrote Rivarola, peace would be forced, but men of decision were sadly lacking; Rivarola, II, 252.

77. U. S., *Foreign Relations*, 1932, V, 119, 124.

78. *Ibid.*, 1932, V, 129-130, 132-136; *Libro Blanco. No Agresión*, 238-328; *Política Argentina*, I, 452-462; Bolivia, *Memoria 1934*, 147-161, 163-168, 170, 173-175.

79. Bolivia, *Memoria 1934*, 162, 171-176; U. S., *Foreign Relations*, 1932, V, 131-132, 135.

80. *Política Argentina*, I, 462-463; U. S., *Foreign Relations*, 1932, V, 218-220.

CHAPTER FIVE

NANAWA—THE BOLIVIAN OFFENSIVE

General Kundt to the Attack

Even in the darkest hours of defeat Bolivian plans envisioned eventual return to the offensive. Lanza's program, the Rivera plan, and the strategic speculations of Salamanca—all had contemplated striking from Ballivián and Camacho against the Guaraní right. When Estigarribia concentrated at Saavedra, leaving only the 1st Cavalry at Platanillos and the small *fortines* to the north, the invitation for Bolivian action was complete.

General Osorio, when removed from his position as Chief of the General Staff, was given command of the II Corps with headquarters at Carandaití. The 8th Division was formed at Ballivián under General Julio Sanjinés to cooperate with the 3rd Division in launching the offensive. This development was eagerly sought by I Corps' General Guillén; on 1 December he advised the General Staff that 2,500 men would be sufficient to retake Platanillos and advance to Toledo if accompanied by a secondary attack at Kilometer 7; on 8 December he tied the 4th Division's projected Alihuatá maneuver to the 8th Division's move through Platanillos to Fernández. Thus Guillén contemplated a double envelopment of Arce.[1]

As an aspect of the II Corps offensive, Osorio brought the 3rd Division down from Ingavi to Camacho by circuitous roads through "27 November" and Picuiba. On 14 December, under the command of Lieutenant Colonel Angel Rodríguez, it expelled the small Paraguayan garrison of Loa. A week later the 8th Division, which had occupied Jayucubás, collaborated in recapturing Bolívar, the Paraguayans retreating to Corrales. Preparations for a concerted attack on Paraguay's westernmost original *fortín* then commenced.[2]

Meanwhile, on 6 December 1932, General Hans Kundt reached La Paz and assumed absolute military power (General in Chief of the Field Army) in the hour when others had halted the Guaraní. Immediately he ordered retreat to Muñoz-Esteros, but directed II Corps to divert the enemy toward Platanillos. Startled, Guillén retorted that the situation was now favorable; I Corps was ready to take the initiative. Kundt then suspended his order, but emphasized that as for future operations, he would communicate these opportunely. After conferring with Lanza on 9 December, Kundt and his predecessor issued a joint directive for the II Corps offensive on Platanillos-Fernández, but ordered I Corps to remain stationary. At Kilometer 7 counterattack was authorized to improve positions. "Instructions," the directive concluded, "must be strictly followed so as not to compromise future operations." Lanza thereupon resigned to give Kundt full freedom, and the latter, possibly to avoid renaming him, thereafter commanded without the aid of a Chief of Staff.[3]

It was commonly believed that General Kundt was able, by his mere presence, to change the course of the war and assure victory. Salamanca, who assumed that Kundt could obviate the need for extensive mobilization and facilitate fighting the war cheaply, succeeded in gaining his adherence to an "economic war." Kundt had commanded the Imperial 40th Infantry Brigade on the Eastern Front during the World War and had acquired a prestigious reputation in the Americas. He was known to have devoted much thought to Bolivia's Pacific problem, and to have considered 20,000 men an ample force for any exigency there. Kundt's ability as a strategist and tactician was greatly deficient. In peacetime his brilliance as an organizer and instructor of troops and his diligent toil and personal demeanor had fostered an illusion of great capacity for field command, but in the Chaco his conduct proved an abysmal disappointment to his adopted country.[4]

Paraguay's reaction to the danger on the right was a reorganization of the army. At Toledo, II Corps was established under Lieutenant Colonel Juan B. Ayala. The functions of the Paraguayan General Staff, of which Ayala had been Chief, were largely absorbed by Estigarribia's staff at Isla Poí. With the establishment of a second army corps, Estigarribia became Chief of the Southern Command (COMANSUR), and the little 3rd Division at Bahia Negra and its lesser dependencies became the Northern Command (COMANOR) under Navy Captain Elías Ayala. The role of the nominal Commander in Chief, General Rojas at Asunción, was reduced in practice to organizing new units and handling administration. Although Rojas longed to assume personal command in the field, he was not supported by the government; it reposed complete confidence in Estigarribia and sought to enhance his authority because "this *jefe* demonstrated from the beginning of the war that he possessed the primordial qualities of a genuine *caudillo* of military command: *Tener una idea*." That idea was to seek annihilation of the Bolivian army as far as possible from nuclear Paraguay.[5]

In answer to the Bolivian 8th Division threat, Lieutenant Colonel Nicolás Delgado, who replaced Estigarribia as I Corps commander, withdrew the 2nd Division from the Saavedra front to Alihuatá-Fernández, and placed the 4th Division in reserve. Heavy rains turned the newly prepared trenches at Kilometer 12 into channels of mud on Christmas day 1932 when, taking advantage of the holiday truce, the 1st Division retreated to defensive positions; its valuable wells were left behind in no-man's land.[6]

After Peñaranda's patrols confirmed that the enemy was entrenched across the *cañadón*, Guillén, obedient to Kundt's verbal instructions and general directive, then issued preparatory orders for an attack. Experience had clearly shown the futility of frontal attacks; the lesson, however, was never to register on General Kundt. Consequently, after final orders from Toro, the Bolivian 4th Division (with artillery and low-level air support) charged 3,135 troops into the hungry fire of the Guaraní (27 December) and left 700 in no-man's land as another tribute to the superiority of defense. Kundt immediately ordered a halt to all attacks, tacitly admitting the restabilization of the contenders at Saavedra despite major Paraguayan withdrawals.[7]

From the beginning General Kundt had resolved to focus his initial attention on Nanawa. Since routes to the Rio Paraguay were blocked by strong forces, he determined to destroy the small 5th Division at Nanawa, eliminate the threat to Saavedra-Muñoz, and open an avenue to the river. This would also enable I Corps to proceed through Rojas Silva-Boquerón and converge with II Corps, advancing through Toledo-Isla Poí, for a grand drive. The projected results were the trapping of the Paraguayan I Corps at Arce-Alihuatá and the destruction of the 5th Division as the necessary military requisites to attaining the political objective. The government, Kundt stated in his second directive (27 December), had promised that "until 20 January it will accept no diplomatic intervention, leaving us for the military operations . . . almost a month." Capture of Nanawa, Corrales, and Toledo could greatly strengthen Bolivia diplomatically. Therefore, the optimistic German promised that although world opinion held Paraguay the victor, Bolivia would have the final triumph.[8]

After reiterating to Kundt the desirability of his own plan for a maneuver from Puesto Sosa to Alihuatá, Guillén issued preparatory orders for the attack on Nanawa. On 30 December the 7th Division captured Fortín Duarte and 8 January 1933 Fortín Mariscal López was occupied. Farther north, the 3rd Division unsuccessfully attempted to surround lightly-held Corrales, captured the *fortín* 1 January, and pursued the fleeing garrison toward Puesto Betty.[9]

Estigarribia anticipated an attack on Nanawa and its sister *fortín*, Ayala,[10] but his army was poorly fed and supplied (due to the problem of transport over muddy roads) and on the defensive all along the front. Therefore, he concentrated on creating exceedingly strong field fortifications under the expert technical supervision of former czarist Generals Belaieff and Ern. If Nanawa fell, Estigarribia planned a rapid retreat to Arce, a flexible defense line from Rojas Silva (Falcón) to Toledo, and reinforcement of Fortín Orihuela to block Kundt from the river. But to prevent Nanawa's loss, the 2,500 men of Lieutenant Colonel Irrazábal's 5th Division (7th and 13th Infantry; 3rd, 4th and 5th Cavalry, artillery battery) constructed barbed wire entanglements, quebracho-protected positions, and extensive trench lines. Machine guns were concentrated to provide the heaviest fire of the war. The old Fortín Nanawa was heavily fortified, for Irrazábal was determined to deny the enemy the moral exhilaration which its capture would afford. By 18 January the Guaraní were ready.[11]

When Toro, Kundt's friend and protegé, saw the master's plan of attack, he received the greatest disillusionment of his life, for the General had not "captured the reality, nor could he adapt himself to the character, of this specialized war." His offensive would threaten only the Paraguayan 1st and 5th Divisions and simply gain ground, whereas an indirect approach through Toledo would have imperiled the entire enemy army. Toro requested use of two regiments from the 9th Division in support of the Nanawa operation; Kundt refused, however, with the result that his vital left was too weak for the mission assigned. There were no reserves, center of gravity, or proper coordination, but Kundt took I Corps under his personal command and on 20 January 1933 launched the 7th Division's 6,000 men (ten infantry and five cavalry regiments, supported by the 2nd Artillery and ten aircraft) against Nanawa.[12]

The Bolivian attack, mounted in the classical three "battles," moved out during the rainy, murky night of 19 January. The left advanced along the too-short Picada Ruck from Agua Rica, mired its guns, encountered thickets of thorny cacti, and was detained from participating in the first day's action. Aircraft bombed and strafed with little success. The center charged into the Paraguayan fire three successive times with negative results. The right was repelled in the late afternoon, and as night descended Kundt ordered his forces to dig in where they stood. Greater determination, preponderant strength on the flanks, and the indirect objective of encircling the *fortín* might have led to victory.[13]

In support of the Nanawa offensive the 8th Division advanced from Platanillos, encountering the Guaraní 2nd Division defending Fortín Fernández. The Bolivians repeated their common errors of inadequate coordination, lack of intelligence, violation of the principle of economy of force, and underestimation of the enemy. An elastic defense easily absorbed their attacks on 20 and 23 January and littered the field with unburied dead. To distract the aggressive Andeans, the Paraguayan 1st Division struck the Bolivian lines across Kilometer 7 of the Saavedra-Alihuatá road, but Peñaranda's 1,500-man 4th Division held firm.[14]

A fresh blow on Nanawa (24 January) abandoned frontal attack, and aimed to cut off the rear of Fortín Ayala. Desperately short of ammunition, Irrazábal received propitious air resupply. The 41st Infantry was for a time successful, but was defeated by Guaraní cavalry attacking from the direction of Puesto Florida. The Bolivian regiment had been too small and weak for its task. Although fighting continued until 28 January, the 5th Division, reinforced to 5,000 and joined by Bray's 4th Division, proved a firm wall against assault. In ten days' fighting, the defenders suffered only 248 casualties against 2,000 Bolivian losses. Nanawa could not be subdued and insufficient troops were available to lay siege. Consequently, Kundt's prestige received a stunning blow; Bolivia suffered a fresh moral defeat.[15]

Farther north, the 7th "San Martín" Cavalry, an element of the Paraguayan 1st Cavalry Brigade at Toledo, had probed Corrales on 13 January. Its repulse raised the spirit of the defending Bolivian II Corps which then began preparation for an attack on Toledo. Unfortunately logistics were highly deficient, even for foodstuffs. The opposing force, the Paraguayan II Corps under Lieutenant Colonel Juan B. Ayala, was physically weak (from epidemic dysentery and typhoid) and materially insignificant, but it gradually accumulated 5,000 men in the 6th Division (5th, 8th, and 14th Infantry), 1st Cavalry Brigade (1st and 7th Cavalry), and 3rd and 4th Artillery. An essentially frontal attack on Corrales (29 January) designed to distract attention from Nanawa was again unsuccessful. Ayala's Corps was clearly unprepared for offensive maneuvers. There was no alternative to defensive concentration.[16]

On 2 February the Bolivian 3rd Division moved on Toledo from Corrales with 3,618 men. Ayala prepared to hold Puesto Betty, a series of trenches and positions across the road, but was forced to withdraw (9 February) due to lack of gas for his water trucks. Moving artillery along the muddy, rain-splattered road was partially responsible for the incedibly slow Andean advance which finally reached the outer defenses of Toledo 16 February. After Bilbao Rioja led his Air Group in a dawn raid, the infantry attacked on the twenty-fifth. Two days later the attackers were nearly destroyed as four successive waves collapsed upon the system of strong points planned by the Russians, Belaieff and Ern. Night assaults had a like result. The superiority over attacking

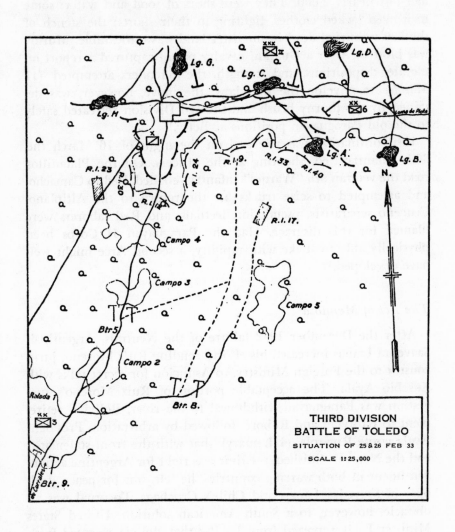

THIRD DIVISION
BATTLE OF TOLEDO
SITUATION OF 25 & 26 FEB 33
SCALE 1:25,000

infantry of fortifications and concentrated machine guns was again proved. An attempt to blast out the earthworks with 65mm. Vickers light guns proved unsuccessful. By 5 March the Bolivians had lost nearly 2,000. They were short of food and water; some men even lacked clothes, fighting in their shorts; the stench of the 700 unburied dead in no-man's land was unbearable. Mutiny was plotted. After a Guaraní cavalry patrol captured a report on morale, dispositions, and strength, the defenders attempted (11 March) to envelop the Bolivians; the move, however, was detained by the thorny brush and the 3rd Division retreated safely to the old Paraguayan positions at Betty.[17]

Insubordination was rife and on the night of 16 March the 30th Infantry fled, shooting at the officers. On the Platanillos road the veteran 9th "Warnes" Infantry rebelled, fled to Camacho, and attempted to seize trucks for the return to the Altiplano. Cruceño separatists, pseudo-intellectuals, and Red laborers were blamed for this disgrace. Had the Paraguayan II Corps been physically able to strike with rapidity, a second Arce might well have developed.[18]

The Act of Mendoza

After the December 1932 failure of the Neutrals, Argentina's Saavedra Lamas increased his efforts, sending Ruíz Moreno, jurisconsult to the Foreign Ministry, to Asunción for secret talks with Eusebio Ayala. The acceptable portion of Ruíz Moreno's suggestion was Paraguayan withdrawal to the river, Bolivian retirement to Ballivián and Roboré, followed by arbitration. President Ayala wrote Rivarola (4 January) that with the front stalemated and the Neutrals finished, the time was right for Argentine action. Sentiment in both warring countries, he felt, was for peace. Jealousy of Saavedra Lamas and Chile's Cruchaga Tocornal was an obstacle, however, to a South American solution. United States Minister Feely reported from La Paz that Bolivia resented fresh Argentine and Chilean pressure and was fully aware that Paraguay was considering a declaration of war in order to oblige the adjacent countries to a neutrality which would halt Bolivian arms transit. Bolivia still favored the 15 December Neutral plan and wished to treat jointly with ABCP and the Neutrals.[19]

To unify the fresh efforts, Cruchaga proposed personal discussions to Saavedra Lamas. The result of their conference of 1-2 February 1933 was the Act of Mendoza, affirming friendship in general terms. Article III embodied the sagacious proposals of Eusebio Ayala for a regional economic conference to consider the mediterranean character of the belligerents, create a transit authority to stimulate exchange, and sign railroad and river conventions. In this manner Ayala had hoped to satisfy what he considered Bolivia's just aspirations without dismembering the Paraguayan Chaco.[20]

An accompanying Secret Act of Mendoza launched an attempt to end the war, exercising friendly mediation and taking into account the "laudable" Neutral efforts. Stipulating withdrawals to the river and Fortines Roboré and Ballivián, and demobilization, it also implicitly provided for double arbitration. A definite proposal, submitted after further soundings, was offered on 25 February.[21]

The previous day at Asunción, President Ayala asked an extraordinary session of Congress for authority to declare a state of war with Bolivia. Undoubtedly, this was timed as a threat in support of the 27 February Paraguayan reply to the Act of Mendoza. This note stipulated that since Ballivián was the main Bolivian supply depot, Andean troops must retire to Villa Montes (the western extremity of the Chaco) in exchange for Guaraní withdrawal to the Rio Paraguay. Troops should be reduced to minimum levels consistent with domestic security in both countries for five years. An international investigation should determine the aggressor and fix his responsibility.[22]

Bolivia's reply (28 February) also advanced conditions: all prior diplomatic acts would be considered nonexistent and would not influence the arbitral verdict; the plea would be defined in accordance with the 3 August 1932 declaration against conquest; the award would be based on the *uti possidetis* of 1810, without consideration of occupation as title; equal compensations would not be considered; the Hayes Award, stipulated the fifth condition would be included in the arbitration zone, which would be bounded by the 21st parallel and meridian of 59° 55'. Although the Roboré-Ballivián *line* was unacceptable, Bolivia withdrew her previous insistence on an absolute cease fire of positions.[23]

Unquestionably, each reply was tentative and provided leeway for bargaining. La Paz could not possibly accept withdrawal to Villa Montes because this would have constituted *de facto* acceptance of Asunción's contentions that the Chaco was a large region possessing natural limits. Likewise, the Bolivian specification of a narrowly-limited, Paraguayan-held area as the arbitration zone was completely unacceptable to Asunción. Bolivia's willingness to accept a cease fire on positions other than those of the moment reflected the repulse of Kundt's offensive against Nanawa, Toledo, and Fernández. It was actually a conciliatory move. On the other hand, she converted Roboré and Ballivián into a fixed, but unacceptable, line. Prior views in La Paz suggest Platanillos-Muñoz as the probable line Salamanca would have granted.

Alihuatá

Like his superiors, Lieutenant Colonel Nicolás Delgado, commander of the 8,000-man Paraguayan I Corps, feared the enemy would seek a victory to impress the Mendoza conferees and bolster his diplomatic position. To deny La Paz this triumph, Delgado reinforced the 1st Division at Kilometer 12 with troops from Fernández, and ordered to Nanawa 400 walking wounded from the Arce hospital. On 16 February a cavalry patrol led by Captain Boris Kasianov clashed with elements of the Andean 9th Division near Puesto Sosa. Since January this force had been forming under Colonel Victorino Gutiérrez in preparation for the maneuver on Alihuatá desired by Guillén. Heavy reconnaissance in the area by the Bolivian Air Force served to warn the Guaraní that a threat was in the offing. Delgado responded by accelerating the construction of defenses at Alihuatá and sending patrols farther afield.[24]

Halted on both right and left, General Kundt had grown interested in the center maneuver which I Corps advocated. He consulted Toro and encouraged aerial reconnaissance, making excellent use of Bilbao Rioja's photomaps. Setting aside past animosities, Kundt returned Bilbao to a field position, assigning him as Chief of Staff of the 9th Division, but unfortunately, against the advice of Chaco vererans, he parsimoniously allotted only 1,500 men for the project, too few to capture Arce or the Guaraní 1st Division! Captain Germán Busch was to turn the latter's left with a squadron of cavalry and menace its rear while the 8th Division feinted at Fernández and the 7th Division again struck Nanawa.[25]

When a Guaraní patrol discovered the advance Bolivian cavalry detachment west of Charata on 8 March, Delgado believed that Fernández was being threatened and shifted troops from Alihuatá. On the tenth a prisoner revealed the pending Bolivian attack, causing the confused Delgado to rush the 3rd Infantry to Alihuatá by truck, but he was too late. The Andean 9th Division advanced early 11 March, took Charata, expelled the garrison of Alihuatá, and cut the road to Arce. Communications with the 1st Division were thus severed except through Gondra and by radio. Delgado hastily formed a large detachment under his Operations Officer, the extremely jingoistic Major Roque Samaniego, to reopen the road through Alihuatá. Meanwhile, Peñaranda's 4th Division lashed the Paraguayans at Kilometer 12, and Busch took Campo 31. Kundt, however, declined to strengthen the 4th Division, leaving it too weak to win. That night Lieutenant Colonel Fernández informed Estigarribia by radio that although he had food for six days and ammunition for three, he was considering retreat. Estigarribia, however, was tempted to destroy Gutiérrez' small division, and therefore ordered Fernández to hold firm while the Gondra road was widened for supply trucks.[26]

Delgado summoned forces from Nanawa to keep the road open. Estigarribia, ever mindful that Paraguay dare not lose her precious, irreplaceable arms and equipment, ordered all 1st Division nonessentials removed to Gondra. On the afternoon of 12 March, Bolivian forces pushed south from Alihuatá, directly threatening Colonel Fernández' rear. His flanks were being infiltrated (albeit by very small forces) while above Alihuatá the Samaniego detachment was contained and forced to dig in. This made more and more unattainable Estigarribia's objectives of surrounding and trapping the Bolivian 9th Division. Despite its small size (1,500), the latter effectively contained both Samaniego and a regiment which Fernández had sent north from Kilometer 12. All the while Peñaranda kept up attacks from Kilometer 7. On 13 March authority from Delgado for retreat to Gondra reached Fernández; the next day he reported he was being surrounded, but Estigarribia replied that if the 1st Division could hold out but three more days, 7,000 men would be brought against the enemy 9th Division. Kundt was indeed very much worried lest this occur. After Peñaranda again struck, using reinforcements and endeavoring to turn the Paraguayan left, Fernández reported (16 March) he feared he would be surrounded that night. He lacked food. Water was difficult to obtain from the wells in no-man's land. His artillery and baggage train already on the Gondra road, Fernández resolved to "sacrifice my own prestige, my career" and save his veteran 1st Division. Consequently, after announcing his intentions, he withdrew, unscathed, by night, leaving behind only a well-filled cemetery in the shade of a giant quebracho tree. Not a single weapon was abandoned; the guns were carried by hand, 20 men per piece. Proceeding through Kilometer 22, Fernández took the new Gondra road on 18 March. Although Peñaranda's 4th Division had been reinforced with walking wounded, it maintained only patrol contact.[27]

Kundt thus lost the opportunity to capture a Paraguayan division. Despite repeated requests from Peñaranda, no attempt was made to block the escape route until after reinforcements belatedly arrived 18 March. Kundt's lethargy and unwillingness to commit forces adequate for the missions assigned permitted the enemy to retreat in good order, luring the 4th Division to positions less advantageous than those it vacated at Kilometer 7. The 9th Division also was too small to capitalize fully its initial success, and was quickly halted. The 8th Division's move on Fortín Fernández failed for the same reason, although it nearly succeeded in surrounding the *fortín* on 25 March. Characteristically, Kundt violated the principle of economy of force, employing inadequate manpower against vital objectives, possibly due to his acceptance of Salamanca's "economic warfare"—so economic as to prevent victory.[28]

Bolivian morale nevertheless soared on the strength of the Alihuatá-Saavedra successes; Paraguayan spirits plummeted. In Asunción, when (20 March) the Press Office reported the 1st Division's brilliantly executed retreat, the people were deeply disturbed, as was the figurehead Commander in Chief, General Rojas. Spoiled by victories, they feared that all was lost in a single reversal. Estigarribia privately felt that Colonel Fernández had become dispirited, and believed that at the very least he should have attacked Alihuatá from the south with his entire command. In the manner of a Great Captain, however, Estigarribia quickly recovered and reacted with decision to adversity, building up Arce while Kundt waited.[29]

As a result of the popular discontent caused by the retreat, President Eusebio Ayala wrote Estigarribia on 18 March 1933, informing him that the Act of Mendoza was a virtual failure because Bolivia, confident of military success, opposed agreement. The war would continue, although Guaraní financial resources were limited. The small gold reserve was already gone, preventing purchase abroad of new supplies. Consequently, it was imperative to maintain an active defense, endeavoring to lure the enemy into destroying himself in attacks. Existing stocks of ammunition would have to last three months. Aircraft could be given only

> the safest missions as the loss of a single plane . . . would cause a terrible impression on this nervous population, which is already sensitive to panic. . . . The people pass from enthusiasm to depression according to the information from the front. . . . In any case [he stressed] you can be assured that my personal and official authority will be on your side in good and, above all, in bad conditions. Not for a single moment have I believed in any intrigue to displace you. . . .[30]

Estigarribia replied that the alarm over the 1st Division retreat was groundless, for Paraguay had lost neither men nor material, only a strip of desert having little value. Since January, obedient to the President's wishes, he had adapted operations to the capability of the nation, gaining resounding successes from the defensive. To maintain the rather extensive front with existing resources, sound intelligence and mobility (by means of trucks,

cavalry, and aircraft) were essential. Since more arms were unavailable—the limiting factor on the size of the army—reserves
must be carefully trained to replace the fallen.[31]

A new tactical situation developed 20 March, when Guaraní
patrols discovered Bolivians working in the woods northwest of
Alihuatá. Delgado alerted the new 7th Division (9th, 12th, and
17th Infantry) and called for aerial reconnaissance. The pilots
erroneously reported that a road was nearly completed to the rear
of Fernández. Delgado warned his forces in that *fortín* and in
Arce, and was well prepared when the weak Bolivian 8th Division
attacked on 25 March. Trenches and quebracho fortifications
had been prepared on all sides, frustrating the belief that the
fortín could easily be taken from the rear. Núñez' 2nd Division
(supported by three bombers) instead began flanking the Bolivians (5 April) obliging their retreat to within 15 Kilometers
of Platanillos. The Andean II Corps had now been defeated both
at Toledo and Fernández, and link-up with the 9th Division at
Alihuatá was prevented. This served to neutralize the threat to
Arce of converging drives.[32]

On 20 March, Colonel Fernández created a detachment under
Lieutenant Colonel Rafael Franco to defend Gondra against
Peñaranda's slowly pursuing 4th Division. The 1st Division was
very weak; after evacuations for illness or combat fatigue, only
1,200 were left for Franco. Delgado desired to employ these forces
against the Bolivian flank at Nanawa, but Fernández was reluc-
tant. His command then passed from I Corps to the new III Corps
(1st, 4th, and 5th Divisions, 2nd Cavalry Brigade, 2nd and 4th
Artillery: 9,000 men) created at Nanawa under Lieutenant Colonel Luis Irrazábal, and was used to defend the III Corps' supply
line running northward through Falcón. Once Peñaranda finally
reached Gondra, a 7 April Bolivian thrust endeavored belatedly
to cut the road above Nanawa. Captain Busch's 5th Cavalry
pushed back outposts below Falcón (Rojas Silva) and closed the
road for four days, but a strong detachment from the Guaraní
7th Division reopened the route; two days later Busch again attained the road but was dislodged, whereupon a new front developed 5 kilometers west of Rancho Ocho (Campo Aceval).[33]

Later, after repeated urging, Kundt permitted the 4th Division to carry out a plan prepared by its Chief of Staff, Moscoso, for taking the road between Gondra and Bullo. This would have served the multiple ends of (1) improving the 4th Division water supply by gaining access to important wells at Pirizal, (2) obliging the Guaraní 1st Division to retreat from Gondra to protect the III Corps' communications with Rojas Silva, and (3) posing an indirect approach to Nanawa itself. After Kundt refused Peñaranda's request for reinforcements, the enemy forced the small 600-man Andean detachment to take up positions immediately west of the road.[34]

Paraguay Declares War

After receiving noncommittal replies to the Act of Mendoza, Cruchaga and Saavedra Lamas requested the Neutrals' support in endeavors to get both belligerents to withdraw their conditions. Paraguay finally agreed. Bolivia, freshly victorious at Alihuatá and Saavedra, informed the ABCP-U.S. (11 April) that discussion of troop withdrawals was premature until the basis for final settlement had been reached. Once this was done, the technicalities of an armistice could easily be determined. On 26 April, Bolivia flatly rejected the Act of Mendoza as merely creating a new status quo "inconvenient for the peace of America," and favoring the Paraguayan aim of converting the status quo into a permanent solution. The act failed to fix the arbitration zone in advance, and in fact assumed a transactional formula for arbitration lines which would ignore rights and titles. Further, Bolivia resented diplomatic pressure which had been brought against her, especially to withdraw her definition of the arbitration zone. Asunción replied (2 May) that Bolivia wished only to discuss arbitration, requiring of her a sacrifical final settlement as a condition to halting hostilities. Paraguay continued to insist on adequate security guarantees, especially demobilization, to assure that she would not be the victim of fresh attacks. La Paz called for continued, joint Neutrals-ABCP efforts looking toward determination of Paraguay's exact pretensions.[35]

The December positions were now reversed. Bolivia was willing to confide in a victorious army, while Paraguay was amenable to

a truce which varied significantly from that suggested by the
Neutrals only in that it afforded greater security by specifying
Andean withdrawal to Roboré and Ballivián rather than behind
the Vitriones-Ballivián line.

Having delayed a declaration of war in the hope that the Act of
Mendoza might succeed, President Ayala now recognized its failure and on 10 May 1933 exercised the authority Congress had
granted him to declare the "Republic in State of War with Bolivia." He hoped in so doing to oblige the ABCP countries to
close their borders to the passage of Bolivian arms. Prior soundings had indicated that Argentina would "decree neutrality of
benevolent application for [Paraguay] . . . and strict for Bolivia."
Chile was, however, believed to be inclined to permit arms flow
to avoid giving La Paz cause to repudiate their 1904 treaty ending
the War of the Pacific. Nevertheless, knowing that Bolivia was
expecting large shipments from Europe, Ayala hoped thus to prevent their delivery. Unfortunately, his action was too late. Stokes-
Brandt mortars and other new weapons had already reached the
front. Chile and Argentina, meanwhile, showed their displeasure
with La Paz by advising that they held her fully responsible for
the failure of their peace effort.[36]

After Paraguay declared war, neutrality declarations were issued
by the adjoining countries. Brazil declined to impede free transit
with either contender as pacted in existing treaties, but she for-
bade foreign enlistments, use of her territory for military operations, or export of war supplies. Her ports were open to the vessels
of both belligerents, and escaped prisoners of war would not
necessarily be interned. Peru issued a similar pronouncement.
Chile decreed neutrality, but permitted Bolivia unimpaired use of
the transit privileges pacted 20 October 1904. The effect of these
policies was favorable to Bolivia, since of the three of them, Paraguay had borders only with Brazil and did not, or could not, make
use of Brazilian routes. On the other hand, La Paz supplied her
5th Division from Corumbá, allegedly receiving contraband.[37]

Argentine, however, lived up to Guaraní expectations and
initiated a neutrality benevolent to Asunción. Her 13 May decree
and implementing directive specified vigilance against use of
communications for war purposes and internment of troops enter-

ing Argentina. Existing river conventions would be respected. She closed the Pilcomayo ports through which Bolivia had always obtained the basic necessities for her forces in the Southeast, explaining that there were no civilian populations in the Bolivian Chaco; *all* goods, under a narrow definition of the term, were therefore contraband. This served to severely handicap Bolivia, who had always required close relations with Argentina to complement her own highly inadequate domestic transport and communications facilities. La Paz, well aware that Paraguay was using the Port of Buenos Aires and even the Argentine railroads, sought clarification of her rights of free transit under an 1868 treaty. This precipitated a lengthy correspondence in which it was made clear that the Justo government would allow Bolivia transit of only purely civilian goods and in the same quantities as before the war.[38]

As soon as Paraguay declared war, Bolivia appealed to the League of Nations, bringing a third successive international force into the Chaco question. Although she had desired new joint Neutrals-ABCP efforts, the unfavorable attitude of Chile and Argentina made such a course impossible. Saavedra Lamas had long sought to be the bearer of the issue to Geneva, but Paraguay's Eusebio Ayala had opposed League interference. He believed that Geneva would do nothing to offend Washington. Secretary of State Stimson had feared that the League, unfamiliar with the problem, would act in haste; in four years' experience the Neutrals had learned the need for patience. But they had failed, and the new administration on the Potomac had little interest in the Chaco War. The dissolution of the Neutrals left the League a clear field.[39]

Brazil was profoundly disappointed at Roosevelt's taking the United States out of the matter, and believed correctly that a League commission would be a waste of time; it would submit a lengthy report and achieve no result beyond designating an aggressor and recommending sanctions. As a compromise, Brazil suggested to the other ABCP powers that they secure from the League a "mandate" for new efforts, thus keeping Geneva out of America. On 4 August, the desired mandate was offered. The ABCP then unsuccessfully sought agreement for submission of the entire Chaco problem to arbitration, with a simultaneous truce under their moral guarantee. Paraguay agreed on 8 September, but Bolivia made her acceptance contingent upon a maximum arbitration zone of 25 kilometers south of Bahia Negra and 61° west. The ABCP, therefore, advised the League (2 October) that they could not accept the proffered mandate.[40]

The Second Attack on Nanawa

For unknown reasons, Kundt failed completely to capitalize the brilliant and audacious Alihuatá maneuver. Although this brought him within gunshot of Arce, he persisted in poorly-conceived frontal attacks on the enemy flanks. Especially strange was his desire to acquire Fernández, an unimportant post which would have been a by-product of the capture or siege of Arce. Yet he maintained the 9th Division at low strength and granted the most important sector only secondary attention. His natural routes lay through Toledo-Isla Poí and Arce-Boquerón, converging for the victory-bringing final drive, but Hans Kundt had inexplicably forgotten strategy, and instead focused his attention on Nanawa, southern terminus of the Paraguayan COMANSUR's sector of action. Even if successful in advancing toward Concepción, his flank would have been exposed and he would have been cut off. Nevertheless, he could not be dissuaded and from mid-April focused on preparations for a full-scale attack on Nanawa, despite Guillén, Toro, Peñaranda, Moscoso, and the host of *jefes* who from experience opposed the plan in favor of a move against Arce.[41]

On 10 May, II Corps ordered the 8th Division (2,000 men) to launch a third attack on Fernández. On the eighteenth, amidst spirited cries of "¡Viva Bolivia!" the Bolivians charged, supported for the first time by the 81 mm. Stokes-Brandt mortar. A withering fire from the strengthened garrison quickly pinned them down. Kundt then ordered a detachment (16th and 41st Infantry, Busch's 5th Cavalry) under Lieutenant Colonel Felipe Arrieta to strike Fernández from the east. The 9th Division, however, had been halted 5 kilometers south of Arce on 13 May, and the Arrieta detachment, supporting it a week later, was severely beaten

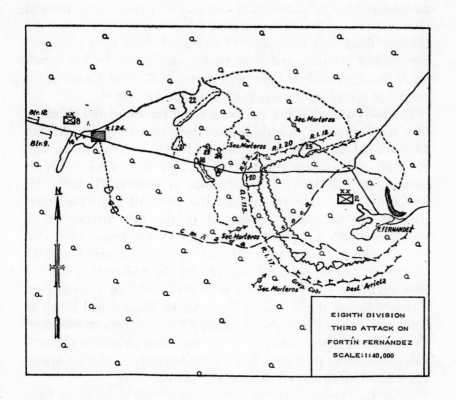

Btr. 12

XX 8 1.

R.I.24.

Btr. 9.

22

Sec. Morteros

R.I. 12

Sec. Morteros   R.I. 20   25

18   24

20

R.I. 115.

Cañada   Sec. Morteros

XX 2

F. FERNANDEZ

N

R.I. 17.

Grup. Cab.   Dest. Arиela

Sec. Morteros

EIGHTH DIVISION
THIRD ATTACK ON
FORTÍN FERNÁNDEZ
SCALE: 1:40,000

by 200 Guaraní. Although the 8th Division again attacked Fernández (27 May) to draw the attention of the defenders, by the time Arrieta engaged on the thirtieth, his remaining 500 men were weak from their unprovisioned march through the brush, and quickly bogged down in what amounted to an extension of the 8th Division's right. A semicircle was pressed around Fernández, but there were too few men to cover the full 5-kilometer perimeter. After failure of an all-out attack (1 June), the Andeans retreated toward Platanillos, harassed by Guaraní bombers, leaving 556 dead and carrying 314 wounded. Had Arrieta's force consisted of the thousand fresh troops with which he had struck Arce, Fernández might have been captured. Instead Kundt again employed forces incommensurate with the mission.[42]

In observations on the reasons for the failure of the third attack on Fernández, Kundt blamed lack of energy by the 8th Division. More astutely, he observed that a common tactical error of *jefes* was employment of a single line of fire with no outposts on the flanks and no troops in reserve. (Indeed, this was a Bolivian error throughout the war. All available forces were almost invariably committed in the first attack.) With regimental CP's fully three kilometers to the rear, the invitation to defeat was complete. In addition, he observed acutely, many *jefes* had no personal contact with their men; they did not even exchange views and ideas with junior officers after engagements.[43] Kundt might have added that he himself had failed to train *jefes* in the use of the traditional Prussian general directive. Consequently, commanders gave minute instructions to subordinates, destroying initiative, but also all too often requiring operations based on situations of an earlier hour.

After its June retreat, the 8th Division was reduced to little more than a battalion, defensively deployed in front of Platanillos for the remainder of 1933. The 3rd Division was only slightly stronger. That Paraguay disdained to attack in force in the II Corps sector is evidence of the great difference in concept prevailing between the contending commands. While Kundt sought to gain terrain, Estigarribia's COMANSUR, reflecting the grand strategy of poverty-stricken Paraguay, concerned itself with the destruction of the enemy, a far sounder objective.[44]

At Gondra, Lieutenant Colonel Rafael Franco's 1st Division opened a breach in Peñaranda's left (16 May), but the Bolivians flanked it, pinned the attackers down with machine-gun fire and their newly acquired mortars, and later recaptured their positions. Along the *cañadón* a war of positions then developed enabling the 4th Division to train its raw replacements.

The rainy season lasted unusually long in 1933—until June instead of ending in March. In addition, the southern winter was exceptionally cold, going below freezing in June. On both sides at Gondra (as well as elsewhere), the combination of cold and rain sickened the improperly clothed fighters, subjecting them to the most miserable kind of war. In Franco's camp malaria was epidemic.[45]

At GHQ late in June, Estigarribia explained the general situation to his major commanders and indicated that the hour had arrived to resume offensive operations. Colonel Franco replied that given the scarce resources of their country, only an overwhelming victory to bring peace was practical. He proposed a maneuver from Pirizal-Gondra to Saavedra (hub of the Andean front) to seize the old enemy positions at Kilometer 7. These would be held in conjunction with attacks by I and III Corps to trap the Bolivian Army. Colonel J. B. Ayala offered a proposal for a drive by his II Corps, reinforced to 12,000, through Platanillos toward Muñoz and Ballivián. Estigarribia listened in silence, but in private stated that Ayala's plan was impracticable for lack of men and trucks. Franco's was good, but the morale of the army was not yet ready for operations requiring the maximum energy of every man.

Paraguayan intelligence indicated that Kundt was about to launch a new blow at Nanawa. Irrazábal therefore spoke with justification of his disturbing situation. Since Ayala's plan would have required weakening III Corps in the face of the enemy's strength, would doubtless have failed for lack of surprise and velocity, and had the inherent weaknesses of all single-thrust strategies, Estigarribia chose instead to shift forces south, getting 9,000 men to Nanawa. He positioned a strategic reserve at Falcón (Rojas Silva), realizing that the pending Bolivian attack would admirably serve his aim of destroying the enemy, and in this case without risking offensive operations. During the lull in fighting, III Corps therefore fortified every "island" at Nanawa-Ayala and mined likely assault routes. Rather complex lines afforded excellent defense in depth.[46]

On 4 July 1933, to coincide with the convening of the League Assembly, Kundt mounted against Nanawa the largest mass frontal attack of the Chaco War. A tunnel had been dug and explosives placed under the edge of the "fortified island" which blocked the center. When this mine was exploded at 0905, nearly 7,000 charged across no-man's land. While overhead the Bolivian Air Force bombed the Guaraní artillery, 32 Andean guns roared, the Tank Group advanced belching shells, and flame throwers spewed burning death. The brave Andean Indians charged through the dust from the mine, which opened a 30-meter crater in front of the "fortified island," and were met by an undiminished Paraguayan fire. In the center, the dead piled up in heaps. The troops became disoriented when what Kundt thought were outposts proved to be the main line of resistance. On the right, improper coordination brought a frontal assault before the artillery had softened the defense; then the infantry was victimized when the guns belatedly opened up. By noon the Andean artillery was out of the battle for lack of shells. The flame thrower operators, unprotected by conventional weapons, were soon killed, rendering their apparatus useless. Bold Guaraní dropped grenades into tanks. On the left, the attack progressed initially, but the *jefes* lacked tenacity at the crucial moment and positions captured were lost to a potent Paraguayan counterattack which utilized innumerable hand grenades.[47]

Although Kundt directed an eight-wave attack (6 July) against the "fortified island," the Bolivian offensive had reached its apogee on the fourth when the German sacrificed the best of his army. Over 2,000 Altiplano soldiers died futilely in front of the III Corps defenses. Ten days later Estigarribia, inspecting the sector, noticed that where fighting had been heaviest, fragments of human bodies were scattered over the ground and in the trees. Masses of bodies and fragments had been heaped and ignited with kerosene. They had been only partially consumed, however, leaving a huge, rotting, putrefying mound of human flesh and bones. "For months this atrocious sight remained in my eyes," he wrote.[48]

With its remaining 5,000 men the Bolivian 7th Division reorganized, at last merging the hitherto tiny regiments to create larger units with two battalions each. It then lay inactive in front of Nanawa until December.[49]

Following the Bolivian defeat, a limited offensive, approved in June by Estigarribia, was launched by Franco's 1st Division at Gondra. On 12 July, Peñaranda's right was turned and his field hospital at Campo Via captured. Although two squadrons of cavalry and service troops rushed to the rear, and the 18th Infantry supported them from the west, the 4th Division was in danger of being surrounded. Water was scarce; the Guaraní called upon the thirsty Andeans to trade their weapons for a few drops. Early 15 July, having opened an escape route to the northwest, Peñaranda withdrew and took up new positions beyond the Guaraní in Campo Via. The Paraguayan operation lifted morale and proved the feasibility of maneuver in the brush. *Movement* returned to the war.[50]

President Ayala, his adherence to a defensive strategy fundamentally the result of confidence in a diplomatic solution, repeated that in view of bright diplomatic propects, unnecessery loss of life should be avoided. Estigarribia was therefore obliged to halt Franco's promising offensive so as not to commit reserves and expand the fighting. Franco dug in along the eastern edge of the woods at Campo Via. Nonetheless, having derived maximum benefit from the active defense, Estigarribia was resolved to return to large-scale aggressive maneuvers.[51]

Kundt, after his second failure at Nanawa, finally turned to the indirect attacks on Paraguayan communications which the Bolivian *jefes* had favored months before. On 5 August, Rojas Silva (Falcón) was briefly occupied; 25 August Pirijayo (Pirizal) was captured by a task force commanded by Colonel Carlos Banzer. After reaching the rear of Franco's division, Banzer asked for reinforcements and more ammunition; typically, Kundt refused, causing the failure of a planned double envelopment. Rancho Ocho was threatened at the same time and major elements of the

7th Division attacked Bullo. Kundt still kept half of the latter unit's 5,000 men idly facing Nanawa when their employment in support of operations along the road to Rojas Silva might have proved decisive. His inept use of his 12,000-man army therefore achieved only transitory success against the doubly numerous, but defensively employed, Guaraní.[52]

The attacks on Nanawa, Toledo, and Fernández indicated Kundt's reliance on mass and his inability to maneuver. His tactics were almost exclusively limited to gaining ground, places, and trenches. He apparently did not understand the lessons of the World War, nor of Boquerón: in the Chaco, as in Europe, defense was vastly superior to attack. Misemploying his excellent Air Force and barred by the jungle from effective use of tanks, Kundt could not overcome the superiority of defensive firepower. He prized ground-gaining above destruction of the enemy and was mentally incapable of indirect approach. Kundt once told Colonel Julio C. Guerrero, a Peruvian military critic, that he intended to base his method of attack on the German experience on the Eastern Front in the World War. Paraguayan intelligence in Europe indicated, however, that Kundt had hurled his brigade against the Russians without artillery support or reserves. "His only order was 'advance,' imparted almost always by telephone at whose use he was very adept." Energetic, but willful and incapable of balanced judgment, he acted without adequate contemplation, and then blamed his subordinates for failure, alleging lack of energy. His principal characteristic was the offensive, often without clearly determined objectives and invariably in violation of the principle of economy of force. In the Chaco these tactics floundered against Paraguay's Russian-inspired defenses.[53]

Another factor in the poor success of the Bolivian offensive was psychological, the human element. The Bolivian soldier, accustomed to the vast open spaces of the austere Altiplano, disliked and feared the thick jungle and easily panicked when he heard "we are surrounded." He was an excellent, stoic, defensive fighter, but the subordinate position of the Andean Indian, unintegrated into the life of his country, made him incapable of the personal initiative which made the Paraguayan a brilliant and aggressive soldier. On patrol the Bolivian re-examined known ground or hid and slept for fear of the brush. Frequently, he was transported from the Altiplano to the Chaco like a beast, unaware of his purpose, and then thrust untrained into combat. He was seldom employed in sufficient numbers at a given tactical moment. Although in the course of the war Bolivia mobilized nearly 250,000 as against 140,000 Paraguayans, her forces rarely possessed numerical superiority.[54]

Summarily, other factors in the failure of the Bolivian offensive were the technical incompetence of *jefes* (having been schooled entirely at home, their ideas were inbred) ; inability of men to acclimate physically to the brush, abominable logistics, Salamanca's "economic war," and the moral deterioration spread by communist-led defeatists. The sum of these factors meant that, commonly, sick, hungry, unprovisioned, disheartened troops were all too often led by half-hearted, inept commanders against strategically unwise objectives. When the impotence of this Bolivian army became palpable, all that remained was for the enemy to administer the *coup d'grâce*.

Notes

1. Vergara Vicuña, II, 434, 547-548, 709; *Bilbao*, 286; Fernández, II, 151-152.

2. Rodríguez, 86; Vergara Vicuña, II, 695-703, 711-715; Díaz Arguedas, *Los Elegidos*, 233-238; Colonel Enrique Vidaurre, *Acciones militares en Toledo y Fernández* (n. p., 1940), 30-32. Osorio had requested 80 trucks in October to move the 3rd Division; Rivarola, II, 240.

3. Moscoso, 159-160; Toro, 30; Díaz Arguedas, *El hombre símbolo*, 40. Kundt used a small personal staff which included Lieutenant Colonel Miguel Candía, Captains Antenor Ichaso and Max España, and Lieutenant Ricardo Rios. Vergara Vicuña, II, 609-619; III, 24; *Bilbao*, 246; Fernández, II, 220; Guerrero, 156; Ayala Moreira, 217-220, 338.

4. Moscoso, 154-158; Vergara Vicuña, III, 1-15, 30, 39; Díaz Arguedas, *El hombre símbolo*, 41, 327; Guerrero, 247. Kundt became a naturalized Bolivian citizen in 1922.

5. Fernández, II, 195-197, 325, quotation 197; J. B. Ayala, 131; Delgado, I, 73; Vergara Vicuña, II, 625-626.

6. Fernández, II, 199-202, 326-327; Delgado, I, 74-79; Vergara Vicuña, III, 49, 70-71. Lieutenant Colonel Arturo Bray took over the 4th Division, replacing Delgado.

7. Fernández, II, 202-215; Delgado, I, 80, says a Bolivian prisoner revealed the pending attack, for which the Guaraní were then fully prepared; Díaz Arguedas, *Los Elegidos,* 201-203; Vergara Vicuña, III, 51-55, 61, 78, 83, 112, 115, 129-130; *Bilbao,* 306. Guillén later attempted to falsely portray the attack as an unauthorized adventure of the 4th Division Command. See Vergara Vicuña, III, 119-124, 133-142. In fact, the attack almost accomplished the end of getting Paraguayans to retreat to Alihuatá; Delgado desired such a move but was strongly opposed by Fernández. The two violently disagreed on tactics, weakening the command of the Paraguayan I Corps; Fernández, II, 217, 339-344. See also Ayala Moreira, 222-234.

8. Fernández, II, 221-223, 227; Vergara Vicuña, III, 183-186; González, 80; Ayala Moreira, 234-236.

9. Vidaurre, *Acciones militares,* 33-40; J. B. Ayala, 150-154; Toro, 31-32; Díaz Arguedas, *Los Elegidos,* 239-241, 245, 248; Vergara Vicuña, II, 593-595; III, 131-132, 139, 148-150, 159-160, 175-178, 188-201; Ayala Moreira, 238-241.

10. The original Fortín Nanawa was west of, but adjoining, the new Fortín Ayala. The names have often been erroneously used interchangeably. The Bolivian attack was directed principally on Nanawa, which formed a 600-meter salient under attack on three sides.

11. Fernández, II, 51, 226; González, 80, 84; Delgado, I, 84, 87, 90-94; General (H. C.) Dr. Stephen Vysokolán, *Batalla de Nanawa* (Asunción, 1958), 17; Díaz Arguedas, *Los Elegidos,* 250; Guerrero, 239; Vergara Vicuña, III, 267-273. Estigarribia (59-62) had studied Kundt's World War record while in France attending the War College. He learned that Kundt was a man of enormous energy, authoritative, self-confident, tenacious, a devotee of constant attacks at all costs. Analyzing the German's record, Estigarribia planned how the man could be made to defeat himself; how his own characteristics could be converted into his downfall.

12. Toro, 33-35; Vergara Vicuña, III, 275, 281-282, 290, 319; *Bilbao,* 329; Ayala Moreira, 243-249. Since Bolivian regiments were really triangular battalions totaling never more than 500 men, the latter (250) places 7th Division strength at 4,000.

13. Fernández, II, 228, 235; Díaz Arguedas, *Los Elegidos,* 251-253; Guerrero, 162-163; Vergara Vicuña, III, 296-298; Ayala Moreira, 251-255.

14. Fernández, II, 238-239; Delgado, I, 85-86, 95-96, 101. See also Díaz Arguedas, *Los Elegidos,* 273-274; Vergara Vicuña, III, 146, 234-252; Ayala Moreira, 257-260, gives casualties as 600.

Bolivian aircraft dropped psy-war leaflets on the 1st Division, which had actually been printed for a strategic psy-war raid on Asunción conceived by Bilbao Rioja. On 13 December tactical leaflets had been dropped saying that while prisoners of war rode the streets of La Paz in automobiles, well treated by all, the 1st Division soldiers were being mercilessly used as cannon fodder by their officers. Surrender, the leaflet continued. Come over to the Bolivian lines, arms raised, and receive an *abrazo* and good care. "Before suffering outrages from your superiors, miseries and privations, entrust yourselves to the Bolivian soldiers!"

Paraguay relied for propaganda largely on her official communiques, spread abroad by the news service. Since these invariably reached the Bolivian population, they were an excellent and cheap medium. Consequently, casualty figures and booty were greatly exaggerated, but places and units mentioned were completely accurate. After such reports met invariable denial, eventual discovery that they were true achieved the desired result of undermining Bolivian morale in rear areas and gaining credence for Paraguayan reports. Fernández, II, 27-29.

In tactical situations, Paraguay employed a "mortarette," a piece of 75 mm. casing held between two pieces of wood. A small charge gave an explosion nearly identical with a mortar, convincing the enemy that great numbers of Stokes-Brandts were at hand; Vidaurre, *Material de guerra*, 167.

15. Fernández, II, 229, 232, 236-237; Estigarribia, 63-65; Delgado, I, 98-99; *Partes del conductor*, 47-49. Also consult Díaz Arguedas, *Los Elegidos*, 267-268; Vergara Vicuña, III, 331-346, 351-360; *Bilbao*, 329; Aponte B., *Cincuenta años*, 180-184.

16. J. B. Ayala, 132-136, 146-147, 155-166; Vidaurre, *Acciones militares*, 46-53; *Material de guerra*, 115, 176; Fernández, II, 240; González, 79, 82, 85-87, 99; Vergara Vicuña, III, 218-219, 224-228, 403-408.

17. Vidaurre, *Acciones militares*, 57-91; J. B. Ayala 167-192; Estigarribia, 67; González, 89-93. See also Díaz Arguedas, *Los Elegidos*, 276-289; Fernández, II, 338, 241-242; Florentín, *Boquerón,* 132. The air attack was a major achievement in that Bilbao's Group took off at Villa Montes during a black night and crossed the Chaco by pilotage, without instruments; Vergara Vicuña, *Bilbao*, 315. At the time, Guaraní sources indicated the Bolivians had 26 fighters, 27 recon-bombers, and 9 tri-motor transports; Rivarola, II, 281. See also Ayala Moreira, 261-265.

18. Díaz Arguedas, *Los Elegidos*, 290-291. The Paraguayan Press Office reported that the 3rd Division had suffered a major disaster; *Partes del conductor*, 62-63.

19. Rivarola, II, 276; *Política Argentina*, II, 3-14; Bolivia, *Memoria 1934*, 185-190; U. S., *Foreign Relations*, 1933, IV, 243-256. White, reflecting the asinine, but prevalent, world sentiment that since Bo-

livia and Paraguay were small, they had no right to war even if their national interests so directed, suggested to Argentine ambassador Espil that the ABCP should "tell Bolivia and Paraguay that the time has come to stop fighting; that they will not let any further military supplies reach them; that they must stop fighting and accept the Neutral proposal of December . . . as the basis for discussion" (p. 253). In late February, Espil proposed a join effort to *force* peace; Argentina would handle Paraguay if the United States coerced Bolivia. White immediately backed down, saying that the United States had no control, economic or otherwise, over Bolivia (p. 275).

20. U. S., *Foreign Relations, 1933*, IV, 288-291; República del Paraguay, Ministerio de Relaciones Exteriores, *Libro Blanco. 1933. Part II, Documentos relativos a los acuerdos de Mendoza y a la declaracion del estado de guerra con Bolivia* (Asunción, 1933), 3-5 (cited hereafter as *Libro Blanco. Acuerdos*); Rivarola, II, 293.

While the Battle of Boquerón was in full fury, Eusebio Ayala outlined with statesmanly perspective his analysis of the Chaco problem; Rivarola was instructed to bring it to the attention of Saavedra Lamas. The Guaraní President, contemplating economic problems, observed Paraguay's mediterranean condition was tempered only by her river and close relations with Argentina. The problem of access to the sea for both her and Bolivia must be solved with broad criteria surpassing the interests and passions of the moment and stimulating continental economic and financial development. For Paraguay, closer relations and an outlet through Brazil for her North were needed to complement the fluvial link with Argentina. "The Republic of Bolivia must obtain equal satisfaction of her legitimate aspirations to communication with the great markets of the world."

Bolivia is a country of many regions; the mineral economy of the Altiplano seeks its exit to the Pacific, the vast Northern plains look to the Amazon, the South to Argentina, and the *Oriente* to the Rio Paraguay. Her communications aspirations unsatisfied by her larger neighbors, Bolivia sought to take the Paraguayan Chaco, which in reality could only ameliorate a small segment of her geographic dilemma.

These complex problems could best be solved by a regional economic conference to conclude agreements on rail, highway, and water transportation to link comprehensively the belligerents with their greater neighbors. Brazil should build an upriver port for Bolivia, while all the Plata countries should join in river improvement to enable 3,000-ton vessels to reach Corumbá. Bolivia should have the right to build oil pipe lines with free zones and facilities where appropriate in neighboring states. Only thus could the vast distances separating Bolivia and Paraguay from world markets be solved. War could accomplish nothing, Ayala concluded, and would only cost

NANAWA—THE BOLIVIAN OFFENSIVE

much blood and ruin both contenders. Rivarola, II, 192-196, 211n-213n; quotation from 212n.

Coincidentally, a report prepared by an Argentine engineer revealed similar general thinking, and was accepted by Saavedra Lamas. This document indicated Bolivia's major problems were a free mineral outlet through Chilean territory, adequate communications between the Altiplano and the lowlands, and an external outlet for her nascent oil fields along the Andean foothills. None of these problems would be solved by a port on the Rio Paraguay. The latter two could better be solved through railroad conventions with Argentina; *Política Argentina*, I, 356-369. Such suggestions were viewed on the Altiplano as an effort by Argentina to avoid the competition of Bolivian oil by acquiring control of its marketing; U. S., *Foreign Relations, 1932*, V, 157.

21. *Política Argentina*, I, 17-21; *Libro Blanco. Acuerdos*, 6-8; U. S., *Foreign Relations, 1933*, IV, 268, 273; Bolivia, *Memoria 1934*, 192-196.

22. *Libro Blanco. Acuerdos*, 9-10, 43-48; Bolivia, *Memoria 1934*, 224-228, 199-200; U. S., *Foreign Relations, 1933*, IV, 272, 274, 276; *Política Argentina*, II, 30-31; Rivarola, II, 301-303.

23. Bolivia, *Memoria 1934*, 197-199; U. S., *Foreign Relations, 1933*, IV, 277-281, 284-285; *Libro Blanco. Acuerdos*, 12-14; *Política Argentina*, II, 32-35.

24. Delgado, I, 95, 100, 106, 109-112; Fernández, II, 243, 332-333. See also Díaz Arguedas, *Los Elegidos*, 309-310; Vergara Vicuña, III, 472-478. Kasianov was killed in this action. It will be recalled that Colonel Gutiérrez was the *jefe* who, while personally seeking a likely site for Vanguardia, was captured in his hammock on the Rio Negro in August 1928.

25. Moscoso, 174-177, 192-194. Bilbao, made the scapegoat for failure of the 27 December attack, had been replaced by Moscoso as 4th Division Chief of Staff in early January (p. 166); Vergara Vicuña, *Bilbao*, 307-313. See also Guerrero, 169; Vergara Vicuña, III, 487; IV, 6-7, 34, 72; Díaz Arguedas, *Los Elegidos*, 298, 312. After reading Kundt's plans for the Alihuatá maneuver, Bilbao raised objections to the small forces involved. Kundt replied, "You have been called to comply with an order and not to give your opinion. Remove yourself to your station in thirty minutes." *Bilbao*, 322.

26. Delgado, I, 119-121; Fernández, II, 247-251; Estigarribia, 68; Toro, 36-38; Moscoso, 178-180; Vergara Vicuña, IV, 76, 101, 107-108, 112.

27. Fernández, II, 252-261, 302-303; Delgado, I, 122-133; Estigarribia, 69-70; Moscoso, 181-186, 195. See also Díaz Arguedas, *Los Elegidos*, 320-321; González, 97; Vergara Vicuña, IV, 114-118, 133; Ayala Moreira, 266-269.

28. Moscoso, 199; Vergara Vicuña, IV, 66, 88, 93-94, 109, 124, 127, 135; Díaz Arguedas, *Los Elegidos*, 453.

29. Moscoso, 197; Estigarribia, 70; *Partes del conductor,* 65; Vergara Vicuña, IV, 154-157.

30. Estigarribia, 71-72; Delgado, I, 138. Rivarola (II, 225-230) had sought a bank loan in Argentina, but after the 1932 offensive halted, the banks refused. He finally secured interest free 8,000,000 Ps Arg. from private citizens and firms doing business in Paraguay. The Guaraní army was receiving 6,000 barrels of gasoline and 400 tons of fuel oil per month from the Argentine Naval Ministry (pp. 340-341).

31. Estigarribia, 72-73.

32. Delgado, I, 138, 143-152; Vidaurre, *Acciones militares,* 99-119. See also Díaz Arguedas, *Los Elegidos,* 299-302; Vergara Vicuña, IV, 40-64, 203-206; Ayala Moreira, 272-274. On 27 March, Delgado received a new Chief of Staff, Major Higínio Morínigo.

33. Delgado, I, 135-137, 140, 144; Moscoso, 198, 201; González, 99; Vergara Vicuña, IV, 138-139, 158, 224; Guerrero, *Peñaranda,* 38.

On 12 April, Franco, the author of Vanguardia and strongman of the abortive October 1931 coup, assumed command of the 1st Division. Fernández had been offered command (28 February) of a new IV Corps which General Rojas proposed to create, still dreaming of acquiring some operational authority in the war; Fernández, II, 197, 247, 268-269; General Rafael Franco, *Dos batallas de la Guerra del Chaco* (Buenos Aires, 1959), 15-16.

On 13 April, Delgado, the victim of malaria, turned I Corps over to Lieutenant Colonel Gaudioso Núñez and went to Asunción; Delgado, I, 153-156; Estigarribia, 74.

34. Moscoso, 208-216; Toro, 39; Vergara Vicuña, IV, 247-252; Colonel Julio C. Guerrero, *Peñaranda* (La Paz, 1940) 40-41; Franco, 18-19.

35. *Libro Blanco. Acuerdos,* 15-21; Bolivia, *Memoria 1934,* 201-212; Rivarola, II, 305-306; *Política Argentina,* II, 35-64; U. S., *Foreign Relations,* 1933, IV, 282, 293-295, 299-311, 314-316, 332. Feely reported 22 March: "Recent military successes and the acquiescence of Chile in the free transit of arms via Arica have greatly strengthened Bolivian confidence in a successful issue of the military campaign" (p. 295). Chile was permitting arms passage because of lack of success in concerting an embargo against Bolivia (p. 286).

36. *Libro Blanco. Acuerdos,* 64-68; Bolivia, *Memoria 1934,* 213-221, 224-230; *Política Argentina,* II, 53-68; Eduardo Diez de Medina, *Conferencias* (La Paz, 1933), 81; Rivarola, II, 246, 249, 287, 314-315, 326-328, 333-335, 346-348, quotation, 251. Rivarola believed sealing Bolivian international supply routes would stimulate peace by enabling La Paz to blame defeat on geographic injustice instead of

military failure (p. 313). U. S., *Foreign Relations, 1933*, IV, 281, 287, 299, 312. From unofficial soundings, Feely believed Bolivia would arbitrate the difference between her narrow arbitration zone and the full Paraguayan claim, excluding the Hayes Zone and an equivalency (p. 315).

37. Brazilian decree is found in DeBarros, 128-138, and Bolivia, *Memoria 1934*, 316-323; Chilean decree, 324-325; Peruvian, 334. Consult Delgado, II, 15; Diez de Medina, *De un Siglo*, 339.

38. For neutrality decree and resulting correspondence, see Bolivia, *Memoria 1934*, 232-316, or República Argentina, Ministerio de Relaciones Exteriores y Culto, *La Neutralidad Argentina en el Conflicto Boliviano-Paraguayo* (Buenos Aires, 1933), 6-66; *Política Argentina*, II, 72-73. Also consult Rivarola, II, 349; Guerrero, 206; Diez de Medina, *Conferencias*, 18-21; Ayala Moreira, 344-365.

39. Rivarola, II, 206, 209; *Política Argentina*, II, 70; U. S., *Foreign Relations*, 1932, V, 243-244, 247; 1933, IV, 332-336. On 1 June, Finot sought to have White revive the Neutral plan of 15 December with Bolivia now willing to retire to Villa Montes. Although this would have made the plan acceptable to Asunción, White would take no action unless Finot put his proposal in writing with official approval of La Paz. Roosevelt, however, desired to "get out of the matter gracefully and leave it to the League and South Americans." Over strong objections of Uruguay, White then led the Neutrals to an act of dissolution 27 June 1933 (pp. 339-345). Paraguay had desired such action since January (p. 259). *Política Argentina*, II, 119.

40. U. S., *Foreign Relations*, 1933, IV, 346-362; DeBarros, 139-140. Brazil had wholeheartedly supported United States interest in the Chaco problem since 1928 as the best hope for a solution. Their cooperation continued throughout the long dispute.

Bolivia's willingness in September 1933 to accept a larger arbitration zone than during the Mendoza efforts was unquestionably due to deterioration of her military situation. In April she was freshly victorious; in September, freshly defeated and her offensive a failure.

The role of the League of Nations has been the subject of a monograph: Margaret La Foy, *The Chaco Dispute and the League of Nations* (Ann Arbor, 1946). The study is inadequate in treating the dispute due to noninclusion of the principal sources. We do not propose here to discuss Geneva's activities in other than a summary fashion.

41. Toro, 39-41; Moscoso, 236-238; Estigarribia, 79; Guerrero, *Peñaranda*, 31-35 (When Guerrero questioned Kundt on his determination to take Nanawa, the General changed the subject, 39-40n); Vergara Vicuña, IV, 237-246, 369-370. Although Bolivia at this time

had only 13,000 troops against at least 20,000 Paraguayans, the defensive strategy dictated by President Ayala left Kundt with full initiative. He could follow lines of his own choosing (p. 295).

42. Vidaurre, *Acciones militares*, 125-145; *Partes del conductor*, 85-88. See also Díaz Arguedas, *Los Elegidos*, 303-304, 371; Vergara Vicuña, IV, 162-176, 296, 300-309, 311-314, 321-322; Ayala Moreira, 278-281. Rivarola (p. 344) wired Asunción 9 May that Bolivia would attack Fernández the following morning and furnished the texts of Kundt's orders for the operation!

43. Vergara Vicuña, IV, 325-329. Kundt himself was kind and well liked by common soldiers, whom he frequently visited at the front and to whom he gave his coca and cigarettes; Guerrero, 246.

44. Vidaurre, *Acciones militares*, 146-148; Vergara Vicuña, IV, 337-342, 348, 355-356, 360; Ayala Moreira, 281-283. Note, however, the dissenting contention of J. B. Ayala (p. 193) that Estigarribia planned to attack Platanillos, but was dissuaded by himself on the ground that the enemy would not thus be destroyed.

45. Moscoso, 207, 217-219, 223, 225; Estigarribia, 75; Benítez, *Estigarribia*, 1st ed., 85; Franco, 20-22. The Paraguayan Press Office reported that Bolivian troops were eating snakes and leather; *Partes del conductor*, 72, 77. Spreading divisive propaganda, it reported that Andeans at Nanawa yelled "Viva Blanco Galindo, muera Kundt" (p. 83).

46. Estigarribia, 75-76; González, 100, 103n; Vysokolán, 19; Franco, 26-35. Reference to this important meeting is conspicuously absent from J. B. Ayala's book. Franco (37) was always critical of General Estigarribia, claiming he should have had "more vision, greater magnitude and ambition." Strangely enough, political foes, even including Franco in 1936, asserted the General had too much political ambition! Franco (38) characterizes Estigarribia as always "a lukewarm, vacillating commander with little imagination and, above all, excessive caution to the extreme of never deciding or risking actions that did not represent almost absolute certainly." These traits, Franco (39) concludes, condemned the Paraguayan commander to mediocrity. While General Franco's opinion merits consideration, it is obvious that a commander of the type he describes could not have led his country to victory.

47. Estigarribia, 77; Toro, 42-44; Moscoso, 235, 241; *Partes del conductor*, 92-95; Vysokolán, 20-24. See also Vergara Vicuña, IV, 283, 374-379, 387, 392-399, 408; Díaz Arguedas, *Los Elegidos*, 339-342; Ayala Moreira, 287-297. Paraguay used grenades in large quantities, as they were manufactured in a modern arsenal at Asunción. This facility worked three shifts making, in addition, canteens, truck bodies, water tanks, and even a few mortars. Vehicle repair and operation was included in this management empire of 22,000 people under Navy

Captain José Bozzano. Lacking such a plant, Bolivia bought all supplies abroad; Rios, 99-101; J. B. Ayala, 78-79.

48. Estigarribia, 78; Vergara Vicuña, IV, 426-427; Visokolán, 25.

49. Vergara Vicuña, IV, 444, 454.

50. Ibid., 469-480; Moscoso, 246-251; Franco, 41-56; Ayala Moreira, 297-298. See also Díaz Arguedas, Los Elegidos, 323-324; Partes del conductor, 99-101; Guerrero, Peñaranda, 51-53.

51. Estigarribia, 80-81.

52. Ibid., 82-84; Moscoso, 256-259. Also see Díaz Arguedas, Los Elegidos, 351-356, 363, 369; Vergara Vicuña, IV, 485-497; Partes del conductor, 106-108. Banzer utilized part of the tank group; Ayala Moreira, 299-300.

53. Fernández, II, 20; quotation, 21; Ayala Moreira, 73-75; González, 94; Vergara Vicuña, III, 212-213; V, 238-242; Guerrero, 196-197.

54. Rodríguez, 80; Moscoso, 164, 221; Pol, 47, 90; Vergara Vicuña, III, 307; IV, 408. See also Urioste, La Encrucijada, 159.

CHAPTER SIX

CAMPO VIA—THE SECOND PARAGUAYAN OFFENSIVE

At the end of August 1933 the aggressive Bolivian army consisted of II Corps, with the 3rd and 8th Divisions reduced to insignificance in front of Platanillos and Corrales; and I Corps with the 7th, 4th, and 9th Divisions deployed in an arc from Nanawa past the Gondra salient and Rancho Ocho to the vicinity of Arce, thence westward to Campo Grande. These forces were opposed by the Paraguayan COMANSUR'S III Corps at Nanawa-Gondra (1st, 4th, and 5th Divisions, 2nd Cavalry Brigade), I Corps at Falcón-Arce-Fernández (2nd, 7th, and 8th Divisions), and II Corps at Toledo-Betty (6th Division, 1st Cavalry Brigade). In the forgotten north, the COMANOR's 3rd Division at Bahia Negra-Galpón looked across the swampy, flooded Rio Negro at the Bolivian 5th Division at Puerto Suárez.[1]

When President Ayala visited GHQ at Villa Militar on 31 August, Estigarribia explained his desire to return to the offensive. He requested 500 new trucks to enhance mobility. Since reserves were already committed against the Bolivian salient at Rancho Ocho-Pirizal, the only route open for action was against the 9th Division, at the moment weakened to about 1,000 men. A double envelopment was envisioned, the one prong on the Andean left at Pampa (or Campo) Grande, the other on the right at Pozo Favorita (Siete Pozos), to converge later on the Alihuatá road behind Colonel Carlos Banzer's 9th Division and complete its destruction. Secondary attacks at Rancho Ocho would support the offensive. Although the plan appeared sound, Ayala did not voice his approval; nevertheless, Estigarribia proceeded to its execution.[2]

At this time Colonel Banzer had three regiments in line from

Pozo Favorita to Pampa Grande. On 30 August the 27th Infantry, astraddle the Arce-Alihuatá road, was briefly surrounded, whereupon the 8th Division made a weak probe at Fernández to divert Guaraní attention from Banzer's weakness. The Bolivian Air Force reported the enemy cutting trails to infiltrate the flanks, but Kundt was unimpressed, believing that the pilots exaggerated. At Gondra, where since July the Paraguayan 1st Division had occupied 24 kilometers of lines, the Andeans attempted a double envelopment. On 7 September, Franco retreated strategically to his former positions, thus shortening his front. By the same act, a dangerous threat was posed to Peñaranda's forces at Rancho Ocho and Pirizal, obliging him to order their withdrawal. These events freed Estigarribia's reserves, giving him full freedom of action and inviting his next move.[3]

On the eleventh he moved his CP to Arce, took personal command of I Corps, and initiated the Pampa Grande-Pozo Favorita moves, employing the reinforced 7th and 8th Divisions. He visited all regimental CPs, spurring the zeal of the *jefes*. On 12 September the Pampa Grande-Alihuatá road was cut behind the Bolivian 2nd and 4th Infantry regiments. Reinforcement of this incursion the following day firmly closed the circle. Water which the trapped Andeans had received on 11 September was issued daily in half rations. In the center the 27th Infantry narrowly escaped encirclement on the Arce road; it was reinforced, however, and counterattacked.[4]

At Pozo Favorita part of the Bolivian 18th Infantry was surrounded on the fourteenth. His disorientation complete, Kundt with a mere 200 men attempted to break the siege laid at Pampa Grande by the 3,500-man Guaraní 7th Division (Lieutenant Colonel José A. Ortiz). While the Bolivian Air Force dropped the Andean narcotic, coca, to the encircled, Estigarribia rushed food and water to his men, urging them to hold firm at all costs. The madness associated with thirst soon gripped the Andeans. Morale deteriorated when a captured sergeant called upon his countrymen in Quechua to surrender and receive water. The afternoon of 14 September, when water was exhausted, both pockets surrendered with 22 officers and 909 men. The remainder of the 9th Division, which had been reinforced to 3,338, thwarted

Estigarribia's plan of annihilation by pulling back. Since Paraguay's casualties had not been light, her army returned to the defense for rest and reorganization.[5]

On 18 September at Villa Militar, to which he had gone to solicit Ayala's approval for continuation of the offensive, Estigarribia was promoted. After a year of war, Paraguay's 25,000-man field army was for the first time commanded by a Brigadier General. At Muñoz another General, Hans Kundt, contemplated flight to Argentina, or suicide.[6]

Peñaranda, Moscoso, Toro, and others stressed that the situation was critical and urged Kundt to prepare to retreat the 4th and 9th Divisions by stages until their lines met in Campo 31. They knew that the Air Force reported a Guaraní road in progress west of Alihuatá. Further retreat, Moscoso stressed, should even be considered to the old bulwark, Kilometer 7, and eventual retirement contemplated to the Platanillos-Magariños line in case of necessity. The General wisely accepted these suggestions, but his addiction to ground made any retreat unlikely. The Bolivian *jefes* unanimously asked Kundt to request Salamanca to mobilize 80,000 men, but the German believed such numbers were beyond the national capacity. Before departing for La Paz on 2 October, he shuffled *jefes,* placing Peñaranda in command of I Corps and giving the 4th Division to Arrieta. Toro was left in acting supreme command with instructions to prepare defenses, but to make no troop moves. II Corps shortly thereafter was turned over to Colonel Rafael Morant; Generals Guillén and Osorio returned to the Altiplano "for reasons of health."[7]

In La Paz, General Kundt was treated as a hero and, apparently whirling in an aurora australis, forgot his resolve to seek more men and equipment. He assured the people that Pampa Grande was an isolated incident without significance and that the possibility of a Guaraní victory was gone forever. He later told Señor Urioste, a government functionary, that Salamanca sat and listened without comment, refusing to speak. If he spoke at all, he allegedly urged Kundt to shorten the front, an admonition which he repeated by wire 17 October. The General dismissed this proposal on the grounds that a shorter front would be easier for the enemy to envelop.[8]

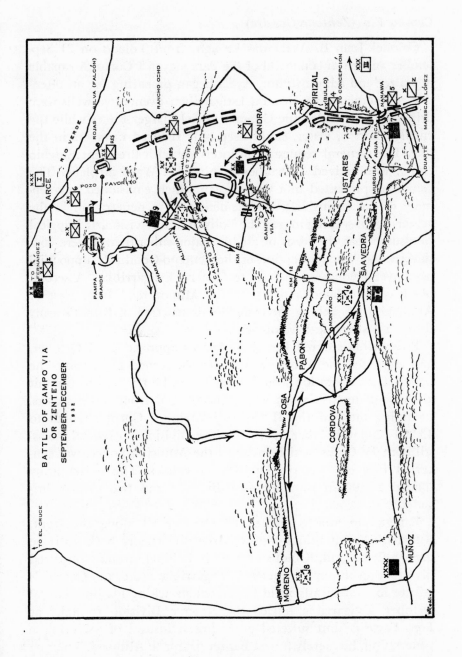

BATTLE OF CAMPO VIA
OR ZENTENO
SEPTEMBER–DECEMBER
1932

Campo Via (Zenteno-Gondra)

Colonel Juan B. Ayala was brought from Toledo on 21 September and given command of the Paraguayan I Corps. A capable organizer and administrator, Ayala began preparing for an offensive contemplated by General Estigarribia: twenty-two wells were drilled. This enabled the Guaraní to field larger forces while the enemy, short of water, could keep only reduced numbers in the line. The General requested an interview with President Eusebio Ayala, who arrived 3 October in his sleek Waco airplane. The command presented him with a plan which envisioned envelopment of the enemy left, complemented by a penetration in the center, again seeking to trap the Bolivian 9th Division. It is logical to assume that the ideas of all his major subordinates were considered, but "the conception of the Zenteno-Gondra [Campo Via] maneuver belongs *exclusively* to General Estigarribia." A second phase contemplated a sweep to the Muñoz road from west of Alihuatá, thus seeking the complete destruction of Kundt's army through a strategic envelopment.[9]

Estigarribia secured President Ayala's approval on 4 October, and requested the trucks essential for the second phase. Since he believed the operation would bring peace, he resolved to commit all his resources. Troops were concentrated from other sectors, including most of the II Corps, bringing I Corps strength to 13,000 (2nd, 6th, 7th, 8th, and Reserve Divisions). General Rojas' stillborn IV Corps, which included the Asunción police, was converted into the Reserve Division at Falcón. The entire army totaled 26,500 in nine infantry divisions and two cavalry brigades.[10]

Paraguayan attacks opened 23 October all along the front. Estigarribia's intentions were to drive the enemy back until he made a firm stand. Kundt's tenacity in holding ground "impaired his situation to our advantage," Estigarribia wrote; the German's failure to strategically yield facilitated stretching his line. On 30 October, Estigarribia hurled the Reserve Division frontally at Pozo Favorita, but suffered grave losses; instead of achieving a penetration, he merely forced Banzer nearer to Alihuatá. To draw Paraguayan attention, the remnant 8th Division made a feeble feint at Fernández, but soon retired. Continued Guaraní attacks in early November were daily and frontal, and forced gradual Bolivian retreat. The use of eighteen regiments against seven smaller Andean units caused the 9th Division to absorb all the scarce reserves in I Corps. By 4 November, Kundt assumed personal direction at Alihuatá, committing additional troops on his left a week later. At Nanawa, a section of Bolivian trenches was lost, and on 12 November the 16th Infantry (318 officers and men) was captured. These actions obliged extension of both the Andean left and right in accordance with Paraguayan planning.[11]

Shortly thereafter Toro arrived in La Paz on leave and immediately made the rounds of his political friends, maintaining that Kundt's incompetence would lead to disaster. Rumors filled the Chaco that the old soldier was a traitor in the pay of Asunción; many could imagine no other answer for his absurd decisions. Others optimistically assumed that he was following a secret plan which would destroy the enemy. Fighting seemed to be everywhere and troops were nervous for lack of information.[12]

The Bolivian Air Force, which dominated the sky and was very active, reported roads, trails, and paths being cut, especially toward the Alihuatá-Puesto Sosa road, but the German General chose to take no action. After 16 November, when Fortín Mariscal López was retaken by the Guaraní, Bolivian lines were stretched to a maximum, with all forces committed. Estigarribia, possessing detailed knowledge of Bolivian troop dispositions gained from tapped phone lines, monitored radio messages, and espionage agents, strengthened his right in readiness for maneuver; he believed that Kundt's fate was now sealed—whether he chose to retreat or fight, the result would be the same.[13] Incapable of any longer resisting frontal pressure, according to the principles of war Kundt should have retired to avoid annihilation, but he had waited too long.

On 25 November the League of Nations' Chaco Commission visited Villa Militar, and heard Estigarribia assert that Paraguay would accept no discussion of the littoral and was determined "to continue the war with the certainty of crushing the enemy." To the assertion of General Freydenberg (France) that war was fickle and could not be absolutely predicted, the Guaraní commander replied, "The destruction of the Bolivian army is a mathematical operation."[14] He had now resolved to shift from frontal to flank attack, aiming to take the enemy in a double envelopment.

Banzer had kept Kundt informed of the exact situation of the left, but in response the German suggested that he "abstain from submitting such alarming reports which the command is sure do not concur with reality." The General, nevertheless, ordered the flank at Charata reinforced from the 4th Division. Colonel Banzer also committed his walking wounded, cooks and bakers, aides and clerks, as final reinforcements. Manpower was especially scarce because Kundt, possibly to reassure the country that all was well, had granted leaves to about 1,500 men. Banzer believed him resolved to hold Alihuatá at all costs because it signified his victory of March. In an effort to save the situation, Kundt belatedly formed a detachment of 400 raw recruits at Puesto Sosa under Major Brandt, a German mercenary, and sent it against the rear of the Paraguayan right, which by then blocked the Alihuatá-Puesto Sosa road at Charata.[15]

Paraguay had assembled all possible forces for the final blow, but Colonel J. B. Ayala procrastinated under diverse pretexts. His subordinate 7th Division commander, Ortiz, had become convinced he was going to do absolutely nothing; Estigarribia believed the man feared responsibility. Ayala had wasted the lives of troops, but was unwilling, despite a perfect opportunity, to begin rounding the Bolivian left. Ortiz offered to assume command with full accountability, but on the night of 2 December, General Estigarribia ordered Ayala not to move another man. The following morning the General appeared at Ortiz's CP and placed him in charge of the right with 14 regiments, advising that he himself would take personal command of I Corps. Immediately, Estigarribia journeyed to Campo Aceval where early 4 December he conferred with Colonels Fernández, Franco, and Irrazábal, outlining the III Corps role. He deferred his own plan for the sector in favor of a proposal advanced by Colonel Fernández. The same day, despite torrential rains, Estigarribia ordered Ortiz to advance from Pampa Grande to the road west of Alihuatá.[16]

The Bolivian situation was now grave. The Air Force furnished semi-hourly reconnaissance reports, which Kundt disdained, terming the pilots "alarmists." Salamanca urged retreat, apprehensive for the units at Gondra and Alihuatá. Kundt vacillated, gave the order, then cancelled it, claiming the situation had improved. On 6 December the Paraguayan double envelopment reached the Alihuatá-Saavedra and Alihuatá-Pozo Negro roads. Kundt placed Banzer on his own ("Proceed according to the situation") to retreat the 9th Division to Campo 31. The only escape route still open—east to Campo Victoria and south to Campo Via—was taken after Alihuatá was fired 7 December. The road was slippery with mud and water, making transport of the artillery difficult. At 0100 Brandt's rear had been blocked at Charata; at dawn, Franco, reinforced with two regiments from Fernández' division, erupted from Gondra, stormed the 4th Division lines, and sealed the Campo Via-Puesto Ustares road. Kundt deliberately concealed this information from him, Banzer charged, and advised La Paz that the retreat had worsened the situation but little. Estigarribia ordered continued advance from Charata by the 3rd "Corrales" Infantry to close the Saavedra road and link up with Franco's 1st Division. At midnight the Paraguayan army occupied burning Alihuatá.[17]

In his effort to sustain the 9th Division's lines and avoid retreat, Kundt had weakened the 4th Division (commanded since November by Colonel Emilio González Quint) to 1,355 men. Pleas for more troops were rejected because Kundt did not believe the Paraguayan army strong enough for action on a broad front. He persisted in the delusion that Estigarribia had no more troops than Bolivia. Consequently, the Paraguayan 1st Division advanced steadily, especially at Campo Victoria where González Quint joined lines with Banzer. The 9th Division retreat had actually facilitated the Guaraní trap by bringing the Andean forces together in a small area. Further, the two menaced divisions were uncoordinated, the 4th depending from I Corps while the 9th was directly under Kundt. In the south the 7th Division had already retired from in front of Nanawa to avoid being flanked by the Guaraní III Corps, which had recaptured Fortín Duarte. Estigarribia, lacking trucks to rush troops toward Puesto

Moreno and Muñoz, ordered his 8th Division to march on Puesto Sosa.[18]

Banzer was resolved to continue his retreat to Kilometer 7, but Kundt ordered a new defense line from Campo Victoria to 3 kilometers west of the Saavedra road in Campo 31. Banzer, however, merged his artillery with that of the 4th Division and continued toward Kilometer 22. On 9 December, Kundt reiterated his order for firm defense. By this time Franco had occupied the woods north of Campo Via, sealing the road from Campo Victoria, and more narrowly confining the Andean forces. With the Guaraní 7th Division at Kilometer 31, Banzer had no ready escape route, and when Kundt advised that a road was being cut toward the endangered forces from Kilometer 25, he pressed the construction of a trail in that direction. González Quint joined in the effort, issuing general retreat orders to the 4th Division. Large, thick trees slowed the road cutting, and soon most of the army, along with 100 loaded trucks, was strung out on the unfinished road. Beneath the burning sun the soldiers suffered. God was a Guaraní, for there was no relieving rain. Thirst, the terror of the Chaco, began to infiltrate the ranks and men slunk away into the woods in search of puddles of rain water.[19]

Kundt, meanwhile, under Guaraní threat abandoned his CP at Kilometer 22 and restored the 9th Division to I Corps. The trapped were cheered by a wire (10 December) that Peñaranda was advancing with troops from Saavedra to assume command of both divisions. Estigarribia immediately ordered his 6th Division to proceed by forced marches from Charata to Puesto Pabón, close the Saavedra road at Kilometer 7, and trap Peñaranda. At 0930 he broadcast that a "triple envelopment" imprisoned the Bolivians, intending thus to lower their morale. On the west side of Campo Via a small relief detachment, sent by Kundt and commanded by Lieutenant Colonel Enrique Frías (former commander of the left at Nanawa), weakly attacked the Paraguayans; however, 200 men from the Guaraní 7th Division closed Kilometer 22, captured two retiring 9th Division tanks, and endangered both Frías and Peñaranda. When Banzer and González Quint learned of this and the similar cutting of Kilometer 16, they ceased work on their escape road because it was leading only to a new trap. They then ordered an attack southward toward Campo Via. Intercepting this message, Estigarribia directed appropriate precautions.[20]

By the morning of 11 December it was clear that escape had failed. The Paraguayan circle actually was incomplete and very weak in places because the 1st Division had not yet contacted Ortiz's forces which had swept around the Andean left. Consequently, before dawn, three battalions of Bolivian infantry escaped. Kundt issued the incongruous order: "Obey order. Destroy material and break." Desperation, however, was prevalent, and the Altiplano Indians were in no condition to fight their way to freedom. Speaking for the doctors, a chaplain informed the commanders that considering the "absolute dehydration of almost all the *jefes*, officers, NCO's, and soldiers" and the existing demoralization, capitulation was necessary. Fifty per cent of the troops were dispersed in the woods. Colonel Luis Irrazábal radioed the beleaguered that they must not destroy their water trucks; if they did, the Guaraní army would not go thirsty to relieve prisoners of war. Banzer and González Quint bowed to the inevitable and surrendered the 4th and 9th Divisions (8,000 men) the afternoon of 11 December 1933.[21]

In addition to prisoners, Paraguay captured 20 spiked guns, 25 mortars, 536 Vickers machine guns and automatic rifles, and about 8,000 rifles. Along with 306 machine guns and 4,830 rifles previously captured, these arms were a bounty to Asunción which, as has been seen, lacked the funds to make new arms purchases.[22]

During the night of 11 December, Peñaranda, who was partially encircled at Kilometer 22, collected the remnants of the Frías detachment and 1,500 stragglers who walked out of the Guaraní trap. With them he worked his way through the woods to Kilometer 7, emerging the next night. Hastily deploying his 2,500 men in the old positions of the previous year, he proceeded to Saavedra, intending to utilize the 7th Division to organize new defenses.[23]

Aware that surrender was likely, Kundt followed Toro's plans and ordered II Corps to reconcentrate at Platanillos. The 7th Division, its rear gravely threatened by the Guaraní 6th and 8th Divisions, was ordered to retire in forced marches. A new

4th Division was resurrected, mainly from the Peñaranda troops, to cover the retreat. Contingents along the Pilcomayo were instructed to fire the *fortines* and proceed to Muñoz. Newly promoted Major General Estigarribia ordered Irrazábal's III Corps to pursue through Tinfunqué to Muñoz. There civilians were hastily departing, and the Andean command prepared to follow.[24]

The morning of 11 December, while Banzer and González Quint debated surrender, the Ministers of War and Defense, Doctors Quiroga and Benavídez, conferred at Muñoz with Colonels Toro and Bilbao Rioja, and Lieutenant Colonels Jordán and Moscoso, to decide the fate of General in Chief Hans Kundt. Bilbao considered the war lost and suggested that Kundt be left at the head of the army to make peace. Toro wished to remove his old friend and save Bolivian dignity. When Peñaranda and his men emerged, he was called to Muñoz, award the "Cóndor of the Andes" and promoted to Brigadier General. Toro, wishing to head off Salamanca's expected appointment of General Lanza, persuaded Kundt to issue orders entrusting command of Bolivia's Field Army to the new General. After advising him not to neglect the left, the old German boarded a tri-motor and roared away into the Chaco horizons, a defeated man.[25]

Colonel David Toro, in a reply to Kundt's comprehensive report to the government, charged (30 May 1935) that the German had had in his hands the sum of power in the field. Kundt had only a small personal staff of ten officers; there was no Chief of Staff, no G-2, and the other sections were more symbolic than real. This contributed to Kundt's loss of political and military reality, and to his conduct of operations with a conviction of infallibility which led directly to disaster. Rarely did he consult experienced Bolivian *jefes*.[26]

In response (30 June 1935) Kundt denied that his powers had exceeded those indispensable for command. In fact, he had been restricted by Salamanca, who reserved the elemental attribute of a High Command, the issuance of General Orders. He denied Toro's charge that he had humiliated his subordinates, and pointed out that Toro himself had frequently commented on the ineptness of many *jefes*. Neither had he disdained critical suggestions, nor hindered written comment. Moreover, no mere Chief of Staff could have avoided the defeat. The old General concluded that he had served honorably and with dignity; his hands were clean before history, which he was confident would vindicate him.[27]

By 1040 hours 13 December the 4th and 7th Division had passed through Saavedra and the *fortín* was afire. At 2015 the Guaraní entered the smoldering ruins. Estigarribia had lost his opportunity to complete the destruction of the Bolivian army. For pursuit, which is really a new attack, fresh troops are desirable. These Estigarribia lacked and this, along with the critical shortage of transport, accounts for his failure to achieve the complete annihilation of the enemy. He did attempt to drive his troops to their last breath. Initially he employed only frontal pursuit, and permitted the 6th and 8th Divisions to tarry at Saavedra and Puesto Moreno for three days while the enemy made good his escape to Muñoz. The latter unit was at the time capable of marching only 2 kilometers per hour, and was not in fighting condition. Therefore, it is probable Estigarribia attempted to entice the Andeans into a slow withdrawal which would have gained time for III Corps' circling pursuit through Tinfunqué.[28]

Paraguay had achieved a tremendous triumph. Unquestionably Estigarribia and President Ayala, convinced that their country was nearly exhausted and that a serious reversal would make La Paz amenable to peace, had committed all available human and material resources. Consequently, as at Boquerón, Estigarribia possessed a numerical superiority which he used, in this case, to grind the enemy down before enveloping him. Failure, however, to completely destroy Kundt's army enabled La Paz to reject peace and continue the war for another eighteen months. Nevertheless, Estigarribia, a little-known Paraguayan, had utterly mastered a Prussian General and in the process demanded recognition as a true master of the art of war.

By employing great numbers—all too often in frontal attacks, however—the Paraguayans managed to sustain enormous casualties. Men spent weeks in the woods, living on Argentine tinned beef, biscuits, and maté, and losing their health. Paraguayan medical figures indicate 12,024 sick and wounded, of whom 2,289 returned to action. In addition, there were certainly many dead. Taking 17,000 as the probable total Bolivian strength in the main theatre, it is evident that the Paraguayan victory, although an impressive show of strength and offensive ability, was achieved at a disproportionate cost.[29]

The Chaco Truce

After the October failure of the Brazilian-led ABCP peace attempt, Presidents Agustín P. Justo and Getúlio Vargas of Argentina and Brazil signed the Act of Rio, 11 October 1933, proposing that Bolivia and Paraguay submit the region between the Rio Verde and 20° South, and bounded by the 62nd meridian, to a joint commission at Rio. If the commission proved unable to define the arbitration zone within thirty days, Justo and Vargas would fix a zone that would exclude the Hayes Award. President Salamanca accepted the plan immediately, but Ayala, committed to exclusion of Bolivia from the littoral—a policy supported privately by Justo—indicated lack of confidence in such a method. On 20 October, La Paz sought Argentine support for a compensatory excluded zone in the northern Chaco. Buenos Aires, which had been following Brazilian initiative, declined to become unilaterally involved. The Rio endeavor definitively failed 11 November when Bolivian Foreign Minister Canelas, who had only been following Salamanca's orders, lost a vote of confidence on this point in the Senate.[30]

The League of Nations had resolved 20 May 1933 to send a commission to solve the question which for many years had troubled the Americas. The ABCP effort to head this off by exercising a mandate delayed the League only six months. On 3 November the Chaco Commission organized itself at Montevideo. The members were Generals Henri Freydenberg and Alexander Robertson of France and England respectively, Major Raúl Rivera Flandes of Mexico, Count Luigi Aldrovandi of Italy, and the Chairman Dr. Julio Alvarez del Vayo of Spain.[31]

At Asunción the important National Commission of Limits, consisting of Domínguez, Moreno, and Zubizarreta, met at the chancellery to decide Paraguay's position. Demobilization and demilitarization of the Chaco were essential. Paraguay must also police the entire region. For arbitration she could produce, with slight modifications, her 1928 propositions at Buenos Aires. The *uti possidetis,* whether of 1810 or 1825, should not be admitted as a basis of defining rights; other principles of international law should be favored.[32]

The League Commission reached Asunción 18 November, and spent the succeeding days visiting the Chaco industries, the Mennonite colonies, and the front. One member flew up river to inspect Puerto Suárez. President Ayala informed the Commission that his country required peace, security, and unrestricted arbitration. Economic questions would be discussed with Bolivia, but she would not be admitted in sovereignty to the Rio Paraguay. Asunción's case was skillfully presented, and the Commissioners were impressed with Guaraní military prowess and Chaco developments. They looked with disfavor on Bolivian pretensions to Bahia Negra, United States Minister Nicholson wrote, and departed well pleased with Paraguay for being "frank, reasonable, cordial, and consistent."[33]

On 1 December the Commission departed for La Paz, arriving on the Altiplano the fifth. They were not permitted to proceed to the Chaco for inspection, but were offered a brilliant recital of the Andean case by Dr. Mercado Moreira. The Commission, after Campo Via, wired Asunción (17 December) that Bolivia accepted troop withdrawal, demobilization, international policing, and arbitration by the Hague Court. This amounted to accession to Paraguay's demands, and she could hardly refuse. Ayala, moving rapidly to seize the initiative, consulted Estigarribia, who "sincerely believed that peace then could be achieved and that an armistice possibly would pave the way." Unquestionably thinking that Salamanca had been brought to a flexible position by military realities, and deeply desirous of peace, Eusebio Ayala wired the Commissioners (18 December) proposing a general armistice 19 to 30 December for meetings in some La Plata capital to consider peace and security. Defeated and demoralized, Bolivia at once agreed to the proposal.[34]

In the Chaco, Peñaranda demanded and received authority to conduct withdrawal to a line from La China to Magariños as he saw fit, where he proposed hastily to form a new army. On 18 December, while Ayala was arranging the armistice, Guaraní intelligence indicated that the enemy was rushing preparations to abandon Muñoz. Estigarribia, wishing to have Muñoz in Paraguayan possession when peace was arranged, ordered occupation of the Bolivian headquarters. At noon 19 December he disseminated the order for an armistice beginning at midnight. That night the 8th Division subjected Muñoz to an artillery bombardment, disrupting the quiet that had prevailed for nearly a week. With flames from the burning *fortín* lighting the way, Guaraní troops moved in. An immediate and critical dispute arose over the exact hour, Peñaranda charging that Muñoz was attacked after midnight in violation of the truce.[35]

Both armies took advantage of the armistice to prepare for possible return to hostilities. Estigarribia directed the building of a new road from Carayá to Platanillos designed to shorten supply lines. He regrouped and rested his forces and shifted troops to balance his lines. On 25 December he agreed to send his Chief of Staff, Colonel Manuel Garay, to Montevideo as military adviser to the peace conference. Since shortage of ammunition and trucks was critical, making a rapid pursuit impossible, Garay tarried in Buenos Aires where, abetted by Rivarola (who had been fronting in the used car business for this purpose), he ordered vehicles in large numbers. To gain time for their delivery, the army agreed to extension of the truce until 6 January 1934, but Estigarribia thought that the enemy, far from being brought to reason by the defeat, was more determined than ever to fight, now seeking vengeance.[36]

At Montevideo the League efforts met an inauspicious beginning when the Bolivian delegation polluted the air by charging Paraguay with violating the armistice. They (Alvéstegui, Escalier, Casto Rojas, and General Blanco Galindo) sought to have this incident made the main topic of concern, implicitly serving notice that Bolivia was not interested in pacting peace. Colonel Garay did not arrive until 29 December, delaying the start of negotiations. President Ayala had sent Zubizarreta and Rivarola as delegates, Efraím Cardozo as secretary, a sure indication that he was yielding to hard peace advocates. Virulent Paraguayans believed they had been obliged to purchase Bolivian withdrawal from the Hayes Zone with blood, and now they refused to withdraw to the river. After visiting Asunción at Ayala's invitation, General Freydenberg reported that settlement of the basic issue was presently impossible. His position, Ayala told Nicholson, was very difficult with now a victorious army and later a Congress to face.

The League Commission sought a truce extension to 14 January, and recommended sending neutral observers to each headquarters to assure respect for the armistice. Bolivia accepted, but Estigarribia would grant only six days. Ayala felt that the Commission inclined toward La Paz, encouraging Bolivian pretensions. The unwillingness of Bolivia to reach security guarantees without prior agreement on arbitration, and Paraguay's attempt to impose a victor's peace, caused the time of the truce to expire without constructive result. The short extension was equally useless and, aware that the enemy army was rapidly reorganizing and receiving fresh forces, and that La Paz had placed numerous arms orders, Paraguay completed her own troop reconcentrations and declined further prolongment. Ayala, however, wired Estigarribia that although so far La Paz insisted upon a sovereign port, hope for an acceptable peace was still good. This could be considered in operations, and if pressure was needed the army would be advised. Estigarribia was pessimistic, feeling that Bolivia had not profited from Campo Via and desired to impose her own terms on the victor.[37]

Reality had once more displaced idealism in the Chaco. La Paz had never intended to make peace, for Salamanca would not contemplate "surrender" while he possessed ample resources—human, material, and financial—to continue the war. He proceeded under the full realization that Paraguay could not invade the Altiplano, and that the farther she advanced the more vulnerable would her communications become. The truce had in fact been opportune for both belligerents: Paraguay because she was physically incapable of completely annihilating the enemy; Bolivia because she was unable any longer to resist Paraguay without pausing to form a new army.[38]

Asunción informed Argentina that she had never admitted the

Rio Paraguay littoral as contentious, and claimed that the nineteenth-century treaties were made without title study and could not constitute precedent. Thus she joined Bolivia, who had long maintained that the early compacts were inadmissible as a basis for recognizing claims of the opponent. Asunción added that Bahia Negra, in view of its isolation below the Rio Negro swamps, could not be used economically by Bolivia as a port and would merely afford her a foothold for military threats to Paraguay. This confirmed the abiding fear for her future security which so vitally conditioned Asunción's diplomacy.[39]

Operations Resume

At the close of 1933 Bolivia had in the field an army of only 7,000 men. Since the beginning of the war she had mobilized and shipped to the Chaco 77,000; of this number, impressive for a small country, 10,000 were prisoners in Paraguay, 14,000 were dead, 32,000 had been evacuated as sick or wounded, 8,000 were serving in the communications zone, and 6,000 had deserted into Argentina.[40]

Bolivia reacted swiftly to the disaster of Campo Via. Utilizing the armistice, she called up the classes of 1917-1920 and the *conscriptos* of 1934. Arms and ammunition orders were placed abroad. Following the establishment of GHQ at Ballivián on Christmas Day 1933, the army was reorganized. The High Command consisted of Peñaranda, with Moscoso as Chief of Staff and Colonel Angel Rodríguez directing operations (G-3). Colonel Toro received command of I Corps (4th and 7th Divisions) with Major Germán Busch as Chief of Staff. II Corps (3rd and 8th Divisions) was commanded by Colonel Bilbao Rioja and Lieutenant Colonel Enrique Vidaurre. Each division consisted of three regiments, the latter raised finally to 1,300-1,900 men. The retreat, which in fact was equivalent to the strategic move envisioned by the prewar Rodríguez plans, served to improve Bolivian communications and worsen those of Paraguay, thus reaching toward a logistic equalization in space.[41]

Paraguay reconcentrated her forces, shifting northward. Colonel Francisco Brizuela's III Corps (1st, 4th, and 5th Divisions,

2nd Cavalry Brigade) remained in the south with headquarters at Muñoz. At Platanillos, I Corps (2nd, 7th, and 8th Divisions) was again commanded by Colonel Gaudioso Núñez, while Colonel Rafael Franco now headed II Corps (6th Division, 1st Cavalry Brigade) at Toledo. The Reserve Division and the 2nd Engineers were Estigarribia's command reserve. Total strength approached 22,000, but the well-filled regiments that had attacked Boquerón now averaged only about 700 men each.[42]

When the armistice ended, the Guaraní resumed their creeping pursuit. Transport still was a grave problem, with heavy rains an aggravation. By 7 January, Platanillos, Loa, Jayucubás, Bolívar, and lesser posts were occupied, and the next day Camacho was taken. Unable to pursue in mass, small advance forces maintained contact with the slowly withdrawing Bolivians. In view of the great length of the front and the small forces available, Toro employed an excellent elastic defense which consisted of small groups in simple redoubts supported by more powerful mobile units. Throughout January 1934 contact was light; the Andeans established a defense line further to the rear, and the Paraguayans crawled along the slippery, viscid Chaco roads.[43]

Estigarribia planned to cover his right with the small II Corps, while pressing the advance in the center and along the Pilcomayo. On 20 January, President Ayala visted the Chaco command (Comanchaco) and informed General Estigarribia that the government would remain "inflexible on the point'of not submitting to arbitration the Hayes Zone and the littoral" of the Rio Paraguay. To Estigarribia's consistent request for trucks, Ayala replied that none would arrive before March. Consequently, unable to proceed rapidly in the main theatre, thinking of the diplomatic aim of forever sealing the enemy from the river, and perhaps dreaming of another sweeping triumph, the commander turned his attention to the 3rd Division. His thought was to capture Puerto Suárez, thus cutting off the enemy 5th Division from its Brazilian supply source, Corumbá. He believed it might then be possible to starve out and capture the 1,300-man Bolivian force.[44]

During the previous dry season, Colonel Delgado had been fearful that the 5th Division would attack him, but in fact reports of a pending offensive had been deliberately planted at Corumbá by Bolivian agents. Delgado worked hard strengthening the defenses of his sector, but he always lacked manpower. In December 1933 a patrol clash produced two prisoners who stated that the Andean troops were in poor condition. The same month, other sources revealed that Altiplano engineers were studying the canal from Puerto Suárez to Corumbá. Delgado apparently was unware that Salamanca had determined to take Bahia Negra, and was futilely seeking a suitable anchorage for small war vessels. Estigarribia, inspecting the sector, found the water again high. An offensive would require 100 boats and 200 trucks to meet the exigencies of both wet and dry seasons and keep the aggressor forces supplied. Unable to divert so much transport from the main theatre, and having surveyed the uninviting terrain, Estigarribia desisted from his plan and returned to GHQ.[45]

On 1 February, Asunción advised him that Bolivia would not renounce the Hayes Zone or the littoral and consequently diplomacy was momentarily hopeless. Estigarribia, therefore, again solicited 500 trucks for a more energetic pursuit. Ever since the truce had ended, feeble efforts had been made against the flanks of the Bolivian II Corps at La China, where the 8th Division (Arrieta) was positioned (by Peñaranda's order) for firm defense of the Andean left. After the report from Asunción, Estigarribia's bombers struck and, once a trail was opened in the thick woods, infantry turned the Andean left, obliging withdrawal. To escape an envelopment (4 February) Bilbao ordered retreat to Pozo Tortuga where the situation was "good." Arrieta complied belatedly, escaping along trails, but his delay deteriorated the situation and on 9 February the II Corps' retreat continued to Tezán.[46]

This permitted another westward Paraguayan advance along the exposed flank of Toro's Corps. Peñaranda at first directed a tenacious defense at Tezán but almost immediately elected a new general retreat. I Corps retired 60 kilometers to a line from Tres Pozos to Chivilar, and II Corps established itself across the Tezán road near Campo Jurado. The front covered about 100 kilometers with a 16-kilometer gap between corps; precautions were ordered against Guaraní flanking tactics. Estigarribia, however, found himself at the momentary limit of his logistic capability and was not disposed to continue the pursuit. Consequently, he probed to define the new Bolivian defense line which by the end of February was firmly established 69 kilometers east of Ballivián. On this line the Andean I Corps rebuilt and trained 7,925 men, and II Corps expanded to 7,342.[47]

Hoping to facilitate advance supply and looking toward an extremely ambitious maneuver, the Paraguayans began a road from Camacho to Cururendá on the Pilcomayo. Estigarribia endeavored to slow the Andean retreat until this project was completed, but this did not prove practicable. His plan was to envelop the entire Bolivian army against the Pilcomayo, obliging it either to surrender or to cross into Argentina and be interned. For this purpose Franco's II Corps was shifted to Camacho, provided with 1,000 mules, and reinforced with the Reserve Division; April, when new trucks were expected, served as the target date for the grand operation.[48]

On 20 March the Bolivian Air Force discovered the "Bengassen" or "Franco" road, as it was variously called, which was by then 130 kilometers west of Camacho. Peñaranda immediately sent the 5th "Lanza" Cavalry to Cañada Cochabamba (80 kilometers west of Campo Jurado), and the 1st "Abaroa" Cavalry to Cañada Strongest (90 kilometers northwest of Cochabamba). Their mission: to explore and block the threatening road.[49]

Meanwhile, in early February a new Bolivian 9th Division began forming at Carandaití under Colonel Francisco Peña for defense of the Picuiba zone. The 18th "Montes" Infantry (about 1,500 men) was placed across the road near Garrapatal at Cañada Tarija. Estigarribia believed that these forces were screening road building south-southwest to intercept his new road, and he determined to destroy them. Since the Andean lines appeared firm, and new trucks were due, he believed the moment right for action. His plan was to destroy the Garrapatal-Cañada Tarija forces, thereby attracting other Bolivian contingents to the area, attack frontally all along the main line, and then launch Franco's II Corps on the grand maneuver.[50]

The 6th Division (Lieutenant Colonel Federico W. Smith) had been slowly advancing up the old road from Camacho toward Picuiba since January. On 20 March it made contact with the enemy at Cañada Tarija, 120 kilometers northwest of Camacho. Four days later fighting began accompanied by the usual Guaraní work in the brush aiming at envelopment. Lieutenant Colonel Angel Bavia had not learned the lessons of two years of war and had no screening outposts on his flanks. His front line was encircled on 26 March. Although still not surrounded, Bavia's second line was nearly powerless for lack of ammunition because he had foolishly placed his entire stock immediately behind the front, and it was now within the pocket. He determined to fight until supplies were exhausted, but (27 March) three lieutenants raised the white flag. Bavia walked into the woods and shot himself. Few prisoners were captured, most of them either walking out or dying in the brush. The next day Garrapatal was occupied, removing a threat to the Paraguayan road and securing the sector; lack of water east of Carandaití obviated further advance.[51]

The Bolivian Political Crisis

With General Kundt's defeat at Alihuatá-Campo Via, President Salamanca reassumed direction of the war, thinking that the disaster stemmed from the excessive liberty he had allowed Kundt. By 2 January 1934 the first friction with the new Peñaranda command arose over the issuance of General Orders for the reorganization of the army. The President reserved to himself the naming of commanders of divisions and above; Peñaranda regarded this as a slur and so informed the Chief Executive. He protested (15 January) the appointment of an Inspector General of the Army, viewing this as an undermining and infringement of his command position. It indicated, he lamented, that he did not enjoy the complete confidence of the President, and was considered incompetent. Reiterating his respect for the constitutional authority, Peñaranda pleaded for powers adequate for the command to cope with the foreign enemy. On 2 February he offered his resignation, in case Salamanca wished to repose his full confidence in another *jefe,* and on 20 March he repeated this offer.[52]

Salamanca correctly retorted 23 March that military posts could not be resigned, and called upon Peñaranda to obey superior authority. He chided him for unpatriotically wishing to resign in the face of the enemy over the triviality of General Orders. The President observed that the latter were within his constitutional prerogative as Captain General. Nevertheless, this seemingly minor issue continued to produce friction and poison relations between the command and the executive.[53]

After the defeat at Cañada Tarija, Peñaranda sacked Peña, charging him with responsibility for the disaster. The Guaraní did not exploit their advantage owing to problems of water and transport; therefore, the sector remained quiet. La Paz, however, was far from quiet. The people were tired of defeats chargeable to incompetent *jefes*, and the patriotic, anxious young cadets of the Colegio Militar staged an abortive rebellion aimed at overthrow of the Salamanca regime. On 5 April, General Lanza put down the revolt, but the foundations of the government were shaken; Salamanca wired Peñaranda that the domestic situation was grave. Disturbed by the event, the General manifested profound indignation over the lack of public confidence in the High Command and the government.[54]

Already with an apparently dangerous threat posed on the left by Cañada Tarija, Peñaranda ordered a new general retreat 25 March. This time the front was considerably shortened by bringing I Corps to within 11 kilometers of Ballivián, while II Corps was situated near Cañada Cochabamba. Frías' 3rd Division, on the extreme left of the army, was charged with blocking the Franco road. This definitively ended Guaraní opportunities for a surprise attack by this route. By 8 April the retreat was complete to a firm line against which Paraguayan advance came to a standstill. Considering the political circumstances, President Salamanca's prompt insistence that Ballivián be sustained was not unexpected.[55]

Salamanca, Dr. Joaquín Espada, and Generals Lanza and Sanjinés arrived at Ballivián by air on 26 April. A briefing revealed that strength was approximately 30,000, but arms were not proportionate. Although 1,000 trucks were needed, the army had only 470, mostly in ill repair. The army wished (1) a uniform censorship to prevent printing of exaggerated reports of victory and defeat in the Paceña press, (2) closing of the Argentine border to reduce espionage, and (3) increase in gasoline supplies to 1,000,000 liters per month. In a conference the following day, the President indicated his intention to leave Espada, a "Chuquisaca lawyer," at GHQ as "Inspector of the Army" to act as his personal observer and middleman. Expressing the view of the *jefes* present, the impetuous Moscoso exclaimed that no *"jefe* or officer would admit the intromission of Doctor Espada in the Command of the Army." "Who are these *jefes?"* the President snapped. *"Yo, uno de ellos, señor!"* retorted Moscoso. The President colored and ordered Moscoso's immediate removal from his post of Chief of Staff. Peñaranda and Salamanca then agreed on Colonel Felipe Rivera as Moscoso's successor. In the ensuing days, however, Peñaranda sought the deposed *jefe's* retention on the grounds that he had participated in operations planning and his continuance was in the interests of victory. This precipitated further unfortunate correspondence with the President and led to increased friction. Unity of command remained unknown in Bolivia.[56]

Cañada Strongest

Upon completion of the April retreat, Bilbao had positioned the 8th Division across the Campo Jurado-Villa Montes road and the 3rd Division in front of the Franco trail. They were 35 kilometers apart, but the 5th "Lanza" Cavalry patrolled the interval. Estigarribia, still confident that a lunge for the Pilcomayo along the Franco road would be successful, accelerated preparations and called for the sending of every able-bodied Paraguayan to the front. Anticipating these moves and wishing to thwart encirclement of the 8th Division (a probable preliminary Guaraní objective), the Bolivian command shifted the 14,000-man 9th Division—the largest ever employed in the Chaco —to a point 35 kilometers above Guachalla. Estigarribia was aware of the location of enemy concentrations and planned accordingly. A feint toward Picuiba would draw enemy forces and hold their attention; pressure would continue at Ballivián; I Corps would attract and hold Bilbao's Corps at Cañada Esperanza, seeking to break through toward the Pilcomayo; II Corps

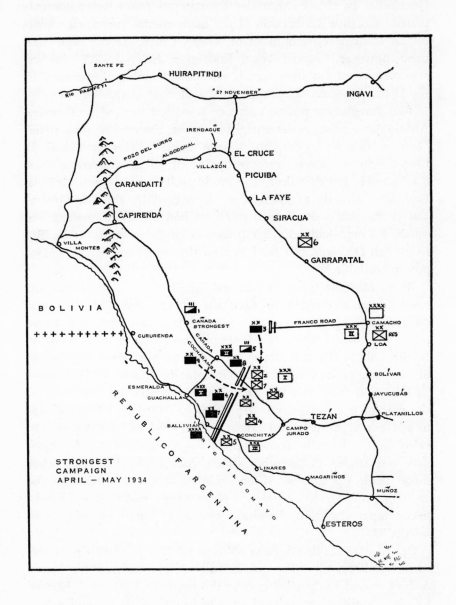

SANTE FE
HUIRAPITINDI
RIO PARAPETI
"27 NOVEMBER"
INGAVI

IRENDAGUE
POZO DEL BURRO
ALGODONAL
EL CRUCE
VILLAZON
PICUIBA
CARANDAITÍ
LA FAYE
CAPIRENDÁ
SIRACUA
XX 6
VILLA MONTES
GARRAPATAL

BOLIVIA
XXXX
+ + + + + + + + + + +
CURURENDA
III 1
CAÑADA STRONGEST
FRANCO ROAD
CAMACHO
XX 3
XXX II
RES
CAÑADA
LOA
COCHABAMBA
XXX II
III 5
XX 9
XX 8
BOLÍVAR
ESMERALDA
XX I
XX 2
XX I
JAYUCUBÁS
GUACHALLA
XX 4
XX 7
PLATANILLOS
XX 8
BALLIVIÁN
XXXX
XX 4
TEZÁN
XX 5
CONCHITAS
CAMPO JURADO
III
STRONGEST CAMPAIGN
APRIL — MAY 1934
LINARES
MAGARIÑOS
RÍO PILCOMAYO
MUÑOZ

REPUBLIC OF ARGENTINA
ESTEROS

would drive south from the Franco road across Bilbao's rear to Guachalla. In this fashion the Paraguayan commander contemplated successive destruction of the main enemy nuclei, culminating in strategic envelopment of Toro's Corps. At the same moment, however, Colonel Angel Rodríguez, Bolivian G-3, planned a maneuver of his own which envisioned luring the enemy to the II Corps sector. Thus a major battle took shape.[57]

The Paraguayan position already possessed marked weaknesses. Although surprise was essential to success, the enemy anticipated Guaraní moves. Inadequate liaison existed between I and II Corps. Franco's forces were incapable of advance at more than 6 kilometers per day along the crude trail. A road from Cañada Esperanza directly to Guachalla, discovered by the Air Group, was to be taken by Franco once he had advanced toward the south. I Corps had only 6,500 men, slightly more than the Bolivian 8th Division, but far less than the combined Andean manpower available.[58]

By 10 May the Guaraní 2nd and 7th Divisions had established contact and attempted to turn the enemy flanks. Bilbao had created strong positions, well defended with redoubts to left and right. Unable to flank, the Guaraní succeeded only in pressing Bilbao back a few kilometers, at a cost of greater overextension of communications lines. The Peñaranda command countered with a road from the 9th Division's concentration area toward the rear of the Paraguayan 7th Division (Ortiz). The plan was to advance vigorously and take the Paraguayans in a double envelopment. Typically, coordination was weak since the 9th Division was under Peñaranda's direct command while the other forces made up Colonel Bilbao Rioja's II Corps. Although the enemy's probable intention was clear, Ortiz, mindful of his mission of attracting him, dismissed warnings: *"no es enemigo, sino miedo."*[59]

On 19 May a 9th Division column cut the road behind Ortiz while artillery, aircraft, and infantry fire paralyzed his front. A dense cloud of dust hung over the battlefield. Colonel Núñez, I Corps commander, ordered each of his divisions to send a battalion to contain the Bolivian incursion. These three small units succeeded in halting the progress of the main Andean body, 7,000 strong! The battalion from the 8th Guaraní Division was surrounded when a second Bolivian column closed the road farther to the rear. Its only source of water was air-dropped ice. Appreciating the seriousness of the situation after close air reconnaissance, Núñez ordered his imperiled forces to retreat. Bilbao, seeing the huge 9th Division halted, directed the 3rd Bolivian Division to move down from the north to complete the trap. This force was detained, enabling Ortiz to escape the night of 21-22 May along a trail cut by the 1st Engineers. Lieutenant Colonel José Rosa Vera, possibly unaware that Ortiz had retired, advised that his 2nd Division (1st, 3rd, 10th Infantry, 9th Cavalry) had defeated the enemy to the north and east and would hold firm.[60]

General Estigarribia initially ordered Franco (20 May) to delay moving for 48 hours and to send a regiment by truck to I Corps. Later he attempted to hasten the movement, but Franco, although he faced but a single regiment, was unable to comply. Vera already was virtually trapped because he had failed to retreat. Nervous and unsteady, he ordered the 9th Cavalry and 10th Infantry to break the Andean lines. When this failed, he personally took command of the 1st Infantry, permitting his division to disintegrate while he walked out. Lack of Andean decisiveness permitted the Guaraní 1st and 3rd Infantry to escape through the brush, abandoning the other forces. On 25 May the latter, as well as the battalion of the 8th Division surrounded on the main road, surrendered. Notwithstanding that Peñaranda had employed over 20,000 men, only 1,556 prisoners and their equipment were taken. Once again deficient command in the execution of offensive maneuvers had cost Bolivia dearly. After cutting the main road, the Andeans lapsed into lethargy, focusing on the single surrounded battalion of the 8th Division. Even so this was Bolivia's greatest victory. Creditable to Colonels Bilbao and Rodríquez, it served to greatly enhance Altiplano morale.[61]

Franco's sluggishness—for he did not move until 27 May—prevented realization of Estigarribia's plan by denying I Corps adequate support on its right, and thus permitted the 3rd Division to close the trap; Vera's refusal to retreat promptly, and the collapse of his division through his ineptness, cost Paraguay men that she could not afford to lose. Had he retreated intact, the Paraguayan offensive might yet have succeeded. Greatly outnumbered and poorly coordinated, however, the Guaraní early lost the initiative. The country was highly disturbed,

> and there were people [Estigarribia wrote] who readily threw upon my shoulders all the blame for this mishap. According to them Cañada Esperanza, the ugly child of disaster, ought to recognize no other father than myself. When I heard of this single fatherhood I could not help contrasting it with the abundant crop of paternal pretenders which the victory of Campo Via had produced.

Peñaranda made no effort to exploit his small triumph, and a period of equilibrium and inactivity set in, marking the end of the long Guaraní offensive which had steadily, albeit slowly, retarded the Bolivians since September 1933.[62]

Notes

1. Lieutenant Colonel Nicolás Delgado, after recovering from malaria, took over COMANOR in June from Navy Captain Elías Ayala. He found Bahia Negra a rude collection of huts with no adequate dock or warehouses. At Olimpo his 300 marines manned positions little changed since 1794. Delgado (II, 5-19) began strengthening defenses with additional small *fortines* strung along the Rio Negro.

2. Estigarribia, 84-86; Benítez, *Estigarribia*, 1st ed., 85; Ayala Moreira, 303.

3. Moscoso, 260; Estigarribia, 89; Ayala Moreira, 302; Vidaurre, *Acciones militares*, 147-148; *El 41*, 40. See also Díaz Arguedas, *Los Elegidos*, 372-373, 377; Vergara Vicuña, IV, 503-506, 549.

4. Estigarribia, 90; González, 110; Díaz Arguedas, *Los Elegidos*, 378-379; Vergara Vicuña, IV, 564-572; Toro, 44-48.

5. Estigarribia, 90; González, 111; *Partes del conductor*, 115; Díaz Arguedas, *Los Elegidos*, 379-381; Ayala Moreira, 304-311; Vergara Vicuña, IV, 573-598; Major Leandro Aponte B., *General Garay* (Asunción, 1956), 2d ed., 70-82. Prisoner totals are based on data supplied the author by Colonel Carlos José Fernández.

6. Estigarribia, 91; Benítez, *Estigarribia*, 1st ed., 87; Díaz Arguedas, *El hombre símbolo*, 43; *Los Elegidos*, 393.

7. Moscoso, 262-266; Toro, 49; Captain Humberto Torres Ortiz, *Campo Via* (La Paz, 1937), 58-59; Vergara Vicuña, IV, 633; Guerrero, Peñaranda, 54; Vidaurre, *El 41*, 89; Díaz Arguedas, *Los Elegidos*, 399.

8. Urioste, *La Encrucijada*, 73; Rivarola, III, 28; Díaz Arguedas, *Los Elegidos*, 393.

9. Estigarribia, 92-93. J. B. Ayala, 193-200, claims that he was the author of the strategy of Campo Via, a legend which has been advanced by General Estigarribia's detractors. González (112-115), for example, accuses the General of incapacity, while Caballero Irala (53-54) supports Ayala's claim. Colonel Ayala asserts that Estigarribia was interested only in a limited drive on Platanillos. Colonel Carlos José Fernández, in a letter to the author from which the above categorical quotation is drawn, points out that a simple comparison of Estigarribia, (p. 93) and Ayala (p. 199), proves that in time and space, Ayala's claims are invalid. Not only did he write González on 5 October that he had just conceived the idea, but also he was then 100 kilometers from Isla Poí where the *previous day* the President had approved the command's plan. As between Fernández and Ayala, a simple comparison of character and scholarly methods leads the historian to the obvious conclusion that J. B. Ayala's claims are without factual foundation.

10. Estigarribia, 94; Rios, 287; Díaz Arguedas, *Los Elegidos*, 416; Delgado (II, 39-40) furnished 2,000 men from Bahia Negra. Rojas resigned his empty title of Commander in Chief in late March, whereupon the supreme command legally, as well as in fact, devolved to General Estigarribia. Rojas' IV Corps never actually came into existence (letter, Colonel Carlos José Fernández to the author).

11. Estigarribia, 95-99; quotation, 95; J. B. Ayala, 203-207; Vidaurre, *Acciones militares*, 151; *El 41*, 102; *Partes del conductor*, 123, 132; Vergara Vicuña, IV, 636-639, 649, 656, 660; Díaz Arguedas, *Los Elegidos*, 406.

12. Toro, 51; Rodríguez, 92; Torres Ortiz, 61. Vergara Vicuña, VII, 673, quotes a Salamanca document warning *Kundt* against "the danger for the country of . . . Toro."

13. Estigarribia, 100-101; Vidaurre, *El 41*, 116-117; Rodríguez, 93; *Partes del conductor*, 134; Rios, 288; Vergara Vicuña, IV, 676. The Paraguayan intelligence system was very good, providing data on Bolivian units, morale, *jefes,* and troop moves. Along the Argentine border, where Andean forces passed on the road from Tarija, agents were particularly successful: Urioste, *La Encrucijada*, 230; Toro, 354-356. An even more startling assertion is made by Ayala Moreira (p. 364) who quotes Dr. Daniel Antokoletz of the Argentine Foreign Office as saying that Argentine army cryptographic sections monitored, deciphered, and forwarded to Paraguay, secret Bolivian radio messages.

14. Estigarribia, quotations, 101-102; Artaza, 88.

15. Vidaurre, *Acciones militares*, 149; *El 41*, 126; Díaz Arguedas, *Los Elegidos*, 417-423; Vergara Vicuña, IV, 665, 690, quotation, 663.

16. Estigarribia, 102-103; J. B. Ayala, 208-210; Caballero Irala, 56; Vergara Vicuña, IV, 661; Colonel José A. Ortiz, *La Batalla de Strongest* (Asunción, 1959), 12; González (pp. 116, 120) claims that Estigarribia took over I Corps only after Ayala had laid the groundwork for the victory. Ayala asserts (p. 211) that Ortiz undermined him by asking the General to take personal command. The bulk of the account given is based upon Estigarribia and upon a transcript from the campaign diary of Colonel Ortiz, in the possession of the author. Corroboration also is found in Colonel Heriberto Florentín, *La Batalla de Strongest* (Buenos Aires, 1958), 22n, stating that in the presence of this officer, Estigarribia referred to Ayala as capable, but requiring the last turn of a thumbscrew to make him act. Colonel Fernández, in a letter to the author, supports the accuracy of the Estigarribia and Ortiz accounts. The latter will be published *in toto* in Fernández' forthcoming book, *La Guerra del Chaco*, III, *Zenteno-Gondra*, which promises to be the most authoritative account to date of this important campaign. Ayala took no further part in the war.

17. Estigarribia, 103-105; J. B. Ayala, 213; Díaz Arguedas, *Los Elegidos*, 418-419, 423-425; Rios, 290; Torres Ortiz, 73-77; González, 117; Vidaurre, *El 41*, 129; *Partes del conductor*, 137-138; Vergara Vicuña, IV, 690; V, 16-18. The allegation has been made that Franco acted on his own. Again, this fable is intended to detract from the brilliance of Estigarribia, and to glorify Franco. "At no time during the Chaco War did Colonel Franco act on his own initiative, i.e., without the prior knowledge of the Comanchaco," Colonel Fernández has written the author. Franco (p. 38) recently dismissed Campo Via as a "fortunate accident."

18. González, 118; Torres Ortiz, 78; Vergara Vicuña, IV, 694, 702-703, 707-708; V, 14; Díaz Arguedas, *Los Elegidos*, 426; Ayala Moreira, 320.

19. Torres Ortiz, 93-99; Vergara Vicuña, V, 37-51, 63, 70-74, 102; Ayala Moreira, 327.

20. Vidaurre, *El 41*, 133-136; *Partes del conductor*, 140; Estigarribia, 105-106; González, 123. See also Guerrero, *Peñaranda*, 56-58; Díaz Arguedas, *Los Elegidos*, 426-428, 433; Vergara Vicuña, V, 85, 92-97, 103-105.

21. Estigarribia, 107; *Partes del conductor*, 141; Torres Ortiz, 105; Rios, 292; Vergara Vicuña, V, 126-137, quotation, 133; Díaz Arguedas, *Los Elegidos*, 429-431; Ayala Moreira, 331-333.

22. Rios, 176-178. Other booty figures vary.

23. Díaz Arguedas, *Los Elegidos*, 433-435; Vergara Vicuña, V, 153; Guerrero, *Peñaranda*, 59. Amusingly, the Asunción Press Office re-

ported that Peñaranda had abandoned his men and fled; *Partes del conductor*, 142.

24. Díaz Arguedas, *Los Elegidos*, 446-447; Vidaurre, *El 41*, 150; Estigarribia, 109. President Ayala, on hand for the surrender 11 December, promoted Estigarribia and numerous *jefes* (p. 108).

25. Díaz Arguedas, *Los Elegidos*, 443-446; *El hombre simbolo*, 144; Vidaurre, *El 41*, 152; Guerrero, *Peñaranda*, 60; Toro, 56-60; Vergara Vicuña, V, 213-228.

Enrique Peñaranda Castillo was thirty-five years of age and had been active in the Chaco for many years. He began his third tour there in 1929, commanding the "Loa" Infantry, which built Fortines Platanillos, Loa, Bolívar, and Camacho, for which he was promoted to Colonel in 1932. He was elected President in 1940; Díaz Arguedas, *El hombre simbolo*, 153-156.

26. Toro, 363-375. See also Ayala Moreira, 341.

27. Díaz Arguedas, *El hombre símbolo*, 47-51; Urioste, *La Encrucijada*, 76-84.

28. González, 121, 129-133; Estigarribia, 110; *Partes del conductor*, 143-147; Vidaurre, *El 41*, 142-149. See also Vergara Vicuña, V, 178; Díaz Arguedas, *Los Elegidos*, 448. In part drawn from letter of Colonel C. J. Fernández to the author.

29. Paraguayan casualties from Vergara Vicuña, V, 151, who quotes Guaraní documents. González (p. 122) lists 8,000. This probably does not include the evacuated sick. Altiplano sources place Bolivian strength at only 13,000. Figuring 8,000 captured and 5,500 who escaped, and allowing for dead and evacuated sick and wounded (which Ayala Moreira, p. 334, places at 2,674), it is obvious that 17,000 is a more accurate number. Rios (p. 288) says 21,000.

30. *Política Argentina*, II, 140-156; DeBarros, 141; Rivarola, III, 25-26, 33-34. Justo agreed with Rivarola that admission of Bolivia to the Rio Paraguay would threaten the future peace of the continent, because vengeful Bolivia would at once create a naval base to implement her aggressive designs (pp. 37-38).

31. *Report of the Chaco Commission*, 5-7; Rivarola, III, 32.

32. República del Paraguay, Ministerio de Relaciones Exteriores, *Libro Blanco, IV Parte, Documentos relativos a la actuación de la comisión especial de la sociedad de las naciones en el conflicto guerrero del Chaco* (Asunción, 1934), 50-51.

33. U. S., *Foreign Relations*, 1933, IV, 368, quotation, 369; *Report of the Chaco Commission*, 8. Ayala presented Paraguay's case four times—in English, French, Spanish, and Italian—so that each Commissioner might hear it, uninterpreted, in his native language (Artaza, 82).

34. U.S., *Foreign Relations*, 1934, IV, 375-378; *Libro Blanco*, IV,

64-65; *Política Argentina,* 169; *Report of the Chaco Commission,* 9; Estigarribia, quotation, 110; Rios, 295; Artaza, 83-86.

35. The belief that Paraguay violated the armistice is prevalent among Bolivian sources: Vidaurre, *El 41,* 159-161; Díaz Arguedas, *Los Elegidos,* 451; Toro, 61; Urioste, *La Encrucijada,* 98. See also *Política Argentina,* II, 175; Colonel Julio Díaz Arguedas, *La guerra con el Paraguay* (La Paz, 1942), 62 (cited hereafter as *La guerra*). Estigarribia (p. 111) and Rios (p. 303) place the hour of occupation at 2300, as do González and Colonel Federico W. Smith who were present. Colonel Fernández assures the author that in his forthcoming book, *La Guerra del Chaco,* III, *Zenteno-Gondra,* he will publish documents that "prove this affirmation."

36. Estigarribia, 112-114; Rios, 246-299; Caballero Irala, 86. Warren, "Political Aspects" (p. 8), mentions the purchase of trucks. Fernández has informed the author that he is not sure the transaction was made *during* the truce, but that it *was* made.

37. *Libro Blanco,* IV, 66-72; *Política Argentina,* II, 170, 176-189; U. S., *Foreign Relations,* 1934, IV, 379-382; Estigarribia, 115-117; Artaza, 87; *Report of the Chaco Commission,* 10-11; Rivarola, III, 46-49.

38. Ortiz, 8; Rivarola, III, 39n.

39. *Política Argentina,* II, 194-195. On 16 January 1934 Saavedra Lamas made a fresh effort, proposing a six months' armistice, troop withdrawals, demobilization, and neutral police, with the whole issue being entrusted to the League if not settled within six months. He observed it was utopian to assume that truce and definitive settlement could be reached simultaneously (as La Paz persistently desired). Transitions in popular opinion in both countries could come only with time. An important factor was the Bolivian belief the war was inspired by a fatal geographic determinism obliging her to obtain a Rio Paraguay port for her future economic survival as a nation. *Ibid.,* 197-201. This program clearly contained the statesmanly ideas of Eusebio Ayala.

40. Díaz Arguedas, *Los Elegidos,* 454; Vergara Vicuña, V, 247. Bolivian deserters in Argentina were aided by a Committee of Deserters led by the communist Tristan Marof. Urioste, *La Encrucijada,* 106-110, 230.

41. Díaz Arguedas, *La guerra,* 66-70; Vergara Vicuña, V, 260-266; *Bilbao,* 349; Estigarribia, 126.

Germán Busch Becerra, at this time upon the meteoric rise of his career, graduated from the Colegio Militar in 1927. He had received the "Condor of the Andes" for explorations of the Zamucos region in 1931, and in recognition of his exceptional talents in the brush. The son of a German immigrant, he attained the presidency in 1937. Díaz Arguedas, *El hombre símbolo,* 336-340.

42. González, 140, 224; Díaz Arguedas, La guerra, 72-73; Vergara Vicuña, V, 269-271.

43. Estigarribia, 121, 123; Díaz Arguedas, La guerra, 75; Vergara Vicuña, V, 257; Partes del conductor, 149.

44. Estigarribia, 122. After Campo Via, Estigarribia became Commander in Chief of the Chaco (Comanchaco). The former COMANOR was effectively reduced to command of the 3rd Division.

45. Delgado, II, 34, 45-66, Estigarribia, 123-125; Urioste, La Encrucijada, 124-125. Delgado later appealed for a spring offensive against Puerto Suárez using large forces, more trucks, and a battery of modern artillery. However, by late March when such an operation became feasible, the Guaraní were too committed elsewhere. The strategic importance of Puerto Suárez for an invasion of Santa Cruz, and its diplomatic significance, were never fully appreciated.

46. Vergara Vicuña, V, 274, 294-300; Bilbao, 358-359; Estigarribia, 125, 127; Partes del conductor, 153; Díaz Arguedas, La guerra, 77-80.

47. Díaz Arguedas, La guerra, 81-82; Vergara Vicuña, V, 304-312, 315-317, 332; Estigarribia, 128-129. Until this time, cattle had been driven along behind the Paraguayan army and slaughtered near the front. Since pasture and water were not available behind the now greatly extended lines, and refrigeration trucks were a luxury far beyond Guaraní capacity, troops had to live on hardtack and maté. This undermined health, required evacuation of scurvy cases, and reduced strength.
Scurvy, grave in the Bolivian army in 1933, fell sharply in 1934; Aurelio Melean, La sanidad boliviana en la campaña del Chaco (Cochabamba, 1938), 137-145.

48. Estigarribia, 129-133; Partes del conductor, 159; Vergara Vicuña, Bilbao, 369-370; González, 143-144.

49. Florentín, Strongest, 18-20; Vergara Vicuña, V, 341; Díaz Arguedas, La guerra, 86. A cañada is a depression where rain water collects. A covering of aquatic vegetation slows evaporation. Such oases were vital, and dictated the location of fortines and concentrations; Vidaurre, El 41, 20. The water was generally potable, but was purified by the Javel method before use; Melean, 78-79.

50. Estigarribia, 133-135; Díaz Arguedas, La guerra, 89.

51. Díaz Arguedas, La guerra, 90-95, 103; González, 142; Florentín, Strongest, 25; Partes del conductor, 163-164; Vergara Vicuña, V, 394-406.

52. Díaz Arguedas, El hombre símbolo, 52-60.

53. Ibid., 63-64.

54. Ibid., 62; Díaz Arguedas, La guerra, 100-101; Vergara Vicuña, V, 407-410.

55. Vergara Vicuña, V, 349, 358-360, 380-383, 390-391; Estigarribia, 139-140; Díaz Arguedas, La guerra, 105-109.

56. Díaz Arguedas, *El hombre símbolo,* 80-86; *La guerra,* 115-118, quotation, 117; Vergara Vicuña, V, 416, 423-427. Guaraní intelligence accurately reported this dissension in the enemy camp; Estigarribia, 143.

57. Estigarribia, 140-141; Florentín, *Strongest,* 22-27; Díaz Arguedas, *La guerra,* 119-121; Vergara Vicuña, V, 435-436; *Bilbao,* 371-372. Cañada Strongest, the usual name applied to this action, is an inaccurate appellation because that place actually lay farther west. The Bolivians refer to the correct locale as Cañada Cochabamba, the Paraguayans as Cañada Esperanza.

58. Florentín, *Strongest,* 22, 26-33, 143; Aponte, *Cincuenta años,* 205-206.

59. Florentín, *Strongest,* 34-45, 57-62, 76; Ortiz, 9; Estigarribia, 146; Vergara Vicuña, *Bilbao,* 375.

60. Florentín, *Strongest,* 48-57, 66-74, 76-80, 95-97, 100; Estigarribia, 146-147; Caballero Irala, 67; Vergara Vicuña, V, 438-464, 471; *Bilbao,* 376-377; Díaz Arguedas, *La guerra,* 123-124; Aponte, *Cincuenta años,* 207-211; Ortiz (p. 9) insists that he advised the 2nd Division of his intentions, Florentín asserts that he did not.

61. Florentín, *Strongest,* 86-92, 98-138, 171; Estigarribia, 148; González, 145; Díaz Arguedas, *La guerra,* 125, 136; Vergara Vicuña, V, 476-479; *Bilbao,* 379-383; Urioste, *La Encrucijada,* 121.

62. Florentín, *Strongest,* 141-148; Ortiz, 6, 11; Estigarribia, 148-149, quotation, 148; Vergara Vicuña, V, 531; *Bilbao,* 391. As the price of their shortcomings, Colonel Núñez and Lieutenant Colonel Vera, and several others were removed from command and subjected to proceedings which did not end until a general amnesty 10 July 1935 freed them. These documents are in part reproduced in Florentín, 224-272. See also pp. 156-223 and 273-281 for other documents of interest.

CHAPTER SEVEN

EL CARMEN - IRENDAGÜE—THE THIRD
PARAGUAYAN OFFENSIVE

After failure of the Chaco truce, the League Commission futilely continued striving to effect peace. Victory at Campo Via had fired Paraguayan extremism; thereafter, many Guaraní insisted on expulsion of Bolivia from the entire natural limits of the Chaco, thus making solution difficult. Consequently, a draft treaty offered by the Commission found no favor at Asunción. A year earlier, Bolivian consent to arbitration by the Hague Court of the respective claims (excluding the Hayes Award and Petropolis cession) might have won Paraguayan favor; now it was scorned because the proposal included withdrawal of the victorious Guaraní army to the Rio Paraguay. Asunción, encouraged by Saavedra Lamas, was certain an indemnity could be wrung from La Paz, and therefore objected to omission of procedures for determining war guilt.[1]

Paraguay's counterproposal was predicated upon President Ayala's opinion that "once a substantial security is obtained, we can negotiate and be generous." Immediate cessation of hostilities with the armies separated by equidistant lines (unofficially, Punta Rieles and Ballivián), Paraguayan policing of the evacuated zone, and arbitration to define the boundaries between Chiquitos and the Province of Paraguay, were the most important points. A conference sponsored by the ABCP should seek a direct solution, while the League Commission fixed war responsibilities. Significantly, Asunción was willing to permit Bolivia to remain reciprocally in a fairly advanced position. This was an innovation in proposals. Ingeniously, Paraguay advocated an economic conference *between* armistice and arbitration. Ayala, who was convinced that the opportunity for peace was magnificent, hoped thus to satisfy La Paz's aspirations by nonterritorial means.[2]

La Paz also rejected the Commission's plan, objecting to exclusion of the Hayes Zone without a compensatory portion of the littoral. She demanded that the arbitration stipulated be detailed and without possibility of delay; consequently, security measures were unimportant and transitory, and could be quickly settled once arbitration was assured.[3]

After a vain attempt to reconcile the contending views, the League Commission sailed for Europe, the latest defeated peace agency. Its efforts had been unrealistic in ignoring Paraguay's victory in the field. The latter's ambitions had, however, grown with Campo Via; talk had become common in Asunción of invading Bolivia, seizing the Andean oil fields, incorporating the entire Chaco, and confining Bolivia forever to the Altiplano by creating an autonomous Republic of Santa Cruz from her *oriente*. While defeat made La Paz more tractable, she maintained her basic condition of a juris arbitration agreement as a prerequisite to an end of hostilities. In fact, unless she did continue the war until this was obtained, the peace would undoubtedly reflect her defeat and end her hope of securing a fluvial outlet.

Charges that the war was motivated by international oil interests were beginning to gain credence, President Ayala, normally levelheaded, now suspected that Bolivia had provoked war in search of an outlet for the production of Standard Oil of Bolivia. As long as fighting had been confined to the old *fortín* line, such allegations seemed foolish, but by mid-1934 oil was becoming a military and a political factor. While oil did not exist in the Chaco Boreal, a broad geosyncline covered with non-stratified alluvial deposits, the Andean foothills are anticlinal formations with usually productive lower Devonian strata. If the Paraguayan army could seize the enemy's refinery at Camiri, his war machine would grind to a halt; in the subsequent peace negotiations the oil fields would be a diplomatic problem. Saavedra Lamas therefore confided to U.S. Ambassador Weddell that the "real issue" was now economic. Western Chaco oil might require a pipeline, making imperative some sort of outlet for Bolivia.[4]

Following Cañada Cochabamba, Bolivia appealed to the League under Article XV of the Covenant, thus terminating Geneva's general efforts and indefinite negotiations. At British urging, the League then concerted an arms embargo against both belligerents. The United States pursued a similar policy unilaterally. La Paz strongly objected, since Paraguay's arsenals gave her an advantage over Bolivia, which lacked domestic arms-producing facilities. What La Paz could only surmise was that Paraguay regularly received artillery shells from the Argentine War Ministry, a source safe from embargo.[5]

In July, Argentina advanced a very general peace plan which was supported by Brazil and the United States. It called for a meeting of plenipotentiaries at Buenos Aires to concert specific peace terms, a definitive cease fire, and adequate security measures. If conciliation were not effected, the issue would be entrusted to the Permanent Court of International Justice at The Hague. Saavedra's plan incorporated two basic ideas: (1) the Ayala concept that an economic conference and transactional discussions could satisfy Bolivian needs without Paraguayan loss of the Chaco; and (2) Saavedra's own great contribution, a gradual transition to peace. This opposed the older view that the war must be ended at once, unconditionally.[6]

Although she had been sounded in May, La Paz manifested resentment that the proposal had been discussed previously at Asunción, and was suspicious of an Argentine peace. Following Brazilian-United States efforts to allay this fear, Bolivia replied that conciliation should be entrusted to the ABCP-Neutrals under the 3 August 1932 principles. (The Continental Declaration, which Salamanca resented at annunciation, grew in favor on the Altiplano proportionally to Bolivia's military reverses.) La Paz further specified that Argentina should, in confidential inquiries at Asunción, secure as a *sine qua non,* recognition for Bolivia of a portion of the littoral.[7]

Renewed Guaraní Initiative

Although defeated at Cañada Strongest, General Estigarribia had continued to contemplate offensive operations. He was certain that turning Peñaranda's left would destroy him. Light contact all along the thinly held front, stretching northward from Ballivián, conceded the Guaraní freedom of action. In mid-June continued pressure on the Bolivian 3rd Division by Franco's Corps brought a strategic retreat. After Peñaranda attempted unsuccessfully to trap the attackers, each side began vigorous road making and broad, advantage-seeking maneuvers in the brush at Cañada El Carmen. Invariably the opponent blocked the trails, preventing positive results.[8]

Attention returned to Ballivián where Toro's I Corps maintained a cordon defense against Colonel Nicolás Delgado's Paraguayan III Corps. On 18 June a salient was thrust into the Bolivian lines; but the Andeans, although employing raw troops (*conscriptos* of 1935), closed the gap and inflicted extremely heavy casualties. This action presaged the danger of attempting to hold Ballivián, a cluster of buildings lacking military importance. La Paz, however, feared that both domestically and abroad its evacuation would signify definitive Bolivian defeat.[9]

The Bolivian command strongly desired to pursue a more militarily sound policy. In May, as a prelude to evacuation, GHQ moved 123 kilometers northwest from Ballivián. On 15 July, after the Guaraní consolidated a new salient, Peñaranda ordered I Corps back to shorter new lines at Guachalla. This would have freed troops for offensive operations, but Toro, with his ear tuned politically to the Altiplano, insubordinately refused, stressing the moral significance of Ballivián. Its loss, he feared, would encourage Asunción's pretensions and prolong the war. Delgado had 9,000 men, some air support, negligible transport capability, low morale, and no reserves; yet Toro, with possibly twice the manpower and matériel, was committed by his political ambitions to passive defense. The moment was critical for Peñaranda's command and personal authority. Instead of acting with decision and sacking the rebellious Toro, who had answered the command with sarcasm and "a kind of benevolent compassion for . . . its ineptitude," Peñaranda weakly bowed to his subordinate's wishes and rescinded the order. Thereafter the die was cast. Colonel David Toro Ruilova was the *de facto* chief of the Field Army, able to force his own desires upon the titular, who bore the responsibility.[10]

The manifest incompetence of the Bolivian command posed an unrefusable invitation to Estigarribia. The Toro-Salamanca passion for Ballivián created an unbalanced front; Toro had 16,000 men in the south, Bilbao's II Corps had only 9,000, and the Reserve 9th Division (Moscoso) numbered 6,000. Comprehending Toro's passive intentions, Estigarribia shifted his main strength northward, increasing Franco's II Corps to over 15,000 against the weaker Bilbao. This provided an ideal opportunity for the long-sought envelopment of the Bolivian left.[11]

After failure of attempts in early July to penetrate the Bolivian lines and reach the Pilcomayo, Estigarribia resolved to launch a strategic feint at Picuiba. Thus the danger to Bolivia of Toro's stubborn defense of Ballivián would be enhanced; the supply lines of Lanza's expanding III Corps at Ingavi-Roboré would be endangered, restraining it from pending action toward the Rio Paraguay; Bolivia's Parapetí-Carandaití region would be threatened, obliging movement of troops away from the heavily manned south. This in turn would invite a new attempt to reach the Pilcomayo from the central front. A second phase, advance from Algodonal toward Camiri, would imperil the enemy's vital gasoline and oil source. To dispose of the perpetual limiting factor, water, Franco therefore sent patrols in search of wells; discovery of potable water at La Faye (28 July) improved the situation.[12]

President Ayala approved as objectives "27 November" and Algodonal, against which Estigarribia proposed to push two columns once Picuiba was occupied. Well-drilling squads were created to follow the advancing troops, since there was no known water between La Faye and Carandaití. A new direct road was completed from the Casado railhead to GHQ at Camacho; 100 new trucks were received; I Corps occupied the II Corps lines, freeing it for the offensive. Small forces at Pitiantuta and Bahia Negra were ordered to converge at Madrejón for a march on Ingavi from the southeast supported by the Air Group. The enemy had demonstrated exasperating resiliency, retrieving himself from catastrophe with frustrating regularity and was presently greatly superior in fire power and numbers. The situation of financially exhausted Paraguay was consequently grave, obliging Estigarribia to seek through bold maneuver for an early end to the war. For this purpose he possessed an energetic Corps commander, Colonel Rafael Franco, who advised that he would be ready to move by 12 August.[13]

In the Bolivian camp, the War Minister conferred with the Peñaranda command on 17 July. Colonel Rodríguez urged an immediate offensive. Despite the President's opposition (for political reasons) to retreat from Ballivián, this was imperative in order to free sixteen regiments for aggressive maneuvers designed to win the war. Otherwise, Bolivia's numerical superiority (35,000 to 21,000 Guaraní) was wasted. The Minister agreed to press this view on Salamanca, but meanwhile Paraguay, with the strategic initiative, forced commitment of the Andean reserves through scattered attacks on the long, static line. Peñaranda "urged" Toro to retreat, but the subordinate retorted: "It is not for poetic reasons that Ballivián is defended, but because its evacuation would crush public morale. . . ." Rodríguez suggested that Peñaranda should resign to save his honor, but in this moment, crucial for his country, General Enrique Peñaranda Castillo was utterly impotent. He agreed (28 July) that Toro could hold Ballivián until it became untenable, an open invitation to disaster.[14]

Franco, in personal command of the reinforced 6th Division, launched his offensive early 14 August 1934, apparently achieving a complete surprise. Only 600 troops under Lieutenant Hugo Pol barred the road to Picuiba. This young officer, unlike the typical Bolivian *jefe,* had deployed his men skillfully along small rises in the terrain, but the more numerous Guaraní quickly pushed back his outposts. To his appeals for reinforcement, the command at first opined that the attack was merely demonstrative and unimportant. Paraguayan bombers struck, and during the hours of darkness the usual envelopment began on the Bolivian left. Pol ordered withdrawal, but the rear was already closed and he succeeded in escaping with only 50 men. Since there were no other significant Andean forces east of Carandaití, Franco was able to continue unimpeded. His fast-moving truck columns reached Irendagüe 17 August, Villazón the eighteenth, "27 November" the following day, Huirapitindi on the twentieth, and captured an enemy battalion at Algodonal two days later. The first phase of the Comanchaco's offensive was accomplished.[15]

Peñaranda belatedly pulled troops out of Ballivián, transporting them by truck toward the Parapetí-Carandaití sector. This amounted to the creation of a new front in the northwest hundreds of kilometers behind the previous lines and made defense of Ballivián even more unwise. Toro attempted to open a 45-kilometer trail toward the Paraguayan rear at Siracua hoping to regain the initiative, defeat an important Guaraní force, and oblige Franco's retreat. After countering this move, the Comanchaco permitted Franco to continue his advance until he reached a string of foothills 5 kilometers east of Carandaití on 27 August. They were the so-called Chiriguanos Mountains, natural limit of the Chaco![16]

As the Bolivians withdrew troops from Ballivián, Guaraní lines stretched thinner, relieving the 8th and Reserve Divisions for use as a reserve. Hauling water from La Faye to Franco's division required all the 100 new trucks and created a logistic difficulty which soon made the advanced position untenable; it likewise imposed a limitation on the ability to reinforce. An armistice, which Paraguay had anticipated would be a status quo of positions, failed to materialize. Estigarribia therefore devised a new plan. Franco was ordered to retreat as slowly as possible, holding the attention of the enemy. Meanwhile, with the southern sector weakened and two divisions free, a fresh opportunity existed to achieve the long-desired penetration to the Pilcomayo by striking heavily at Cañada El Carmen.[17]

On the diplomatic front, Saavedra Lamas stated that if Bolivia insisted on a littoral zone, "he would end the whole matter." The Argentine Foreign Minister was fully committed to the proposition that Bolivian appearance on the Rio Paraguay would pose a threat to the peace of Buenos Aires, as well as of Asunción, because of the Altiplano's bad faith. Brazil, however, promised confidentially that she would endorse Bolivia's claim to a river port once a conference convened. On 17 August, Paraguay accepted the original Argentine proposal unconditionally, closely supporting her diplomatic move with Franco's drive toward Carandaití, which was "made with the proposition of creating a favorable situation in case of an armistice." Saavedra Lamas then attempted to interpret the proposed arbitration clause as embodying acceptance of the statutes of the Hague Court, Article XXXVI of which entrusted to the Court determination of the scope of litigations submitted. Since this was a patent attempt to secure what amounted to the double arbitration which Asunción had favored since 1929, La Paz declined further reply pending the return of President Salamanca from a Chaco visit.[18]

Renewed Tension in the Bolivian Command

President Salamanca visited the Chaco for the third time on 29 August. His previous visit (5 June) had introduced a Czech mission contracted to advise the army. This, foreseeably, led to new tensions between executive and command and culminated in a telegraphic exchange in which Salamanca asserted the command had lost the "sympathy of the people," to which Peñaranda replied that the government had "lost the confidence of the army." By the end of August, however, peril momentarily smoothed relations.

To the President, Colonel Rodríguez stressed the need for prompt retreat to Villa Montes-Carandaití, asserting that peace should be sought. Toro arrived, unfortunately, and assured Salamanca that Ballivián could be held; the situation was not desperate, and his offensive on Siracua would remove the danger. The President, who could not conceal his nervousness and fear over the turn of the war, grasped at the optimism of Toro and accepted his plan, which in reality had already failed.[19]

The Chief Executive wished to remove Chief of Staff Colonel Felipe Rivera to a post at La Paz and replace him with Colonel Bernardino Bilbao. Although Peñaranda and Rivera were willing, the sinister power behind the command, Colonel Toro, vetoed such a position for Bilbao. Peñaranda, wholly under Toro's spell, then reneged on his agreement with the President, asserting that the change was "occasioning a division in the bosom of the army." The ultimate result of the subsequent dispute, occasioned by General Peñaranda's inability to command Colonel Toro, was tragic for Bolivia.[20]

In view of the dispute over Rivera's reassignment, Salamanca visited the Chaco for the fourth time on 23 September. Peñaranda, because of resentment against the President at GHQ, met him at Villa Montes. In a violent meeting, the President charged the General with leading a rebellion against him. They shouted their respective constitutional rights as Captain General and General in Chief. Salamanca's son, Rafael, drew a revolver; Peñaranda stepped back and went for his own sidearm, and only the intervention of the Ministers averted bloodshed. The General then explained his position, leaving little doubt that he was unable to command his subordinates; he compromised instead of giving firm orders. Further, he deemed it his burden to maintain harmony between *jefes* and government.[21]

The weakness of Peñaranda and his utter misunderstanding of his own proper role is so patent as to require no comment. To this impotent pusillanimity, the Paraguayan command offered a perfect contrast. There Estigarribia tolerated no hint of insubordination, removing from the Chaco all officers (such as Colonel Juan B. Ayala) who, however competent, disputed his authority. Neither was there dissension between President and command in the Guaraní camp. The close cooperation of President Ayala and Estigarribia lent added strength to the country and was in no small measure responsible for the outcome of the war. Their relationship is typified by an incident related by Estigarribia. On 23 August, Ayala visited the Chaco, highly desirous of taking Ballivián. The General disagreed, preferring continued indirect approach to frontal attack. Ayala asked, "What would you do if I directly ordered the troops?" Without hesitation Estigarribia replied that he would have but two courses: "Obey as a subordinate of the President of the Republic, the constitutional Commander in Chief of the armed forces of the nation, or request my release."[22]

Meeting on 24 September, Peñaranda and Salamanca considered Toro. Removed momentarily from the Colonel's influence,

Peñaranda agreed that Toro's lack of discipline was grave and vowed he would settle the matter. After lengthy discussion, Peñaranda and Salamanca reached accord on the reassignment of *jefes*: Moscoso to become Chief of Operations, Rodríguez to be promoted to Brigadier General and placed in command of the 2nd Division at La Paz, General Guillén to take over the 1st Division at Oruro (and consequently, local purchase of supplies from Chile), and Rivera to stay on as Chief of Staff.[23]

The presidential party then accompanied Peñaranda back to GHQ for a few days. Vice-President Tejada Sorzano met with the *jefes*, seeking to improve their relations with the President. He stressed that the latter had only one desire—national victory. In a memorandum, Moscoso asserted that the army accepted the Captain General in his legitimate role, but objected to his meddling in details of command and operations. On behalf of the army, Moscoso respectfully solicited retention of Rodríguez. Peñaranda, typically inconstant, took this occasion to repudiate his agreement with the President, and sided with the *jefes*. Salamanca therefore returned to La Paz, rightly convinced that the sole solution was replacement of the inept, impotent Peñaranda command.[24]

Shift of the Diplomatic Front

While Salamanca was visiting his troublesome army in late August, his Guaraní counterpart informed the United States Minister that he was willing to arrange for a Bolivian port. "Bolivia owns many millions of acres of oil lands," he said, "which are not involved in the Chaco dispute. Pipe lines to the river would provide Paraguay with cheaper gasoline." This would have more advantage to the litigants than Argentina's notorious desire to acquire control of marketing the oil. To Rivarola, however, Ayala emphasized that a *sovereign* Bolivian oil port would endanger their country's security.[25]

Saavedra Lamas had no desire to see Paraguay and Bolivia arrive at agreements to which Argentina was not a party. On 28 August, while Salamanca was flying to the Chaco, he finally conveyed officially to Rivarola the *sine qua non* of Bolivia "in order to assert the impartiality of his attitude." A week later, with Salamanca's confidence restored by Toro, Bolivia made counter-suggestions which Saavedra Lamas deemed irreconcilable with the peace formula. These sought to limit titles to "those emanating from the Spanish crown," to make cessation of hostilities dependent on a conciliation agreement, and to expand the mediation group to include the ABCP-Neutrals. Should conciliation fail, La Paz wished guaranteed juridical arbitration in accordance with the 3 August 1932 declaration and the *uti possidetis juris* of 1810. It will be recalled that Bolivia interpreted the latter broadly against all occupations, regardless of date. Saavedra Lamas merely transmitted these proposals to Asunción. There, Ayala insisted that peace should consider military reality and not theories rendered inapplicable by Andean aggression. The mediators, he felt, must proceed with more "energy, decision, and authority."[26]

After Toro convinced Salamanca (29 August) that the military situation could be ameliorated, the colonel flew to Carandaití to form a detachment of six regiments with which (5 September) he attempted a double envelopment of Franco's 6th Division at Pozo del Burro. Estigarribia ordered the Reserve Division to Algodonal, but Franco, with mixed courage and bravado, advised that he would soon escape. On the night of 8 September he withdrew silently by a trail through the brush, leaving 14 trucks, spiked artillery, and 78 automatic weapons, and taking Toro so by surprise that on the following day the Bolivian Air Force was still dropping surrender leaflets into the now empty circle.[27]

Toro blamed his humiliation on poor aerial reconnaissance, but assured Peñaranda that he would pursue and capture the enemy. On 11 September he ordered construction of a direct road to La Faye, communications center and source of water for Franco's entrenched forces at Algodonal. At the same time, in the Bahia Negra sector, Paraguayans with soaring spirits took Vanguardia and Vargas. Morale in Franco's II Corps (6th and Reserve Divisions) was much lower, due to the extreme shortage of water (one-half pint per man per day) and the retrograde movement in progress. Estigarribia sternly insisted on slow retreat in the interest of operations at El Carmen. There, Bolivian forces retreated 10 kilometers, nullifying the latest Guaraní attempt at penetration, but Toro continued eastward, fully complementing the enemy strategy.[28]

Paraguayan finances were in an especially desperate condition. Money was unavailable for needed aircraft, and the arms embargo made their acquisition unlikely. Trucks needed for war on an expanding front could not be purchased for lack of funds. Attempts to borrow money in Argentina seemed unrewarded. Peace continued elusive. Providing for the army and 14,000 Bolivian prisoners was straining the economy. Discouraged, the President asserted that Paraguay was in her worst moment, broke, in disfavor with the League, and under Argentine pressure to accept Bolivian modifications to the peace plan. He went to GHQ convinced that neither side could obtain a decisive victory in the field. After conferring with Chief of Operations Lieutenant Colonel Raimundo Rolón, the President remained skeptical of the Comanchaco's latest plan, but Estigarribia explained that the critical national and military situation obliged energetic action—Paraguay could not remain stationary. Every available man and every last peso (for trucks) must be committed to win the war. An armistice, he informed the President 16 October, "does not present any advantage to us."[29]

Toro, meanwhile, concerted a fresh double envelopment, aiming to converge 5 kilometers east of Algodonal. On 22 September the road was closed between the 6th and Reserve Divisions and, although the northern column did not complete the circle, Toro's aircraft dropped surrender leaflets. The 6th Division broke out (23 September), concentrating fire and successive assault waves on a battalion of the 3rd Cavalry. The 200 Bolivians died in their positions, but the Guaraní, taking heavy casualties, escaped into the brush to fight another day. Toro was again left foolishly clasping air.[30]

Saavedra Lamas had permitted peace efforts to gravitate once more to Geneva, despite expressed opposition of Brazil and the United States to further meddling in American affairs by the League of Nations. Against the backdrop of Toro's advance upon the enticing, slowly retiring Guaraní, the belligerents presented their cases to the League. Neither embodied new titles. Paraguay, candidly revealing the reason for her insistence on security as a condition to peace, said:

> There is no reason not to suppose that, the very day after this war is ended, Bolivia will begin to prepare her revenge, with the certainty that time will repair her losses more rapidly than those of Paraguay.

Bolivian appearance in sovereignty on the Rio Paraguay would enhance this threat, and was therefore wholly unacceptable to Asunción.[31]

The Bolivian statement tacitly admitted aggression at Pitiantuta, but stressed that La Paz had been willing to settle the incident. Paraguay, however, chose to complicate matters with counterattacks. Bolivia now sought definitive "final settlement of the dispute and absolutely refuses all dilatory procedure." She modified her previous position, however, agreeing that armistice and "final acceptance of the procedure for the solution of the dispute shall be simultaneous."[32]

Preparations for Maneuver

Colonel Aquiles Vergara Vicuña, newly arrived Chilean mercenary, found the Bolivian command convinced that the "failure" of Franco's offensive had left the Comanchaco prostrate and incapable of any new action. Northward movement of Andean forces brought predominant strength to pose a threat, for the first time, to the Guaraní right. Moscoso's I Corps (4th, 8th, 9th, and Reserve Divisions) covered the entire old front, but still possessed greater strength than Delgado's opposing Paraguayan III Corps.[33]

While Paraguay remained passive in October only for lack of human and material means, the Bolivian command was rendered stationary by the type of dissension which contributed so greatly to its ultimate defeat. The chief actor was, predictably, the archinsubordinate, Colonel David Toro Ruilova, at this time commanding the Cavalry Corps (1st and 2nd Cavalry Divisions) at Carandaití. By exaggerating the strength of Franco's II Corps, Toro endeavored to draw ever greater forces to his sector, making it the principal arena for future operations. He opposed

Rodríguez' plan for a balanced offensive at Strongest-El Carmen and from Carandaití, intended to defeat the weaker enemy, force him to retreat, and free the Reserve Division for cooperation in a converging drive on Camacho. Toro sought authority only to capture Franco's detachment at Villazón, portraying such a move as maximally advantageous and promising to avenge Campo Via.[34]

Peñaranda bowed to Toro (23 October), issuing a directive to Cavalry and II Corps for converging attacks toward Picuiba and "27 November." The variant stemmed in part from the Guaraní capture of Ingavi (5 October), which implied an invasion of the Department of Santa Cruz. Capture of Picuiba would paralyze the enemy threat to El Carmen, while advance of Bilbao from Santa Fe through "27 November" with 8,000 men would negate danger to Santa Cruz and relieve pressure on Lanza's weak III Corps (5th and 6th Divisions) at Roboré-Puerto Suárez. The plan reflected Toro's opposition to an offensive by Moscoso at El Carmen, but was compatible with a G-2 report (Colonel Victor Serrano) that Estigarribia was deeply concerned for his thinly held line. Serrano reasoned that he would therefore soon be obliged to shorten the front through a general retreat in the north. If this failed to occur within fifteen days, it would confirm that Paraguay had succeeded in mustering more troops and would launch a fresh offensive in mid-November. Strategic intelligence concurred, for Salamanca advised GHQ (26 October) that Estigarribia was preparing an audacious blow and general offensive to begin within twenty days.[35]

After accepting the new plan, Toro demanded II Corps (Bilbao) as reinforcement in order that he might capture Franco's two divisions at Villazón. Although he already possessed superior strength and material, Toro persuaded General Sanjinés to intercede with the command on his behalf. In a grossly insubordinate document on 27 October, Toro asserted that the least results of his plan would exceed the best expectable from that of the command. In the interest of victory, Bilbao agreed (28 October) to lend Toro additional troops. Peñaranda, ever the moderator but never the commander, then "ratified" the agreement of his subordinates and accepted Toro's plan for a major maneuver by the Cavalry Corps seeking to (1) capture Franco, (2) relieve Guaraní pressure on El Carmen, (3) negate the threat to Roboré by II Corps taking "27 November," and (4) advance toward Camacho.[36]

Camacho, as the common objective of Bolivian plans, reflected a September report prepared by the Czech mission. The document held forth greater promise for an offensive in the north than in the south, and misjudged Guaraní objectives as simple conquest of the Chaco. Actually, the aims it deemed sound for Paraguay—Villa Montes, the Camiri oil fields, the Villa Montes-Santa Cruz road, and Puerto Suárez—coincided with those of the Comanchaco, although the latter labored under grave handicaps in translating aims logistically into reality.[37]

At Buenos Aires, secret negotiations between Rivarola and the Argentine government reached a successful climax in early October when £180,000 was deposited to Paraguay's account in Paris. A direct, interest-free loan, for an unspecified term from Justo's government to Asunción, it was followed on 27 November by a second installment bringing the total to 4,000,000 Ps. Arg. The loan was made covertly from the Treasury through middlemen. Due to a favorable exchange rate, Paraguay realized a profit of 600,000 Ps. Arg. in the conversion. This money enabled Asunción to buy more trucks and other essential ingredients for a resurgence of the war machine.[38]

Estigarribia already had toured the front (27 October), conferring with Fernández (I Corps) and Lieutenant Colonel Eugenio Garay (8th Division) regarding their role in the perennial plan to destroy the enemy at El Carmen. Although the Bolivian Reserve Division had only three regiments covering a 20-kilometer front, Comanchaco thought twice that number were engaged. Arriving at Picuiba, Estigarribia learned that water squads had struck unlimited, potable water at Irendagüe, solving Paraguay's problem in that sector. Since the bulk of Guaraní trucks had been required to transport water from La Faye to Franco, this discovery was immensely important. Estigarribia was therefore able to reiterate his order for a slow II Corps retreat, luring Toro toward Picuiba. Franco was also alerted to cooperate at El Carmen if necessary. Having concentrated the maximum number of men and amount of equipment available, and having prepared painstakingly over a period of months (as was his wont), Estigarribia now was ready to gamble Paraguay's fate on a single, well-calculated throw of the dice.[39]

El Carmen

After receiving the 3rd Division from Bilbao, Toro prepared a double envelopment at Villazón. The northern column, consisting of the 3rd Infantry and 2nd Cavalry Divisions, and the 1st Cavalry Division which formed the southern column, were to converge at Irendagüe. This served to greatly overextend the perimeter of envelopment. Heavy rains delayed the operation until 6 November, whereupon weak forces made frontal attacks as the envelopment progressed, closing on 9 November. The Paraguayans, undismayed by this maneuver, began a trail southeastward. After thrusting a gap through the Andean lines (late 10 November), the two light Guaraní divisions poured out toward Picuiba. Meanwhile, Caballero Irala's 2nd Engineers (reinforced) had attacked from Irendagüe, covering the retreat. Toro was left with only 400 prisoners, but he seized 50 nearly new trucks. With 12,000 men he had been unable to capture 5,000 Guaraní, and what he had portrayed as a decisive battle turned into a minor engagement.[40]

Toro attributed the result to the month's delay in gaining approval, and to lack of adequate reserves. He ordered pursuit toward El Cruce, where link up was effected (13 November) with motorized elements of Bilbao's 7th Division, which had advanced almost unimpeded from Santa Fe through "27 November." Had principal strength been kept with II Corps (as Bilbao had desired), Picuiba could have been taken and the probability of capturing Franco's advanced forces would have been enhanced. But most significantly, Toro had drawn the entire Bolivian command to his false belief that Estigarribia, wishing to hold Villazón, had committed decisive forces. This fallacy misdirected Bolivian attention, and perfectly complemented the more important Paraguayan maneuver under development at El Carmen.[41]

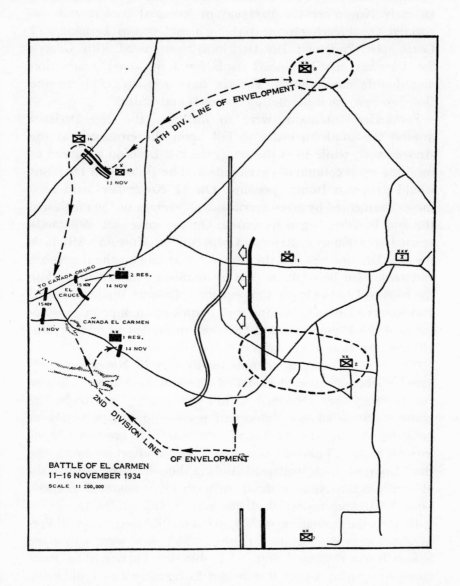

BATTLE OF EL CARMEN
11–16 NOVEMBER 1934

SCALE 1: 200,000

8TH DIV. LINE OF ENVELOPMENT

2ND DIVISION LINE OF ENVELOPMENT

13 NOV

TO CAÑADA ORURO

EL CRUCE

15 NOV

14 NOV

CAÑADA EL CARMEN

1 RES.

14 NOV

2 RES.

14 NOV

15 NOV

8

There the Bolivian Reserve Division (Colonel Zacharías Murillo) had long been poorly situated with both flanks open. In early November the Paraguayans localized its left and discovered the breach on the right. Colonel Carlos Fernández' I Corps (1st, 2nd, and 7th Divisions), reinforced with Garay's 8th Division, hastily pushed roads for a projected penetration and double envelopment. For six days a patrol explored the Bolivian rear, carefully noting all roads and trails.[42]

Fernández' intentions were to infiltrate the 2nd Division around the south in order to fall upon the crossroads at the Andean rear, while from the north the 8th Division advanced to meet the main column of envelopment. The 1st and 7th Divisions would maintain frontal pressure. On 11 November, with regiments augmented by green recruits to an average of 550 men each, the 2nd Division began its march. On the same day, Peñaranda created a 9,000-man Reserve Corps under Moscoso. Although the 2nd Division reached the Bolivian rear late on the thirteenth and took Murillo's CP, it proved unable to immediately close the road to Fortín Oruro. Consequently, Colonel Walter Mendez' 2nd Reserve Division, coming up by truck to attempt an envelopment of the Paraguayan 2nd Division, succeeded in joining Murillo in time also to be trapped.[43]

The two Paraguayan columns finally met 15 November. Estigarribia thought they had failed; he did not know whether enemy troops yet remained within the circle. That night the truth began to emerge. Important prisoner groups were taken, revealing that at "the cry 'Pilas in the rear!' . . . everybody [had] lost his head." The next morning a feeble effort to break the thin Guaraní circle collapsed and (although there were available rations for seventeen days), prisoner totals mounted to 4,000. Over 2,500 Andeans perished; the rest walked out.[44]

In a rapid maneuver with 4,500 men, Estigarribia and Fernández achieved a brilliant triumph. Not only were important enemy forces destroyed and invaluable—for impoverished Paraguay—equipment captured, but also Estigarribia's long objective of a break-through to the Pilcomayo was realized. The road at last lay open. The weight of the numerous prisoners impaired pursuit, however, absorbing transport to rush them to the rear.

Already 15 November, Frías began retreating his outflanked I Corps, and on the seventeenth Paraguayans entered Ballivián. The Bolivian defense system was shattered and the front dislocated, but most important were the moral effects. In both countries, as well as abroad, Ballivián had been a symbol of Andean resistance; it stood for the ability to mount an offensive and return to the original theater of operations along the old *fortín* line. Its loss signified Bolivian defeat, expulsion from the Hayes Zone, and forfeiture of the Chaco Boreal.[45]

Estigarribia ordered pursuit by I and III Corps, and directed the 8th Division to cover their advance against the parallel threat of the Cavalry Corps. Toro, he assumed, would also retire, but he did not. To the end, Toro had opposed the decision to abandon Ballivián. More than any other man, he was responsible for its conversion into a moral symbol, for holding it at the expense of offensive operations, and consequently for the shattering effects produced by its loss. He now considered El Carmen a transitory tactical development, asserting that in a few days he would take La Faye, threaten Garrapatal, and "remedy the stupid negligence of 'Moscosito.' " Yet the Cavalry Corps was detained in front of Picuiba until the Paraguayans abandoned the place for strategic reasons on 20 November, retiring southward 9 kilometers. Estigarribia, with quickness of mind, then ordered the 8th Division toward La Faye for a fresh maneuver.[46]

In the South, III Corps reached Guachalla on 21 November and halted for lack of transport, but I Corps (Fernández) broke the new Bolivian lines at Cañada Oruro on the following day and persisted in the direction of Ibibobo. The Andean retreat continued, covered by Busch's 8th Division and by the Bolivian Air Force which relentlessly bombed and strafed the advancing Guaraní. Despite the extent to which his right was being opened, Toro refused to retreat, still assuming that he could fall upon the Guaraní flank and convert El Carmen into a startling triumph. His men, however, were exhausted from their long advance and incapable of such operations, and he was obliged to pause. A more efficacious maneuver would have been a rapid drive by a reinforced II Corps through Ingavi and into the heart of the Chaco far to the Paraguayan rear, but Toro would have

vetoed an offensive by Bilbao. In fact, he again requested II
Corps as reinforcement for his own projected attack toward
Garrapatal.[47]

Overthrow of President Salamanca

Peñaranda's failure to remove Rodríquez after Salamanca's
September visit to the Chaco led to the definitive break between
the two leaders. On 22 October, Salamanca assured Peñaranda
that his sole concern was to avert a ruinous disaster. Bolivia had
been expelled from all but small parts of the Chaco; in this
situation the nation, not men, was important. The command,
he wrote, acted as if "military assignments are intangible personal rights, even when necessities of discipline and of defense
demand convenient changes." The exchange of recriminations,
misunderstanding, lack of discipline, and hatred between President and General, Díaz observes, led Bolivia down the road
to defeat, culminating first in the overthrow of Salamanca and
finally in loss of the Chaco.[48]

After El Carmen and the loss of Ballivián, Salamanca decided
the time had come to make a clean sweep of the command and
to install others with less egotism and more energy and compre-
hension. This seemed the last chance to save Bolivia from defeat. Fearing revolt on the Altiplano, Salamanca set out (21
November) for the Chaco against the wishes of his cabinet. At
Santa Cruz his party was met by General Lanza who, unaware
of the President's purpose, asserted that the situation was not
lost; a new line might be formed by a new command. At Villa
Montes on 25 November, Colonel Rodríguez met the party, but
Salamanca declined to hear his report, dismissing him as "no-
body."[49]

The day before, at Geneva, the League Assembly had approved
a report which recommended that hostilities should end within
six days of an armistice, troops should withdraw within ten,
military construction should halt for 150 kilometers on each
side of the military positions, and a neutral commission composed of the ABCP, Uruguay, and the United States should meet
at Buenos Aires within a month. If the peace conference failed

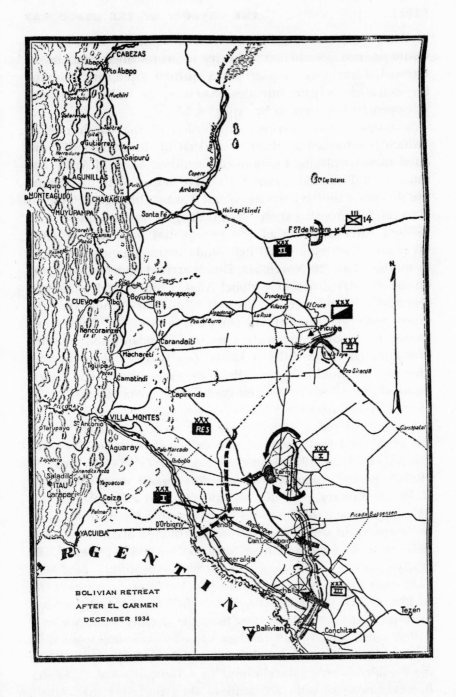

BOLIVIAN RETREAT

AFTER EL CARMEN

DECEMBER 1934

to effect final agreement within two months, the Hague Court would assume jurisdiction. Security measures might also be arbitrated. Clearly, the report was a distinct diplomatic triumph for defeated Bolivia, but demonstration of military capacity was essential if it were to be capitalized.[50]

Salamanca, after hearing the opinion of the Czech mission (which "conformed as always with that of the command") dictated an order placing Lanza in command of the Field Army, and summoned Peñaranda from GHQ. He hoped thus to improve the desperate military situation, but Lanza, although assured by General Sanjinés that there was no danger, feared a military rebellion. After members of the presidential party had received his report, Rodríguez wired Peñaranda setting momentous events in motion. Late 26 November, Busch arrived and briefed Lanza on the military situation. Colonel Añez, Chief of Staff designate, also appeared and accepted his new role. That evening the *jefes* dined with the presidential party. War Minister Canelas returned from conferring with Toro at Carandaití, and reported that although Toro disliked Lanza (and coveted the command himself) he would support Peñaranda's removal. The diners assumed that all would be well once Lanza personally visited the often insubordinate *jefe*.[51]

Lanza "enjoyed a formal resistance among his comrades of the army" apparently stemming from his *civilista* policies while a member of the 1930 Junta. As Salamanca's War Minister in 1931-32 he had imposed economies on certain wasteful and extravagant military expenditures, and required an unprecedented strict accounting of funds. This affected *jefes* directly, since commanders in the Chaco and other colonial areas were given cash to make local purchases of supplies and equipment. By falsifying expenses (such as an alleged expenditure of 20,000 *bolivianos* for a bridge across the Río Verde at Arce which was in fact a 20-foot log structure built by *conscriptos* from local materials), the corrupt emerged from the frontier wealthy men.[52]

Peñaranda already had reached Villa Montes accompanied by Colonels Díaz Arguedas and Serrano. When Sanjinés read him the President's order, the chubby, inept General asked, "*Cuántos hombres tiene su policia?*" Sanjinés then suggested that Rivera be called as "his presence is necessary here." Upon his arrival, the Chief of Staff agreed that they could not tolerate such treatment by the President of the Republic. "This is infamy," Rivera snorted, "and it is necessary to castigate them [the politicians]." Late that night, after conferring with Busch (who had slunk from Salamanca's table like Judas to conspire with his enemies), the *jefes* determined to take violent action to protect and perpetuate their incompetent command. Rivera accordingly set out to bring troops from the front.[53]

The next morning at the air strip, supposed engine trouble prevented Lanza from flying to GHQ. Añez, who had not eaten, suggested breakfast at the President's quarters, an isolated house chosen deliberately by Sanjinés. Observing soldiers about, Lanza obtained weapons, still fearful of rebellion. At 0630 Rivera returned with the 300-man 4th Artillery Group and quickly surrounded the house. Sanjinés and Añez stood by, arms folded, while Lanza exchanged harsh words with Rivera and Busch who had arrested both him and the President. Soon Peñaranda appeared in the garden, allegedly intoxicated, shouting, "Now we are going to show this rabble to be men!" Soldiers seized Lanza and shoved him into a car. "I am ashamed to be a Bolivian General," he muttered. Later the President emerged and remarked cynically, "This is the only maneuver in which they have been successful."[54]

Having captured the government, the plotters were joined by a host of *jefes*, many of whom had never seen the front, to deliberate on a new regime. Among those present were Peñaranda, Sanjinés, and General Adalid Tejada Fariñez; Colonels Rivera, Rodríguez, Frías, Gutiérrez, and Aliaza; Lieutenant Colonels Jordan (Air Force Chief), Serrano, Vidaurre, Añez, and Díaz Arguedas; and Major Busch. In view, Sanjinés said, of the delicate international situation, it was imperative to preserve constitutionality by elevating Vice-President Tejada Sorzano. It was agreed this would avert the impression abroad that the army was politically ambitious and would obviate the problem of gaining recognition for a *de facto* government. Accordingly a committee was formed to obtain Salamanca's resignation.[55]

The President quietly resigned after Rodríguez threatened

to pact immediate peace if he refused. Salamanca, a patriot, had at once recognized there was no other way to avert a disastrous civil war in front of the foreign enemy. That afternoon (27 November) the *jefes* again met, augmented by Toro, Bilbao, Ichaso, and others. The command stipulated that Tejada Sorzano must be subject to military control and be required to turn the government over to the army after the war. After Salamanca agreed to sign a revised resignation on the promise of his personal liberty, the *jefes* addressed a wire to General Blanco Galindo at La Paz, stating their recognition of Tejada Sorzano as President. Of all the Bolivian *jefes,* only two—both disciplined responsible men far beyond the common Altiplano breed—failed to affix their hands to this treasonous document: Bilbao Rioja and Moscoso.[56]

Tejada Sorzano was (since the November 1933 death of General Montes) the leader of the Liberal Party, well known for its pacifistic leanings and policy of cooperation with Chile in the Pacific. He wished peace, but an honorable one. After the cabinet approved his ascension (28 November), he formed a coalition government of all parties. On 4 December, he (an avid partisan of peace) took the realistic step which Salamanca (the *guerrista*) had always refused, and decreed general mobilization. A program of vastly expanded military spending commenced. Relations between government and command were now harmonious, as indeed they might be, for Tejada well knew his source of power. "Militarism, which has not been capable of repelling the foreign enemy, has already imposed its domination in Bolivia," Salamanca wrote on Christmas Day 1934.[57]

True to their promise, the *jefes* set their prisoners at liberty. With all his faults Daniel Salamanca was a patriot who placed the interests of his country first. He had not wished hostilities, but had only desired to prevent Paraguay from gaining control of more of the disputed Chaco. He later wrote that the war was provoked by military insubordination and conducted in insubordination by an inept command moving from disaster to disaster, in time forfeiting all the Chaco. When war came, he had assumed that the entire nation would rally, and for a time it did. He had considered the army capable of winning, but recognized his presidential responsibility to intervene when it displayed incompetence. In this he took no arrogant pride, for he was a modest, retiring figure, never jealous of his high office. When he read the text of the peace which Tejada's government signed in June 1935, Salamanca exclaimed, "The Protocol has killed me." He deemed it an arrangement catastrophic for Bolivia, which in time would mean renunciation of all the Chaco, because Paraguay, in possession, would never consent to an arbitration of law. Militarism and *caudillos* he saw in the offing for his Andean patria. It is doubtful if he ever understood that his own policies in 1931-32 set in motion the events which led to this end. The prospects for Bolivia were a sore tribulation to his spirit, and on 17 July 1935 he lay down and died. Perhaps, as many have written, he died of a broken heart.[58]

Irendagüe

In the southern sector of the front, meanwhile, retreat continued toward the foothills of the Andes; nevertheless, Toro persisted in the belief that advance by his 12,000-man Corps could restore the previous situation. His flank was exposed on the right by approximately 100 kilometers, but he remained convinced that he could force the Guaraní to retreat at least to Garrapatal. This strategy was theoretically plausible. While the advance of the Paraguayan I and III Corps endangered Toro's rear, in like manner his own position at Picuiba threatened theirs. If he could strike southward powerfully, most of the enemy army would be strategically enveloped against the Pilcomayo—the Estigarribia plan in reverse! In practice, Toro's intentions violated the principle of the objective in that his goal was unattainable, and the principle of security, as will be shown. Until 8 December the High Command, lacking any plan of action, simply reacted to the enemy. Probably, the *jefes* were too much absorbed with president-making to attend to military matters. This left Toro free to follow his own designs. General Estigarribia, in a demonstration of his mastery as a strategist, had succeeded in luring the Bolivian forward to a point where he could be destroyed by greatly inferior Paraguayan forces.[59]

After the victory at El Carmen, Estigarribia reinforced Franco's fatigued II Corps (6th and Reserve Divisions—5,500 men) with the 1st Division, and ordered Garay's 8th Division (1,800 men) to La Faye. Franco had only 25 trucks, all used for hauling water, and there were no shells for his artillery. Nevertheless, since Bolivian attention had been drawn to I and III Corps, and prisoners planted by Franco had informed the enemy that II Corps was too exhausted to move, it was unlikely Toro's rear would be well guarded. Estigarribia therefore prepared probably the most brilliant conception of his career. Doubtless remembering the October 1917 British capture of Beersheba, he dwelt upon the fact that Toro's sole source of water was the Guaraní-drilled wells at Irendagüe. He therefore ordered the 8th Division to advance through the brush, hacking a trail with machetes, and seize the Cavalry Corps water supply. On 6 December colorful old Colonel Garay, with a challenging cry in Guaraní (Rise up my sons, and let's go to die together in Irendagüe), began his march. The Reserve Division already was turning the enemy left in a complementary maneuver, while in the north the 14th Infantry was advancing from Ingavi toward "27 November," and from the southwest the 1st Division was moving on Villazón.[60]

Toro, from his remote CP at Carandaití (140 kilometers distant), learned on 7 December that the enemy was noticeably more active, probing to fix the Bolivian positions. The 6th Division attacked frontally while the Reserve Division began turning the left. Aircraft reports, on which Toro heavily relied, indicated that the enemy was cutting a trail northward. On the right flank, where the Guaraní had been active all day, jefes failed to keep the distant Toro informed. Late in the afternoon—Bolivian positions having been determined earlier by patrols—Garay passed his men through between the Andean 7th and 2nd Cavalry Divisions. Toro belatedly ordered the enemy trail blocked at 2340, shifted troops for depth on the right, and called for more aerial reconnaissance.[61]

At 0105 8 December, Toro learned that Irendagüe was under attack. He ordered the 130 soldiers there present to man defenses —thinking they faced only a small enemy raiding party bent on destroying the wells—ordered reinforcements to advance from the west, and directed the 7th Division to cooperate. Although only a single 200-man Paraguayan regiment had reached Irendagüe, they cut telephone lines to the 7th Division and imperiled the cavalry divisions. These forces wished to retreat because they were threatened by the Guaraní effort to envelop their left. Toro was unable to believe that large forces could advance 40 kilometers through solid brush within a single day, eluding Bolivian patrols and posts. Consequently, he approved retreat to El Cruce but ordered a division to Irendagüe, where he hoped to convert defeat to victory by capturing the Garay forces.[62]

At noon, flying over the front, Toro dropped orders reiterating his desires and promising water from "27 November." The Cavalry Corps had received neither food nor a full water ration the previous day; the retreat to El Cruce occurred under a burning sun, exhausting and dehydrating the soldiers. In view of the physical condition of their men and fearing envelopment, the acting divisional commanders resolved to continue the withdrawal to "27 November" unless water arrived. Toro charged them with the disaster, asserting that they needed only to proceed 15 kilometers to Irendagüe, expel the far weaker enemy, and receive abundant water. Watching from the air as his men moved ant-like, Toro furiously demanded that his orders be obeyed. He overlooked the physical condition of the men and the developing Paraguayan maneuver aimed at their annihilation, failed to supply the water the soldiers required, and was not personally present to lead his Corps.[63]

Again, 9 December, Toro dropped orders seeking to stimulate the *jefes* to obey instructions. At this time the cavalry divisions were well on their way north, and the orders fell among disorganized stragglers and their Guaraní pursuers. In a stirring tribute to the Paraguayan soldier, Toro challenged:

> The enemy troops have demonstrated they can live months lacking almost every element. Yesterday they effected a march of 40 Kilometers by trails on foot to attack Irendagüe with maximum audacity and energy.

Furiously he berated the *jefes* for disobedience, vowing to hold the culprits to courts-martial. He was unware of, or unwilling to accept, the fact that men without food or water for days pass beyond the control of their commanders.[64]

Peñaranda realistically ordered general retreat at noon on the ninth. For once Toro obeyed, for he had no choice. The 7th Division, which had withdrawn in good order, was to defend Carandaití; the 1st Cavalry Division was to reorganize and await fresh troops at "27 November." Meanwhile, the Paraguayans faced the most horrible spectacle of the Chaco War as they advanced along roads filled with Andean troops insane with thirst, who sucked blood, drank urine, and "implored on their knees a little water, urine of the soldiers or gasoline from the [Paraguayan] trucks to appease the thirst that devoured them." Many stumbled away into the brush, staggering, crawling, to collapse and die. Others "marched and marched and marched with their swollen tongues protruding from dry lips, and one by one they fell down and [their fellows] marched on leaving them to die." Toro claimed that only 1,635 were lost; Asunción asserted that over 4,000 died of thirst and 3,000 were captured; a realistic figure would probably be about 3,000 total Bolivian casualties. Finally, on 11 December, God took mercy and the skies opened with heavy rains. That evening Paraguayan cavalry occupied "27 November."[65]

The scope of the combined victories of El Carmen and Irendagüe was evident for everyone except the League of Nations, whose unrealistic actions served to encourage continued Bolivian resistance. Desperately poor, Paraguay partially reoutfitted her army with the large booty from these battles. Along with purchases made with a new 2,000,000 Ps. Arg. loan, the Guaraní were made ready to invade Bolivia and deliver the *coup de grâce*. For Bolivia, her army retreating into the Andes, the defeats meant loss of the Chaco and the war.[66]

Freshly defeated and expelled even beyond her western 1907 status quo line, Bolivia accepted the League's latest proposal on 10 December. The plan embodied La Paz's consistent desires, quite probably due to disgust in Europe with Paraguay for seeking to retain the fruits of her hard-won military successes. Asunción responded, therefore (18 December), that the proposal was in essence only a prolonged truce. It left the armies on a war footing and exposed the littoral of the Rio Paraguay to a contention the Guaraní did not admit. His eye on the feverish, bellicose, victory-wild populace, Ayala pointed out that there was no provision for constitutional ratification by Congress, nor a procedure for fixing war guilt.[67]

Four days later Bolivia charged Paraguay's insistence on security, and a cooling-off period before final settlement, was a mere continuation of her historic desire to regularize encroachments through passage of time. For this purpose, Asunción demanded demobilization and limitation of the Bolivian army to small numbers, prohibition on arms purchases, and a nonaggression pact "which would enable Paraguay to evade forevermore the settlement of the actual dispute."[68] Despite two and one-half years of war and defeat, La Paz still viewed the military as her instrument of policy in seeking reintegration of the Chaco.

Foreign Minister Luís A. Riart at once elaborated Paraguay's objections, mainly to the lack of adequate, permanent security guarantees. Since most male Guaraní were in the army, demobilization was essential for the restoration of the economy; the army's financial burden was ruining the nation. Consequently, Asunción insisted, renewal of the war must be made an impossibility. "Unless Paraguay obtains absolute security in reward for her titanic efforts, her destiny as a nation must remain precarious." The League chose, thereupon, to consider Paraguay's request for modification of the plan as a rejection, and moved in January 1935 to lift the arms embargo on Bolivia, recommending that it was Paraguay's duty to refrain from waging war! In response to this nonsense, Paraguay left the League in February, in the process effectively expelling Geneva from further participation in the Chaco dispute.[69]

Ibibobo

After the Cavalry Corps' disastrous retreat, the 7th Division, which had retired intact, formed a defense line across the road to Carandaití. The 1st Cavalry Division, "a reduced contingent of troops that arrived at the Parapetí without arms and in extreme exhaustion," was reorganized at Santa Fe under Major

Busch. With the Chaco already lost, Peñaranda resigned (11 December) to give President Tejada a free hand. The President decreed general mobilization and prepared for a maximum effort to save the territorial integrity of Bolivia. A new war had in fact begun. Having won the Chaco Boreal, Paraguay now prepared to invade the Bolivian departments, capture the oil fields, and/or take Villa Montes. As the general retreat continued, the Paraguayan army approached the foothills where the pre-Columbian campaigns of the Guaraní against the Aymara and Quechua had floundered.[70]

From mid-December, the Bolivian command attempted to stabilize a defense line from the Pilcomayo at Ibibobo northward along the foothills to Carandaití. When the Paraguayan III Corps (Delgado) neared Ibibobo, it began explorations and heavy patrolling. In the hills Andean troops were thinly spread; there was an 8-kilometer gap between the 8th and 9th Divisions where the rugged terrain alone was deemed adequate to block the flatland enemy. Well aware of the excellent results obtained by advancing even small forces to the Bolivian rear, Delgado pushed the 5th Cavalry through the foothills during the rainy night of 27 December. The following afternoon, closing the Palo Marcado road enveloped about 2,000 Bolivians.[71]

The Andeans attempted to escape by crossing the flooded Pilcomayo, and 200 were drowned. After failure of belated, feeble efforts to break out, the surrender of units commenced. Using only 2,380 men, Delgado achieved an important triumph through audacity, skill, and surprise in maneuver, capturing over 1,200 men and a large booty at a cost of 46 wounded. The road to Villa Montes was reopened and the Bolivian retreat resumed to another line from Palo Marcado northward to Capirendá. At Villa Montes, 1934 closed with the command contemplating abandonment of that last foothold in the Chaco as the Paraguayan advance continued, apparently undaunted by the foothills of the Andean cordillera.[72]

General Estigarribia's command, after several months of effort, had for the third successive year produced major victories just prior to the beginning of the summer rainy season. In this campaign, Estigarribia reached the fullness of his stature as a Great

Captain, relying exclusively on the strategy of indirect approach to defeat a doubly numerous Bolivian army. His victories at El Carmen and Irendagüe demonstrated true genius; the former in the execution with surprise of a penetration and double envelopment; the latter by strategically mastering his opponent, and by exploiting water to oblige him to retreat disastrously. Along with Delgado's single envelopment of Ibibobo, these actions constitute model maneuvers. The results were decisive: Bolivia was definitively expelled from the Chaco plains and her departments were exposed to the invasion which the Paraguayans, now flush with victory, demanded of their government and army. The concept of just defense (the expulsion of the invader from historic Paraguayan territory) vanished; it was replaced by lust for conquest—a thirst for the blood of the mortally wounded enemy. The lure of the Camiri oil fields replaced for Asunción the colonial promise of the wealth of Potosi, and posed a counter aspiration to La Paz's longing for salt water.[73]

Notes

1. *Report of the Chaco Commission,* 42-46. The Commission (p. 47) indicated that a Bolivian port was feasible from an engineering standpoint in the Petropolis cession. Also note U. S., *Foreign Relations,* IV, 33-61; Bolivia, *Memoria 1934,* 606-607; Rivarola, III, 63, 72-75.

2. *Report of the Chaco Commission,* 62-66; Rivarola, III, 65, 70-71, quotation, 66; *Libro Blanco,* IV, 109-117; U. S., *Foreign Relations,* 1934, IV, 63.

3. *Report of the Chaco Commission,* 66-67; U. S., *Foreign Relations,* 1934, IV, 64.

4. U. S., *Foreign Relations,* 1934, IV, 52, 65; Rivarola, III, 180-182. Separatism of Santa Cruz was an old problem for La Paz, but it was fanned by Asunción's clever psychological warfare. See Enrique de Gandia, *Historia de Santa Cruz de la Sierra* (Buenos Aires, 1935).

5. U. S., *Foreign Relations,* 1934, IV, 68, 70, 260-261, 289; Rivarola, III, 99-104.

6. U. S., *Foreign Relations,* 1934, IV, 141-146; Bolivia, *Memoria 1934,* 779-780; *Política Argentina,* II, 229-233; Rivarola, III, 154.

7. Bolivia, *Memoria 1934,* 781; U. S., *Foreign Relations,* 1934, IV, 150-157; Rivarola, III, 136-138, 145-150, 158-159.

8. Estigarribia, 151-153; Vergara Vicuña, V, 510, 534-543, 548, 557; González, 146-147, 151-156; *Partes del conductor*, 175-180; Caballero Irala, 97-110.

9. Delgado, II, 81-83; Díaz Arguedas, *La guerra*, 142-143, 174; Vergara Vicuña, V, 584, 587-590; Urioste, *La Encrucijada*, 103. Delgado (II, 73-77, 205) took over III Corps 20 June from Colonel Brizuela, who assumed command of the Northern Sector at Bahia Negra. The same command changes, an outgrowth of Strongest, brought Colonel Carlos José Fernández to command of I Corps on 7 June; Florentín, *Strongest*, 226.

10. Toro, 70, 393-395; Delgado, II, 79-80, 89-91, 97-108; Aponte B., *Cincuenta años*, 225-226; *Partes del conductor*, 182-184; Vergara Vicuña, V, 570-575, 614-621; Díaz Arguedas, *La guerra*, 150-151, 167-168, 174-175; *El hombre símbolo*, 144-146, quotation, 144.

11. Vergara Vicuña, V, 630-631; Díaz Arguedas, *La guerra*, 142; Delgado, II, 95, 232-233.

12. Estigarribia, 152-160, 163; Delgado, II, 109-122, 134; Letter, Colonel Fernández to the author. Lanza was supplied from Santa Fe through "27 November." Actually his was an impotent threat since, for reasons of personal dislike, the command denied him significant troops for his potentially sound operation; Urioste, *La Encrucijada*, 127-128. Salamanca had belatedly grown interested in the north and the limited objective, the Rio Paraguay, which the army had advocated two years before; Díaz Arguedas, *La guerra*, 360-361.

13. Estigarribia, 160-165; Rivarola, III, 108-109, 135; Aponte B., *Cincuenta años*, 242; Delgado, II, 127-135, 231. Florentín, *Strongest*, 22n, says Estigarribia remarked that Franco was always in action, whether for good or bad, and never questioned the means.

By war's end, Paraguay had drilled 95 wells in the desert area; Benítez, *Estigarribia*, 2d ed., 104.

14. Díaz Arguedas, *La guerra*, 175-178; Benítez, *Estigarribia*, 2d ed., 81; Vergara Vicuña, V, 633-634, quotation, 633.

15. Estigarribia, 166; *Partes del conductor*, 189-191; González, 159-160, 205. Delgado (II, 151) denies the allegation that this offensive was the brain child of Franco, insisting that it came from Estigarribia himself.

16. Estigarribia, 167-168; *Partes del conductor*, 192; Díaz Arguedas, *La guerra*, 206-207; Toro, 71-72.

17. Estigarribia, 168-171; Delgado, II, 146-153; Caballero Irala, 110; Rivarola (III, 183, 201) provides intelligence of Bolivian movements which was obtained by Argentina air reconnaissance. See also Silvio Macías, *La Guerra del Chaco* (Asunción, 1936), 80-81. The strategy narrated is from Estigarribia. Delgado (p. 152) says Estigarribia intended to unite II Corps (Reserve, 1st and 6th Divisions) at Picuiba for a fresh offensive to take the Camiri oil fields.

18. U. S., *Foreign Relations,* 1934, IV, 158-184; Rivarola, III, 141-142, 149, 160-161, 178, quotation, 183.

19. Toro, 74-77; Díaz Arguedas, *El hombre símbolo,* 88-95, quotations, 93; *La guerra,* 214-215; Aponte B., *Cincuenta años,* 234-239. In June, Salamanca received a new military mission contracted in Czechoslovakia. Although the members were able, well-versed advisers, the native *jefes* were extremely suspicious and hostile; Vergara Vicuña, V, 558-620.

20. Díaz Arguedas, *El hombre símbolo,* 96-99, quotation, 99. Toro was not alone in disliking Bilbao, but made his distaste more open. Bilbao later wrote that his relations with other *jefes* were cold and indifferent, and he had not a single friend in the command; Vergara Vicuña, *Bilbao,* 407.

21. Díaz Arguedas, *El hombre símbolo,* 99-111.

22. Estigarribia, 168.

23. Díaz Arguedas, *El hombre símbolo,* 111-122; *La guerra,* 229-230. Peñaranda believed Toro a brilliant strategist, and therefore was apparently awed by him; Vergara Vicuña, VI, 457.

24. Díaz Arguedas, *El hombre símbolo,* 123-135; *La guerra,* 231.

25. U. S., *Foreign Relations,* 1934, IV, 186; Rivarola, III, 180.

26. U. S., *Foreign Relations,* 1934, IV, 188-193, quotations, 188; Rivarola, III, 185-186, third quotation, 181.

27. Estigarribia, 172; Macías, 85-94; Toro, 77; González, 161; Díaz Arguedas, *La guerra,* 217; Vidaurre, *Material de guerra,* 110.

28. Estigarribia, 173-174; Delgado, II, 159-167; Toro, 87; Díaz Arguedas, *La guerra,* 218-219; Vergara Vicuña, VI, 7; *Partes del conductor,* 194-196.

29. Estigarribia, 172-174, 176-177, quotation, 177; Benítez, *Estigarribia,* 1st ed., 99; U. S., *Foreign Relations,* 1934, IV, 199-203; Rivarola, III, 68, 187-192.

30. Estigarribia, 175; Macías, 93-98, 137; Toro, 80; Aponte B., *Cincuenta años,* 229; González, 161-162; *Partes del conductor,* 200; Díaz Arguedas, *La guerra,* 220-223. The Bolivian leaflets, alleging that Estigarribia was using the troops to further his political ambitions, sought to undermine morale by convincing them they were without hope: "You will die of thirst and hunger or by the action of our arms—not only are you completely surrounded; we have also taken your rear guard post and after tonight all the trucks and carts from Camacho will fall into our power." (p. 222)

31. *Statement of the Paraguayan Case,* 46-49, quotation, 46; also note especially U. S., *Foreign Relations,* 1934, IV, 88, 92, 97, 106, 210-216. Ayala, too, objected to the League, which he considered anti-Paraguayan; Rivarola, III, 204.

32. *Statement of the Bolivian Government's Case,* 26-29, quotations, 29.

33. Vergara Vicuña, a graduate of the Spanish War College and former Chilean cabinet member, was the most famous of a group of Chilean officers contracted by Bolivia in June, to the great consternation of Asunción; Vergara Vicuña, VI, 17-23. See Rivarola, III, 114-134.

34. Vergara Vicuña, VI, 27-41, 49.

35. *Partes del conductor*, 203-205; Díaz Arguedas, *La guerra*, 263-264; Vergara Vicuña, *Bilbao*, 392-394; VI, 47-50, 56.

36. Toro, 88-91; Vergara Vicuña, VI, 52-54, 57-68; *Bilbao*, 395-400, 403, 405; Díaz Arguedas, *La guerra*, 237.

37. Díaz Arguedas, *La guerra*, 232. Even the Salamanca government was at this time optimistic that Camacho would be taken; Urioste, *La Encrucijada*, 133.

38. Rivarola, III, 166-174, 192.

39. Estigarribia, 177-178, 187; González, 167; Vergara Vicuña, VI, 161. Five wells, operated by truck engines, were drilled at Irendagüe; Urioste, *La Encrucijada*, 131. Eugenio Garay, brother of Blas, was a popular old Guaraní hero, 62 years old when the war began; Benítez, *Estigarribia*, 1st ed., 105.

40. Toro, 93-94; Díaz Arguedas, *La guerra*, 238-241; Estigarribia, 178; *Partes del conductor*, 205-207; Vergara Vicuña, VI, 72-81; González, 164; Caballero Irala, 123-129.

41. Toro, 95-97; Díaz Arguedas, *La guerra*, 242-243; Vergara Vicuña, VI, 82, 84, 91-93. Vergara, who observed interrogations, says Paraguay had unarmed raiders behind Bolivian lines to disrupt communications. When captured, they "revealed" that main Guaraní attention was concentrated on the Irendagüe area, thus corroborating (seemingly) the false premises which Toro had inculcated in the High Command, (pp. 99-100).

42. Estigarribia, 178; Vergara Vicuña, VI, 105, 133, 158, 163-168. Vergara (161-185) quotes an article by Captain Francisco Chaves del Valle, Commander of the Paraguayan 10th Infantry during this action. The article first appeared in *Revista del Ejército y Armada* (Asunción, 1939), Nos. 14-16. I Corps strength was 9,000, excluding the 8th Division; Colonel Victor Ayala Queirolo, *El Carmen* (Asunción, 1959), attached document.

43. Díaz Arguedas, *La guerra*, 247-248; Benítez, *Estigarribia*, 2d ed., 83-84; Vergara Vicuña, VI, 135-141, 168-178; Ayala Queirolo, 40-52. Frías assumed command of I Corps vice Moscoso.

44. Estigarribia, 179-182; quotation, 180; Benítez, *Estigarribia*, 2d ed., 84; Díaz Arguedas, *La guerra*, 249; Vergara Vicuña, VI, 143, 179-185. To the south the Paraguayan circle was held by only three men per 500 meters! (p. 174). Vergara (p. 140) also says the Bolivian collapse was due to the early capture of the *jefes* in their CP's, thus destroying effective command.

On 15 November the Chief of Staff of the barely created Reserve Corps was ambushed and maps he carried were captured. The Bolivians always blamed their defeat on this loss. Estigarribia correctly points out that his maneuver was already in full development *before* this event. Nonetheless, the strategic defeat was facilitated by one of the maps, size 31 x 19, which detailed all Andean dispositions from Ballivián to Picuiba with air and ground annotations; Ayala Queirolo, 93, 56-61.

45. Estigarribia, 181-183; *Partes del conductor*, 207-210; Vergara Vicuña, VI, 193-198. "The soul of the victory of El Carmen," writes Ayala Queirolo (p. 69), "was the commander of I Corps, Col. Carlos J. Fernández."

46. Estigarribia, 183; Vergara Vicuña, VI, 110-122, 200-202, quotation, 110; Toro, 103-105; Caballero Irala, 132-134. In fact, Moscoso had not actually taken control of the Reserve Corps when El Carmen occurred.

47. Vergara Vicuña, VI, 211-212, 221-223; *Partes del conductor*, 212-214; Toro, 105-109; Díaz Arguedas, *La guerra*, 258-261. See also Lieutenant Thomas Wewege-Smith, *Gran Chaco Adventure* (London, 1937), 155-156.

48. Díaz Arguedas, *El hombre símbolo*, 140-141, quotation, 140. This monograph, recent, thorough, containing numerous documents, and written by a bystander at Salamanca's overthrow, far surpasses any other data available. Colonel Díaz was Historical Officer of the Bolivian Command.

49. *Ibid.*, 157-161, 280. In part, this portion is Lanza's account as quoted by Díaz. Salamanca's version begins with page 279. Also consult Urioste, *La Encrucijada*, 136.

50. League of Nations Publications, Political, 1934, VII, No. 13, *Dispute Between Bolivia and Paraguay. Report as Provided for under Article 15, Paragraph 4, of the Convenant*, 6-9; Rivarola, III, 209-212.

51. Díaz Arguedas, *El hombre símbolo*, 161-165, 184-185, quotation, 284. For Toro's views, see Vergara Vicuña, VI, 267-270. Añez had been II Corps Chief of Staff.

52. Urioste, *La Encrucijada*, 125.

53. Díaz Arguedas, *El hombre símbolo*, 167-170, quotations, 168 and 170.

54. *Ibid.*, 165, 171-178, 286, quotations, 174, 176, 178. Lanza's account ends with page 172. Díaz then takes up his personal recollections. Salamanca blamed Rodríguez for the plot, but knew the cooperation of Toro was essential. He later wrote: "The Command had never realized an operation better prepared nor as brilliant," (p. 287).

55. *Ibid.*, 180-185.

56. *Ibid.*, 186-204, 288-289, proceedings of meetings, and Díaz' per-

sonal account. Rodríguez told a member of the party regarding Salamanca: "Yesterday for him I was no one. Now for us he is no one," (p. 294). See also Vergara Vicuña, *Bilbao,* 413.

57.　Díaz Arguedas, *El hombre símbolo,* 207-233, 251, 264, quotation, 289; Diez de Medina, *De un siglo,* 346. Note also Urioste, *La Encrucijada,* 170. When informed of Salamanca's overthrow, Estigarribia (p. 185) wrote in his diary: "The great obstacle for the advent of peace has disappeared."

58.　Díaz Arguedas, *El hombre símbolo,* 258-280, quotation, 266. Urioste, who had close relations with the Salamanca government, wrote that when war began people and parties were unanimous in support of reprisals on Paraguay, but when defeats occurred they attributed them solely to Salamanca; *La Encrucijada,* 221.

59.　Vergara Vicuña, VI, 233-236, 241, 248; Franco, 62-64.

60.　Franco, 67-71; Caballero Irala, 135-136; Aponte B., *General Garay,* 111-114; Ernesto Andía, *En el pais de los heroes* (Buenos Aires, 1947), 109 for quotation; Vergara Vicuña, VI, 287-288. Franco (p. 66) again claims the authorship of the strategy and says (p. 77) written confirmation of nonexistent verbal orders was received three days after the victory. Fernández has told the author this is incorrect.

61.　Toro, 113-146; González, 172; Macías, 132; Vergara Vicuña, VI, 287-288, 293-296, 304, 317-320, 330-331, 352-354. Vergara had respectfully suggested earlier that Toro place his CP closer to the front and for his pains was reassigned to I Corps (p. 188). There is no doubt that Toro's distance and the presence of the cavalry division CO's at his headquarters were serious factors in the defeat. Further, Toro was allegedly wenching and debauching himself while his men were being annihilated; Urioste, *La Encrucijada,* 140. "Play, women and alcohol have been the great enemies of the country in the war," Urioste wrote, referring to the pastimes of most *jefes.* The headquarters of Bilbao was the exception (p. 190). By contrast, at Estigarribia's staff mess, milk was the variant to water; Benítez, *Estigarribia,* 1st ed., 92.

62.　Toro, 147-153; Macías, 134; Vergara Vicuña, VI, 356, 362-365; Franco, 72.

63.　Toro, 154-182, 198; Caballero Irala, 138; Estigarribia, 186; Vergara Vicuña, VI, 291, 378, 391-394, 412. Toro (p. 185) reprints documents from his G-4 indicating that the Cavalry Corps actually had received water in adequate amounts during the previous three days. The same documents seek to fix total strength at 5,291, an obvious falsehood.

64.　Toro, 189-210; Caballero Irala, 139-140; quotation, 140; Vergara Vicuña, VI, 437, 471, 479, 494.

65.　Toro, 185, 213-220; Franco, 73; Caballero Irala, 141-145, first quotation, 142; Wewege-Smith, second quotation, 223; Macías, 128,

139-142; *Partes del conductor,* 217-218; Vergara Vicuña, VI, 407, 429, 438-443. Vergara (p. 502) places total Cavalry Corps casualties at 2,384. Considering both cavalry divisions were immediately reorganized with full strength, they obviously were not annihilated as Asunción claimed. Placing the Paraguayan claims in their diplomatic, political, and military context, it is apparent that they were deliberate exaggerations for psychological warfare purposes.

66. Rivarola, III, 192-197.

67. League of Nations Official Journal, Special Supplement No. 132, *Dispute Between Bolivia and Paraguay. Records of the Special Session of the Assembly,* 73-77; Bolivia, *Mensaje 1935,* 3; U. S., *Foreign Relations,* 1934, IV, 123; Rivarola, III, 213-220.

68. Special Supplement No. 133, 40-43.

69. Special Supplement No. 133, 44-48, quotation, 48; League of Nations Official Journal, Special Supplement No. 134, *Dispute Between Bolivia and Paraguay. Appeal of the Bolivian Government under Article 15 of the Covenant,* 55; U. S., *Foreign Relations,* 1934, IV, 132-134; Rivarola, III, 223-224, 231-248.

70. Toro, 310-311; Díaz Arguedas, *La guerra,* 284-285, 290-293; Vergara Vicuña, VI, 504; Franco, quotation, 72; Rivarola, III, 192-193; Bolivia, *Mensaje 1935,* 12, 67. A new loan was made with the Central Bank for 50,000,000 Bs. Restrictions on world tin production facilitated general mobilization without pain to the vital mining industry; *Mensaje 1935,* 21. Note also *El Banco Central de Bolivia durante la Guerra del Chaco* (La Paz, 1936), 156.

71. Macías, 146-147; Vergara Vicuña, VI, 592-597; Díaz Arguedas, *La guerra,* 262, 278. The trapped forces were the 8th Cavalry, 2nd Infantry, and the 9th Artillery, elements of the 9th Division.

72. Vergara Vicuña, VI, 598-605, 615-616; Díaz Arguedas, *La guerra,* 280-281; *Partes del conductor,* 221. Rios (p. 302) places prisoners at 1,717, booty at 1,800 rifles, 15 mortars, 420 automatic arms. Paraguay's victorious 1934 campaign was not without cost. The number of soldiers evacuated was 13,683. Total casualties were probably about 17,000 from May to December 1934. Vasconsellos, *Memoria,* 39.

73. Benítez, *Estigarribia,* 1st ed., 117-118. Rios (p. 302) places total Bolivian casualties in these actions at 17,000 men.

CHAPTER EIGHT

THE BOLIVIAN COUNTEROFFENSIVE

After the defeat at Ibibobo, Bolivian President Tejada Sorzano, accompanied by a group of Generals and Ministers, visited Villa Montes. He probably wished to replace the entire command, but was patently incapable of dislodging it. Peñaranda was retained and Colonel David Toro, through the intercession of his political friends, returned to his 1932-1933 position, Chief of Staff. "Disoriented and optimistic as always," Toro appeared to have been rewarded for his failures with a higher post.[1]

With the command confirmed, a new line was established based on the defense of Villa Montes. With its arsenals, depots, and communications lines, this town was the last major Chaco foothold of Bolivia. Its loss would have opened the road to Tarija and, because of Bolivia's poor communications system, would have left the lowlands at the mercy of the Guaraní. After other *jefes* refused the responsibility, Bilbao and Moscoso were entrusted with Villa Montes' defense. Artillery concentration was unprecedented; 25,000 men were employed; field fortifications were extensive; caltrops were used. Morale rose in response to sound leadership. The Pilcomayo, included in Bilbao's Southern Sector Command, was made impassable to the enemy by the 4th Division which was sprawled along the south bank.[2]

The Comanchaco's intentions were to cut the Villa Montes-Santa Cruz road and bisect the enemy army. After heavy patrolling, I Corps fixed upon the Andean 3rd Division at Capirendá, extreme left of the Southern Sector. Fearing a double envelopment of the division, General Carlos Quintanilla, restored to the war as Commanding General of the Central Sector at Carandaití, placed strong forces on its left. Nevertheless, on 11 January 1935 the Paraguayans surrounded two regiments, killed

330 and captured 200, and obliged fresh retreat. On the fifteenth the Andean 19th Infantry partially escaped envelopment by the Caballero Irala Detachment at Huirapitindi, and the next day Paraguayan troops attained the banks of the Parapetí, historic limit of Asunción's Chaco claim. On 23 January, Franco's II Corps entered Carandaití.[3]

These rapid actions shattered the nascent defenses of the Santa Fe Detachment (former Bolivian II Corps) and Central Sector, forcing wide retreat to positions deeper in the Serrania de Aguarague foothills. Defenses were prepared across strategic passes to hold the Paraguayans back from the Camiri oil fields. But by espionage, Guaraní agents in Buenos Aires obtained detailed Standard Oil maps of the region, better data than the Andeans themselves possessed.[4]

While the Caballero Detachment mopped up small towns on the east bank of the Parapetí, the Guaraní-speaking ethnic remnant of ancient invasions welcomed the Paraguayan troops and supported them enthusiastically. From Carandaití, Franco drove toward Boyuibé on his way to the oil fields, a step in the proposed economic defeat of Bolivia. On 28 January, Boyuibé fell and the Villa Montes-Santa Cruz road was severed. Ten days later II Corps turned the flank of the defenders of the Ñaincorainza pass, but the arrival of the 1st Cavalry Division left the Guaraní greatly outnumbered. Defeated, Franco's men retreated on 11 February, frustrated in their attempt to reach Camiri.[5]

Thwarted in the indirect approach which success for Franco would have entailed, the Comanchaco attacked the Villa Montes defenses on the thirteenth with 5,000 men. Bilbao's single squadron of aircraft harassed them, and reported their center of gravity, the Capirendá road. Fortifications and artillery met the assailant, who lacked shells for his own guns. Consequently, the attack progressed little until on 16 February a 3-kilometer salient was created near the mountains on the Andean left. Employment of reserves, close air support, and an artillery bombardment halted the advance. Four days later successive assault waves accomplished nothing more than extremely heavy Guaraní casualties. In March the bulge was closed by the Bolivians. Estigarribia had wished to capture Villa Montes to clear the Chaco and open the way for an invasion of Tarija. The Paraguayan attempt to take the town had been unwise, however, since Bilbao had twice the strength in strong defensive positions; unfortunately, Estigarribia therefore violated an elemental lesson of the war and was severely chastised.[6]

While attention focused on Villa Montes, II Corps was restrained from fresh endeavors to seize Camiri, halt the flow of gasoline to the Bolivian war machine, and hold the oil fields as a material guarantee of a postwar indemnity. Having failed in the south, Estigarribia returned to this objective. On 8 March, in the narrow valley between the Aguarague and Charagua ranges, Franco struck the enemy 7th Division. After five days, attacks failed definitively, leaving numerous Paraguayan dead. On the ninth, Andean forces surrounded a battalion of the 15th Infantry and obliged it to surrender. This raised Bolivian morale and confirmed that the addition of a third dimension, elevation, had confounded the dexterous maneuvers which the Guaraní had perfected in the Chaco plains.[7]

Colonel Franco then formed a detachment under Colonel Eugenio Garay (2nd Division and González Detachment, 2,600 men) to attack Charagua. Faced with a Paraguayan threat along the Parapetí, the Peñaranda command resurrected the II Corps (2nd Division and 3rd Cavalry Division, about 5,000 men) under Colonel José E. Anze. Despite numerical inferiority, Garay crossed the Parapetí into Bolivia proper and captured Coperé (5 April) after bombing had destroyed Andean communications lines. Pushing the 3rd Cavalry Division before him, Garay advanced toward the Charagua-Santa Cruz highway. On 12 April he turned the enemy's flank at the village of Carandaití Moza, and drove through the pass to Charagua. Three days later, in cooperation with the 8th Division pressing from the south, the city was occupied. Peñaranda then re-established the Cavalry Corps at Boyuibé, and replaced Quintanilla in command of the Central Sector with General Guillén.[8]

Charagua had been evacuated in hopes of luring Garay and the 8th Division up the road toward Santa Cruz; there, with greatly extended communications, they could have been annihilated. In fact, the Paraguayan thrust was more apparent than real due to lack of trucks. Unfortunately, panic in Santa Cruz (where traditional separatism was opportunistically fanned by Asunción), obliged a premature counteroffensive to remove this nascent threat. The plan envisioned (1) breaking the Paraguayan lines at Boyuibé and advancing to Mandeyapecuá, there to face any reinforcements from the south, (2) double envelopment of Franco by the Cavalry and II Corps moving on a broad front, and (3) diversionary attacks at Villa Montes. The Peñaranda-Toro command hoped thus to destroy the enemy in the north and, by rapid advance, to oblige a Paraguayan retreat to the former Ibibobo-Capirendá-Carandaití line. From this position, with vastly superior forces, the Bolivian army would wage an active defense. With his long supply lines and shrinking human potential, the enemy would be forced to waste himself.[9]

General Guillén had proposed a double envelopment of the Paraguayan Reserve Division, but his forces lacked shoes and clothing, as well as essential communications equipment. Consequently, when he opened the offensive on 16 April his 15,000 men were not really fit for such operations. The primary aim was the Casa Alta-Machareti road used by Franco for troop movements. On the seventeenth, Guillén's advance was general, but the Guaraní evaded the trap and retired in good order. On 20 April, Mandeyapecuá was taken, the Paraguayans withdrawing toward Carandaití.[10]

At Villa Montes, where Paraguayan lines formed a crescent from the Pilcomayo northwestward around the town to the mountains, a limited offensive was directed against the Guaraní right. Attacks 14-16 April broke the lines along the Camatindi road, but an attempted penetration and envelopment failed against fierce resistance. On the nineteenth the Bolivians took Tarairi, obliging Colonel Fernández to retreat his entire front in that area. The Andean success was nevertheless limited and at the cost of heavy casualties. Despite lesser manpower, the Paraguayan lines were no weaker than the Bolivian, making further attacks at Villa Montes unpromising.[11]

The light Paraguayan II Corps forces retreated toward Carandaití, but contained their pursuers in the mountain passes; Peñaranda therefore chose to go on the defensive in the central sector, while pressing the attack along the Parapetí. To counter Guillén, Franco had ordered the 8th Division south from Charagua. Only the small 2nd Division remained, and on 21 April, Paraguay's five-day occupation of the town came to an end. Carandaití Moza was evacuated and on the twenty-third the 8th Division was surrounded near Cambeiti. The Paraguayan 3rd Division (8th Cavalry, 21st Infantry) was rushed from Bahia Negra, no other relief forces being available. An attack by the González Detachment failed to free the 8th Division, but on 28 April it broke the extensive perimeter held by the Andean 7th Division and escaped toward Santa Fe on the Parapetí. Once again Bolivian disregard of the principle of economy of forces had lost a promising opportunity.[12]

The war was turning, at least momentarily, in favor of Bolivia. Rugged terrain prevented the brilliant Paraguayan maneuvers of the plains. The cold reduced effectiveness. Asunción was financially exhausted. The treasury was empty. Levies on export receipts had already been tapped for a year in advance. Manpower was nearly spent. Home production was kept up only by prisoner-of-war labor. Sixteen-year-olds, old men, and reclassified former rejectees made up the last 6,000 recruits. When the 3rd Division was shifted from Bahia Negra, it was replaced with boys under Naval command. Bolivia, with her greater population, had been able, even after the 1934 defeats, to muster a new army of 50,000. Paraguay, whose proud regiments had been 1,600 each at Boquerón, now fielded small units of 250 to 400, albeit mostly veterans, and totaling 15,000. Her triumph in expelling Bolivia from the Chaco extended greatly her communications, and absorbed more and more manpower in support functions. In the next rainy season, logistics probably would have obliged a general retreat. The titanic war effort had exhausted the nation; the people were tired of the prolonged struggle. The army had been re-equipped with captured arms, but had no aircraft with which to destroy Camiri or the single bridge across the Pilcomayo at Villa Montes. The army was entirely dependent upon Argentina for artillery shells—3,000 were obtained in March—and for gasoline requirements of 1,500,000 litres per month. La Paz, on the other hand, had expended huge sums on her new army. Command remained, however, a vital factor; in this respect Paraguay was palpably superior.[13]

As the river rose dangerously, the Paraguayans retreated briskly in the Parapetí sector. The Andean 3rd Cavalry Division crossed the stream on 2 May, attempting a hastily conceived envelopment in cooperation with the frontally pursuing 7th Division. This threat kept Caballero Irala moving retrogressively from the enemy, who had been ordered to clean up both banks of the Parapetí by 10 May (for diplomatic reasons) and advance toward Huirapitindi and "27 November." Excessive caution and lethargy of these Andean II Corps troops permitted the Paraguayans to slowly retire, luring their pursuers back onto the plains where they could be destroyed. The Guaraní had, nonetheless, definitively lost the Parapetí by 13 May, and formed a new line in front of Huirapitindi.[14]

In the north, which had been quiet throughout the war, the Bolivian command also undertook an offensive in April. After Salamanca's overthrow, the III Corps, which really consisted of but three regiments and a single airplane, passed to General Raimundo González Flor. On 24 April his 6th Division enveloped Paraguayan forces at Pozo del Tigre, 15 kilometers north of Ingavi. Although the Guaraní soon escaped, the Comanchaco was threatened from a new direction, adding to the gravity of the situation.[15]

Armistice Negotiations

Following a year's fruitless effort by the League of Nations to effect peace, Argentina and Chile, who were unwilling to embargo Paraguay, began confidential inquiries in February. Predictably, Asunción's conditions were an immediate armistice, troop withdrawals, settlement of the basic issue as a boundary and not as a territorial dispute, and a commission to fix war responsibilities. To Rivarola, Ayala indicated peace should be forced "on the basis of military results." Bolivia, "to avoid the occupation of Santa Cruz and the certain separation of the province . . . will admit concessions," he asserted, relying upon skillful psychological exploitation of Altiplano fears. Although La

Paz suggested modifications, her government and command were quite favorably disposed toward an end to the war. On 1 April 1935 the United States was invited to join the peace moves. Two days later Ayala assured Rivarola that "we (including General Estigarribia) want peace promptly." Paraguay had no intention of advancing farther. Her wants were filled, but Bolivia dare not realize this or she would be more determined. Once a peace conference convened, President Ayala added, Argentina should secure adherence to an order of points: security—demobilization and a ban on arms purchases—first, then consideration of the basic question.[16]

In early May, President Tejada went to Villa Montes to confer on the armistice proposals. Peñaranda wished to continue operations in search of the Ibibobo-Capirendá-Huirapitindi line, thus hoping to recoup the old, Bolivian-settled portion of the Chaco and save the oil lands. Tejada spoke of a peace without victor or vanquished, of the hazard of further war to the economy and life blood of the nation, and stressed that the settlement would be by juris arbitration.[17]

After the newly constituted mediatory group (ABCP, Uruguay, and the United States) had invited the Foreign Ministers to Buenos Aires for negotiations, Bolivian Chanceller Tomás Elio and Bautista Saavedra tarried (13 May) at GHQ for briefing. Colonel Toro admitted that the army desired peace, if it were without victor or vanquished. He asked time to continue the offensive and asserted no indemnity could be paid. Saavedra observed that the prisoner issue might necessitate payments, but this must not jeopardize the imperative requirement of a fluvial outlet. Dr. Elio agreed, saying that the army's present victorious postion would facilitate peace, although a complete military solution seemed impossible. At Buenos Aires, Brazilian protection might open new avenues, but a peace prepared by the pro-Paraguayan Casa Rosada should be avoided.[18]

To counter the Bolivian offensive, Estigarribia placed Franco in full command of the Parapetí sector (4 May), while he took personal command of forces assembled at Carandaití. On 16 May, catching Peñaranda completely by surprise, he pushed his 6th

Division across the mountains by trail and fell upon Mandeya-pecuá. The 3rd Division, transported from Bahia Negra, joined along the Cuevo gorge for a northward movement against the flank of the enemy II Corps pursuing Franco. A parallel blow by the latter on 17 May failed to progress, despite lessened Bolivian will to fight and die when the air was gravid with the magic word "peace." Five days later Estigarribia infiltrated the rear of troops shifted south against him, shattering a Bolivian counter maneuver. Guillén consequently prepared to place twelve regiments on defense, releasing only nine for offensive operations on both the Cuevo and Parapetí fronts. Allegedly, the Peñaranda command then prepared to launch a "second phase" offensive to realize the Ibibobo-Huirapitindi line as the minimum acceptable for peace.[19]

Already Paraguayan Foreign Minister Riart, Efraim Cardozo, and Chief of Staff Colonel Manuel Garay had reached Buenos Aires. When the Andean delegation, mostly Liberals, arrived, Foreign Minister Elio was at its head and the intransigent Saavedra was merely a delegate. The latter thought that Elio simply sought to remove the enemy from Bolivia proper, a tacit confession of impotence. Elio, however, indicated to his delegation (21 May) that the government's position was a port above Olimpo, juridical solution, and the 3 August 1932 Continental Declaration against conquest. If an equitable, honorable peace could not be had, they would withdraw, for the country was capable of prolonging the war awhile longer.[20]

A week later, Elio brought the delegation together to inform them that talks with the mediators had revealed that to them simple "cessation of hostilities was a primary object." Colonel Rodríguez (G-3, representing the army) observed that the army did not wish a truce until it had secured both banks of the Parapetí, pushed the enemy back to Huirapitindi, and opened the vital Villa Montes-Boyuibé road. Saavedra agreed that a truce could be dangerous for Bolivia, opening the way for an end to the war without guaranteed juridical arbitration. Probably a practical solution under pressure would result. Argentina's diligence for peace implied that Paraguay's situation was desperate.

The consensus of the meeting, therefore, favored a maximum truce of fifteen days, to be entered upon only with extreme caution. Arbitration remained the rigid Andean position.[21]

Meeting separately with Elio and Riart, the mediators (27 May) sought a truce to facilitate arranging an armistice. Riart accepted in principle pending Elio's reply. The Bolivian delegation, however, continued to think in terms of simultaneously convening the arbitral court and ending hostilities. They proposed a thirty-day truce under supervision of a neutral military commission. On 31 May the mediators offered a modified formula which Elio accepted. Paraguay then demanded guaranteed cessation of hostilities prior to considering the basic issue. Bolivia at first refused, insisting on an arbitration agreement before demobilization, but on 3 June, Elio agreed to accept Guaraní security demands "provided Paraguay would formally agree to submit [the] Chaco dispute for arbitration to the Hague tribunal, failing success of direct negotiations." The certainty of obligatory arbitration if direct talks failed was Tejada's *sine qua non* to peace.[22]

Elio pointed out, in the decisive 5 June meeting of the Bolivian delegation that, practically, the Chaco had been lost. The problem was now to prevent dislocation of the Bolivian departments. Mediation must not fail through the kind of inflexibility which had characterized Salamanca's diplomacy. Bolivia fought alone against an enemy of proved capability. To continue the war was to invite definitive disaster. A nation could not base her policy upon fantasy.

Saavedra disagreed, maintaining that the pressure of the mediators was inspired by Guaraní urgency, and meant delaying arbitration until later, or worse, forever. The Andean situation was not yet so bad as to require this; the army could still be reinforced, whereas Paraguay was exhausted and bankrupt.

Other delegates (Zalles, Diez de Medina, and Calvo) voiced opposition to Saavedra, asserting that the struggle was being prolonged at the cost of the nation's economic future and the sacrifice of a generation. Bolivia had rejected magnificent propositions. Her triumph at Geneva was only moral and could not save her.

La Paz must assure herself peace, save the departments, and work toward a better future. Lamentably, she could not even secure inclusion of the *uti possidetis* of 1810 in a peace protocol, because Paraguay would block the word "juris," enabling her later to allege a *de facto* case to Bolivia's detriment.

Colonel Rodríguez expressed himself in favor of the last formula of the mediators, stating that Salamanca had begun the war unprepared and had disdained the realistic objectives of the General Staff. To mount an energetic offensive now would require (1) 50,000 men, (2) 500 new trucks, (3) funds and supplies—which the country could not afford, and (4) a competent command—which she did not have. Colonel Rivera (representing the Auxiliary Staff at La Paz) agreed, reminding the civilian delegates that plans could not always be translated into victory in the field. Money was unavailable, the last reserves were old men and boys; it was not possible to prolong the war.

The consensus was evident. Bolivia must make peace, admittedly because she was a defeated country.[23]

The Bolivian counteroffensive had demonstrated no real power. In the Parapetí sector, due to indecisive command the 10,000-man II Corps was held at bay by Garay's 3,500 Guaraní. Conditioned by years of defeat, the Andeans feared that the enemy was leading them into a trap. To such low morale indeed could be attributed many Bolivian defeats. There was deficient cooperation among units and the usual reticence on the part of patrols. Taking the offensive as a whole, it suffered from absence of a center of gravity; attacks were made at Ingavi, the Parapetí and the Central Sectors, and demonstratively at Villa Montes. Consequently, the III Corps forces were too weak, while the Central Sector and Parapetí alternated troops and attention. This failure, aggravated by the incompetence of the Peñaranda command, made it very doubtful that Bolivia, even with huge forces, would ever have been capable of defeating the agile Paraguayans. On the other hand, exhaustion of Guaraní resources made conquest of Altiplano vitals an impossible dream. The only alternative to stalemate, therefore, was peace.

Throughout the war, Estigarribia had conceded his subordinate commanders freedom of action, and their audacity and fearless courage were major factors in victories. Peñaranda, on the other hand, like Kundt, absorbed functions of lower echelons, destroying initiative and tactical flexibility; his command was confused, neglected security, and rarely acted with boldness or achieved surprise. The greater talents of others were ignored by vacillating, bumbling Enrique Peñaranda, who yielded perpetually to the counsels of Toro.[24]

A contributing factor to the Bolivian defeat was poor employment of air power. Although La Paz spent considerable money for the most modern aircraft, and enjoyed absolute air supremacy throughout the war, the air arm was too often directed against poorly evaluated targets. The transport branch, using trimotors, performed excellent service. Use of fighters for reconnaissance missions frequently achieved good results, but ground commanders were prone to ignore air intelligence. Aircraft were usually employed ineffectively against troops, trucks, and other close support targets. While Argentine protests prevented bombing of Puerto Casado, the Air Group early in the war should have been used on Paraguayan supply lines—the railroad, the Asunción docks, and the river traffic—where it could have contributed more efficaciously to the campaign. Later, Guaraní advances placed these targets beyond the range of operations.[25]

While Paraguay also lacked air doctrine—and her *jefes* commonly misunderstood air power—General Estigarribia was more discerning. Had he possessed the equipment, his perspicacity might well have enabled him to parley air power into total victory. Unfortunately, the arms embargo prevented the shipment from France of the aircraft Estigarribia needed.

Elio had already gone to the mediators, however, with a new project aimed at arbitration and seeking inclusion of Ecuador, Mexico, and Venzuela in the conference. His proposal provided for prisoner exchange, limited armies of 6,000 each, and specified that the terms of arbitration must be settled before the military commission proceeded to the front to effect security guarantees. Dr. Riart offered a Paraguayan plan which "promoted" settlement of the question of limits, or as an alternative, a *compromiso arbitral*; it sought to fix war responsibilities, and reduce armed forces to 4,000 men each.[26]

At Ingavi, small Paraguayan forces had been expanded into an 800-man regiment. On 1 June, with peace negotiations deadlocked, they attacked the Bolivian 6th Division; the Andeans commenced an envelopment, but four days later were themselves encircled. Since III Corps had always been weak, no reserves were available at Roboré to help shatter the trap. The 14th Infantry attempted to break out, but the Paraguayans shifted with pressure, permitting the Bolivians to exhaust themselves in the forest. When water came into play, the latter surrendered on 8 June. The Guaraní then forced retreat upon those who had escaped and the remnants of the 6th Division. Estigarribia released exaggerated statements of the extent of the Andean defeat, providing close, timely support for the diplomats of Buenos Aires.[27]

Elio consequently accepted peace at 0200 of the ninth. It involved, Saavedra lamented, the defeat of Bolivia's interests. Her position was neglected; there was no guarantee the Hague Court would ever receive the question. Even if it did, not arbitration juris but a *compromiso* would be considered. This assured Paraguay's victory and obviated the possibility that Bolivia would have her day in court. She could take no new action against Paraguay's complete *de facto* occupation of the Chaco without being the provocator of another bloody war. Elio declined to hear the reservations of Saavedra or to place those of President Tejada before the mediators because he had given his word of acceptance.[28] Dr. Tomas Elio had moved a long way from the bellicose young minister who in 1929 threatened war if Bolivia did not receive a £1,000,000 indemnity for Franco's attack on Vanguardia.

The protocol, formally signed on 12 June 1935, contained five articles and a supplement. The first requested the mediators to convene a peace conference to settle issues incident to ending hostilities and to promote solution of the basic issue by direct agreement or arbitration at The Hague. If direct agreement proved impossible, the "arbitral compromise" would be drawn under auspices of the conference, which would also seek agreement on prisoner exchange, economic development, and a system of "transit, trade and navigation" to ameliorate the geographic situations of the belligerents. The conference would create an international commission to fix responsibilities of every kind arising from the war.

The second article provided for cessation of hostilities on the basis of present positions. A twelve-day truce would provide the military commission time to fix intermediate lines between the armies. This truce could be extended by the conference until security measures were effected. The military commission was empowered to modify lines as deemed advisable and maintain separation under guarantee of the conference.

Article II was concerned with security measures and included demobilization of standing armies to 5,000 each within 90 days of the military commission's fixing of lines. No new equipment might be purchased, unless indispensable for replacement, until the signing of a peace treaty. The parties were bound to non-aggression, and the war would be declared terminated by the peace conference upon completion of the work of the military commission.

Article IV stated: "The declaration of the third of August 1932, regarding territorial acquisitions, is recognized by the belligerents."

The final article established the instant for the cease fire as 1200 hours 14 June 1935, Córdoba local time.

The supplementary protocol requested the military commission to arrange the cessation of hostilities and to fix lines. After ratification within ten days, the provisional cease fire would become a truce.[29]

Almost exactly three years from Moscoso's attack on Pitiantuta, the Chaco War came to a close. The cost was high for the two poor, lightly populated nations. Bolivia suffered 52,397 killed. She lost nearly 10,000 deserters. Over 21,000 were captured, of whom 4,264 died in captivity. The net loss to her population was therefore roughly two per cent—over 65,000 youth. From 1932 to 1935 her paper currency increased twenty-five per cent. By 1935 loans to the government by the Central Bank reached 370,000,000 *bolivianos* (approximately $228,660,000). Levies on export receipts of the mining companies had gone to finance foreign arms orders. Consequently, doubling of the world price of tin during the war contributed directly to the Bolivian effort. Large sums were wasted, however, due to corruption in arms and supply contracts, and extortion among paymasters.[30]

Paraguay, in a monumental example of fiscal astuteness and responsibility, financed the war largely upon a cash basis. This feat was accomplished by expropriation of export proceeds, issues of paper, loans in Argentina totaling 16,626,072 Ps. ($5,542,026), and a 3,000,000 Ps. gold surplus ($4,900,500) built up by Eligio Ayala. The cost of the war was a stupendous sum for a country of Paraguay's meager resources. The cash outlay by Asunción was 76,218,865 Ps. gold ($124,503,515). The country was aided by the huge war booty captured—28,000 rifles, 2,300 automatic weapons, 96 mortars, large ammunition stores—whose value was over $10,000,000. In human terms, of 140,000 men shipped from Asunción, about 36,000—three and one-half per cent of the population—fell in the Chaco Boreal.[31]

Notes

1. Vergara Vicuña, VI, 632-633, quotation, 639; Toro, 304; Díaz Arguedas, *La guerra*, 294-295; Rivarola, III, 225. At this time the Peruvian, Colonel Julio C. Guerrero, and the Czech mission were incorporated into the command. Peñaranda was promoted to Lieutenant General; Bolivia, *Mensaje 1935*, 68.

2. Vergara Vicuña, VI, 580-583, 618-624, 627, 634-635, 679-681; VII, 20-21; *Bilbao*, 412-433; Toro, 309; Rios, 321; Major Juan Esteban Vacca, *Notas de la pasada guerra del Chaco* (Buenos Aires, 1938), 310. Bilbao had I Corps, plus the 4th Division, 5th Cavalry, independent artillery, and Headquarters troops. Typical of his method was a 24 January order that *jefes* familiarize themselves with their subordinates and men, instilling confidence; orders would be executed without comment; inept *jefes* would not be tolerated. Realistically, Bilbao viewed defense as a tactical and *moral* problem; *Bilbao*, 436-442. Villa Montes had been built as the headquarters of the German Staudt Company, concessionaire of 400 square leagues of Bolivian Chaco; Díaz Arguedas, *La guerra*, 310.

3. Díaz Arguedas, *La guerra*, 297-298; Estigarribia, 190-193; *Partes del conductor*, 223-225; Vergara Vicuña, VI, 633, 636, 648-654; VII, 93-115; Caballero Irala, 154-162. Caballero (147-152) had the 2nd Engineers and 14th Infantry, 1,100 men.

4. Vergara Vicuña, VI, 661-671, 686; Toro, 305-307; Díaz Arguedas, *La guerra*, 301-304; Major Pablo H. Barrientos Gutiérrez, *La contraofensiva del Parapetí* (Santiago, 1936), 115.

5. Estigarribia, 192-194; Caballero Irala, 169-170; *Partes del conductor*, 226, 229-230; Vergara Vicuña, VII, 118-120, 126-127; Díaz Arguedas, *La guerra*, 305-306, 325.

6. Estigarribia, 194-195; Vergara Vicuña, VII, 4, 35-76, 164-166, 175; Bilbao took over the Southern Sector Command on 20 January 1935 (p. 17). Díaz Arguedas, *La guerra*, 310-314; Rios, 322; Rivarola, III, 263.

7. Vergara Vicuña, VII, 135-143; Toro, 314; Díaz Arguedas, *La guerra*, 307-309, 350-351; Rios, 325, 331-332; González, 175-176; Rivarola, 264-265.

8. Vergara Vicuña, VII, 182-193, 203-215; Rios, 325; Barrientos, 123-126; Díaz Arguedas, *La guerra*, 326-330; *Partes del conductor*, 233-237; Caballero Irala, 174-183. Major Antonio E. González had taken over Caballero's detachment, the latter assuming command of the 2nd Division (p. 173); González, 177-178.

9. Toro, 315-322; Barrientos, 135; Vergara Vicuña, VII, 260-265; Díaz Arguedas, *La guerra*, 331; Rivarola, III, 263.

10. Toro, 323; Estigarribia, 201; Vergara Vicuña, VII, 250-251, 257, 276-299; Guerrero, *Peñaranda*, 103; Díaz Arguedas, *La guerra*, 332-336.

11. Vergara Vicuña, VII, 355, 365-371, 386; Barrientos, 116; Díaz Arguedas, *La guerra*, 343.

12. Estigarribia, 204; Barrientos, 117, 147-181; the latter, a Chilean mercenary, was II Corps G-3; Vergara Vicuña, VII, 308-315, 340, 391, 395, 425; Guerrero, *Peñaranda*, 103; Caballero Irala, 184-186; Díaz Arguedas, *La guerra*, 338; Rios, 326-327.

13. Estigarribia, 195-199; Rios, 308-309, 316-319, 330, 333; González, 187-194; Vergara Vicuña, *Bilbao*, 445-446, 448; Rivarola, III, 247, 266. During 1935, evacuation of 11,866 Guaraní occurred; Vasconcellos, *Memoria*, 38. Adding probable dead brings losses to around 15,000.

14. Barrientos, 181-279; Caballero Irala, 187-195; Díaz Arguedas, *La guerra*, 445-449; Vergara Vicuña, VII, 392-393, 398-399, 438-439, 454, 471-472, 482; Estigarribia, 203.

15. Díaz Arguedas, *La guerra*, 365-366; Vergara Vicuña, VII, 228, 634-638; *Partes del conductor*, 240-242; Macías, 193.

16. U. S., *Foreign Relations*, 1935, IV, 7-8, 12-14, 21, 26, 31; U. S. Delegation to the Chaco Peace Conference, *The Chaco Peace Con-*

ference (Washington, 1940), 45-47; Rivarola, III, 248-258, quotations, 265, 275.

17. Toro, 327-330. The counteroffensive cost Bolivia most of her 1935 military expenditure, which equalled $22,000,000. *Armaments Yearbook*, 1939, p. 36.

18. *Politica Argentina*, II, 350; U. S., *Foreign Relations*, 1935, IV, 57; Toro, 331; Bautista Saavedra, *El Chaco y la Conferencia de Paz* (Santiago, 1939), 43-45.

19. Estigarribia, 204-206; Díaz Arguedas, *La guerra*, 354; Caballero Irala, 197-199; *Partes del conductor*, 246-249; Guerrero, *Peñaranda*, 110-118; Vergara Vicuña, VII, 546-548, 554, 577, 585-587; *Bilbao*, 453.

20. Saavedra, 47-52; Díez de Medina, *De un Siglo*, 352; Rivarola, III, 282.

21. Saavedra, 53-62; U. S., *Foreign Relations*, 1935, IV, quotation, 63.

22. Saavedra, 63-80; U. S., *Foreign Relations*, 1935, IV, 64-70, quotation, 68.

23. Saavedra, 82-91; Vergara Vicuña, VII, 671-672; *Bilbao*, 448-449.

24. Vergara Vicuña, VII, 451, 460, 484, 500, 509, 526, 542, 624-625; *Bilbao*, 468; Franco, 39, 61; Vacca, 309. Informed that the war had ended, bewildered General Peñaranda lamented: "It is very disagreeable. I don't like this peace. We must continue the war." Guerrero, *Peñaranda*, 121.

25. Díaz Arguedas, *La guerra*, 183-185; Melean, 59; Terán Gómez, 332; *El Banco Central*, 74.

26. Saavedra, 92-102; U. S., *Foreign Relations*, 1935, IV, 71; Rivarola, III, 292-294.

27. Estigarribia, 208-209; *Partes del conductor*, 250-252; Macías, 195-196; Toro, 337; Díaz Arguedas, *La guerra*, 370-377; Vergara Vicuña, VII, 644-646, 652, 655, 659-665; Rivarola, III, 289-291.

28. Saavedra, 105-128; U. S., *Foreign Relations*, 1935, IV, 73-75.

29. U. S., *Foreign Relations*, 1935, IV, 76-77; *Politica Argentina*, II, 363-366; *Peace Conference*, 49-53; República Argentina, Ministerio de Relaciones Exteriores y Culto, *La Conferencia de Paz del Chaco 1935-1939* (Buenos Aires, 1939), 29-33; Rivarola, III, 298-301.

30. Díaz Arguedas, *La guerra*, 398-399; Bolivia, *Mensaje 1935*, 73-87; *Bolivia*, 1934, No. 1, 15; 1936, No. 9, 17, 19; Robert M. Morris, "Bolivia," *Bulletin of the Pan American Union*, LXX, February 1936, 169-171. For a detailed account, see *El Banco Central*.

31. Rios, 11, 176-178, 261; Benítez, *Estigarribia*, 2d ed., 102, 126; República del Paraguay, Ministerio de Defensa Nacional, *Breve resumen de la campaña del Chaco* (Asunción, 1935), 48; Colonel Ramón César Bejarano, *Antecedentes de la guerra con Bolivia* (Asunción, 1959), 41. Gold pesos converted at $1.6335.

Paraguayan loans in Argentina

1933	Private citizens, Paraguayan Light and Traction Company, Paraguayan Industrial Company, and other firms doing business in Paraguay	10,000,000 Ps.
1934	Argentine Treasury	6,626,072 Ps.
	Argentine Pesos	16,626,072
	U. S. Dollars (at unofficial rate, 3:1)	$ 5,542,026

CHAPTER NINE

THE PEACE CONFERENCE

After debate in the respective legislatures, the Protocol was ratified by Paraguay and Bolivia on 20 and 21 June. The military commission visited the front, conferred with the commands, and traced lines which required each army to retire 25 kilometers. The Bolivian command, although thus thrust across a mountain range (a virtually impossible position in case war resumed), gained partial Guaraní evacuation of the oil zone and the Boyuibé-Villa Montes road. With these steps accomplished, the Chaco Peace Conference convened on 1 July and extended the truce.[1]

The military commission then proceeded to demobilize the contending armies. Saavedra Lamas, dominating the Conference, procrastinated on other projects until each belligerent's ability to resume fighting had been destroyed. In four stages the Bolivian army by 15 September released 54,105 men. Paraguay, although her front-line forces had been small during 1935, demobilized 46,515. Each former belligerent was left with a standing army of about 5,000. Reductions in force having been accomplished without incident, and truce lines determined, the commission reported (31 October) that the security phases of the Protocol had been accomplished.[2]

A prisoner committee had been created on 19 July, but it quickly developed that Paraguay desired an exchange man for man, the vast overage which she held being retained until peace was signed. These prisoners she apparently hoped to hold as hostages until Bolivian intentions were unmistakable, or until La Paz yielded on the boundary issue. Since she held about 17,000 (after the release in May of Cruceños to stir up separatism of Santa Cruz) in contrast to only 2,500 Guaraní in Bolivian hands, her bargaining position was good. When Elio delivered rigid demands (originating with Saavedra) for prompt and complete repatriation, the project was for the moment at an impasse.[3]

The views of both Bolivia and Paraguay were heard 31 July on the basic question. Paraguay, with Saavedra Lamas' favor, would never allow Bolivia a port and insisted that she had won the war and the entire Chaco. Elio proposed what amounted to the Ichaso-Benites treaty or, as an alternative, arbitration of the whole region. Two weeks later it became clear that he intended to force direct negotiations into a deadlock and then demand that the Conference secure arbitration. Since the mediators had no intention of allowing the Conference thus to be ruined, they procrastinated in order to avert discussions until after demobilization was completed. Saavedra Lamas' old view was gaining favor that time must be allowed for passions to cool. Neither side would yield from its extreme point of view; and Paraguay, already in physical possession, could prevent legal solution simply by intransigence.[4]

The Conference offered a comprehensive proposal on 15 October which declared peace restored and drew a border from 20° 14' on the Rio Paraguay to the Pilcomayo at 22°. A free zone for Bolivia at Puerto Casado and the use of the Casado Railroad was provided, Zubizarreta, chief of the Paraguayan delegation, having previously accepted these ideas. Embodied in the plan were an unfortified zone stretching 30 kilometers on each side of the border, amnesty for war criminals, immediate exchange of prisoners, and renewal of diplomatic relations.[5]

Bolivia was given a "psychological port" at Puerto Caballo (just below the mouth of the Otuquis) "without her access to the river being of such a nature as to be dangerous to Paraguay." The site was "of equally [as] little use as Bahia Negra." The free port at Casado was, however, of some real commercial worth and coincided with the thinking of Paraguayan statesmen ever since Domínguez offered it to Cano in 1906.[6]

The mediators learned on 18 October that Zubizarreta and Rivarola (the other Paraguayan delegate) deemed the proposal too preposterous to consider. They insisted on the entire Chaco,

refused to arbitrate any portion under Asunción's control, and
due to the wording of the Protocol could not be coerced into
arbitration. It began to dawn on the mediators that Paraguay
had signed the Protocol only to secure international maintenance of the status quo and demobilization of the Bolivian army.
Her diplomatic triumph was now apparent.[7]

The formal Paraguayan reply, according to Gibson, was "a
categorical rejection . . . couched in sarcastic and insolent terms."
It expressed "most formal dissent" to admitting Bolivia to the
littoral, giving her part of Paraguay's holdings, or considering
her "aspirations" against Asunción's "realities." Zubizarreta asserted his country's rights even to the zone which Brazil had
ceded to Bolivia at Petropolis and alleged that "the 12 June
protocol created a status quo which is the basis for the cessation
of hostilities" and the conciliatory process. The Conference proposals offered Paraguay nothing she did not already possess; she
would never conclude the war by concessions to the aggressor
who had provoked it.[8]

Bolivia, replying on the same day, alleged that the Protocol
had restored the dispute to its previous status, without prejudice
of either contender, through inclusion of the principle of non-
recognition of territorial conquests. The Chaco remained liti-
gious in entirety and awaited settlement by the Hague Court.
A direct settlement should be based on possessions of 3 August
1932. An ample littoral had been granted to La Paz in all the
nineteenth-century treaties; she could not now be limited to
only a small zone above Bahia Negra. She should be given sovereignty *"por lo menos"* to Olimpo.[9]

The tone of the replies was startling. Bolivia, who had started
the war and lost it, sought a settlement which Paraguay had
rejected in the prewar period as harsh. La Paz even sought restoration of 3 August 1932 possessions, at which moment she had
held the reprisal *fortines* and Huijay (Carayá)! Paraguay had
modified her traditional stand only in endeavoring to sustain a
new status quo reflecting extension through the military instrument of her hold in the Chaco. In view of these extreme
positions, the Conference postponed the basic issue in the hope

that time would modify attitudes. Forthcoming elections in each country and the abject weakness of the Tejada Sorzano regime made this the best course.[10]

After a period of negotiation, the Conference secured a pro- tocolized act 21 January 1936 confirming obligations of the 12 June 1935 Protocol, continuing security stipulations in force until peace should be signed, and providing for prisoner ex- change. This amounted to Asunción's trading the prisoners for a fresh guarantee of the status quo, a diplomatic victory of the first order. Her long contention that each country must pay the cost of maintaining its prisoners was also recognized, netting her £132,232.[11]

Paraguay had been firm on the prisoner question, determined that these men would never again fight in the Chaco. Reaching agreement on the issue proved fatal for the regime of Eusebio Ayala. Demobilization had been difficult, especially for reserve officers. Controversy raged over Estigarribia's life pension of 1500 Ps gold per month. *Jefes* who had been in disagreement with the command during the war, and consequently relegated to unimportant posts, were bitter. After what was considered the soft agreement of January, discontent finally coalesced in a rev- olution led by Colonel Franco and the conspirators of 1931. The sound rule of the Liberal party came to an end (17 February 1936) and the architects of victory were imprisoned and later exiled.[12]

Franco recognized the prisoner agreements, and repatriation consumed the first half of 1936. Bolivia returned 100 officers and 2,478 soldiers; Paraguay delivered 349 officers and 16,825 men.[13]

In Bolivia a united front of leftist groups was formed in Jan- uary which had close connections with Colonel Toro. The Gen- eral Staff had retained all wartime restrictions, as well as control of the oil fields and all roads into the Chaco and Santa Cruz. Rival to Toro's leftists and the army clique was the Legion of Ex-combatants, the veterans group, who idolized Colonel Bilbao Rioja, "the only higher officer who came through the Chaco campaign with the respect and admiration of the rank and file . . . Bilbao and Toro are born enemies." Elections were scheduled for 31 May, but Tejada's extreme weakness and inability to cope with postwar problems made Toro's ascension an expected event. On 17 May the army cashed its mortgage on Tejada's political life, and was in absolute power after the dust had settled; Enríque Finot was in the Foreign Office and Diez de Medina in Buenos Aires. With truth it was said on the Altiplano "that the Command responsible for the loss of the Chaco has received the government as its reward."[14]

After correspondence and discussions with the new governments, an agreement on policing was signed on 9 January 1937 at Buenos Aires. Free transit was provided on the Boyuibé-Villa Montes road (previously a sore point with La Paz) ; travel without inspection was permitted parties of five or less trucks provided they possessed a road permit. Bolivia assumed the expense of highway maintenance. Each country was authorized civil policing in her zone, but an absolute prohibition on shooting (including hunting) was imposed. Military observers were placed at Camatindi. The regulations for implementing the agreement were accepted by both in May 1937, and in September the Conference put them into force.[15]

Dissatisfaction over the allegedly soft attitude toward Bolivia manifested by the agreement culminated in the ouster of Franco on 15 August 1937. The coup, led by Colonel Ramón L. Paredes, veteran commander and at the moment chief of Chaco forces, brought a restoration of the Liberal party. Dr. Félix Paiva, the new President, returned Zubizarreta, well-known advocate of a hard policy toward Bolivia, to the Chaco Peace Conference. On the Altiplano the 14 July removal of Toro by Busch had no marked effect on the Buenos Aires delegation. Zubizarreta, however, rejected the security regulations (20 October) , whereupon they remained in effect only by a tenuous *modus vivendi*.[16]

Already in December 1936 new exploratory talks on the basic issue were carried out by Cruchaga Tocornal of Chile, Macedo Soares of Brazil, and Braden of the United States. They determined that Paraguayan opinion would be satisfied if Bolivia was denied a port. While La Paz demanded the latter, the majority of her people could not distinguish a free port from a sovereign outlet. Finot, although personally admitting that the former

would meet Andean needs, stated that the Toro regime viewed
a sovereign port as a *sine qua non;* he insisted too on receiving
the Boyuibé-Villa Montes road. Soler and Isidro Ramírez, then
the Paraguayan delegates, accepted the proposals as a basis for
discussion. Thereupon the committee presented maps, sounding
the minimum territorial demands. They discovered that Bolivia
would not tolerate a frontier with Paraguay across from her trans-
Pilcomayo region, nor across the Parapetí. Finot suggested that
La Paz might purchase the port she required, but Ramírez was
immovably opposed. On 24 December, Paraguayan Foreign Minister Juan Stefanich arrived, saying he did not believe opinion
in either country was ready for settlement. Stefanich posed a
new demand: Paraguayan participation in exploitation of western Chaco oil.[17]

After a normal change of government in Argentina removed
Saavedra Lamas from the Conference, strong efforts were again initiated in March 1938 to conclude the Chaco issue. Following
lengthy, unsuccessful preliminary explorations, the foreign ministers, Diez de Medina and Cecilio Báez, were invited to Buenos
Aires on 16 May. Paraguay at last seemed ready to negotiate a
final settlement. On the twenty-fourth, Braden informed the ministers that the Conference was making its final proposal; peace
must now be accepted. Intransigence would alienate every mediator. With the changed attitude of Argentina, the mediators at
last were in harmony, and Rivarola admitted that Asunción
would have to yield.

The proposal offered on 27 May drew a line from Esmeralda
on the Pilcomayo northward to "27 November," passed between
Ravelo and Ingavi, thence to the Rio Paraguay at 7,500 meters
above Bahia Negra. Bolivia should pay Paraguay an indemnity
of £200,000. In explanation, the Conference stated that the
desert region between 61° and 63° served as a natural frontier,
protecting valuable zones and settlements. The coast above Bahia
Negra gave Bolivia her desires, but preserved the town to Paraguay.[18]

Although deploring the fact that the proposal ignored her
rights, Bolivia accepted on the thirty-first. Paraguay objected to
giving her any littoral, still viewing Andean appearance on the

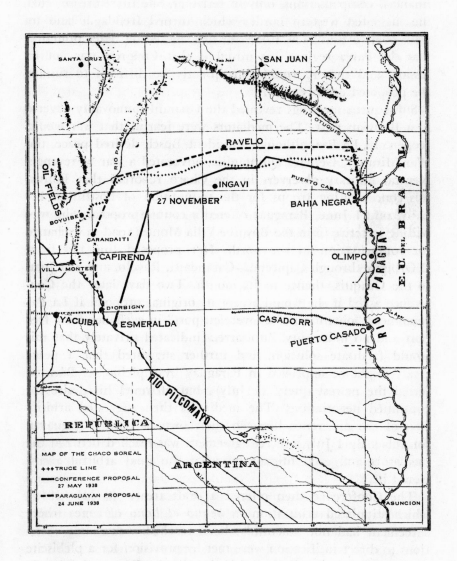

MAP OF THE CHACO BOREAL

+++ TRUCE LINE

CONFERENCE PROPOSAL
27 MAY 1938

PARAGUAYAN PROPOSAL
24 JUNE 1938

river as a perpetual menace to peace. In private, Zubizarreta made clear that Paraguay had no interest in either economic or financial compensations, only in territory. She therefore rejected the suggested western border which turned Irendagüe and its wells over to Bolivia as a base for new aggression. Báez protested that the Paiva regime was unstable, that Congress was not in session, and that it would consequently be difficult to sustain the proposed arrangement.[19]

Subsequent meetings revealed the Guaraní immovably adverse to a Bolivian port. The mediators were fearful that war would reopen. In La Paz, although President Busch desired peace, the War Minister, General Quintanilla, advocated a war of revenge. Neutral military observers in the Chaco reported that Bolivia was concentrating troops for the resumption of hostilities. Finally, on 24 June, Paraguay offered a counterproposal. She was willing to retire from the Boyuibé-Villa Montes road in exchange for compensation in the north. Her proposed line ran from D'Orbigny through Capirendá, Carandaití, Ravelo, and San Juan to the Otuquis, thence to its mouth. Two days later the Conference asked if she would accept its original proposal if La Paz renounced "obtention of a sovereign port" in exchange for a free port and no indemnity. Zubizarreta indicated privately that this would facilitate solution, and further suggested that a peace treaty might be approved in Paraguay by a plebiscite. Báez rejected the newest query (1 July), but affirmed his desire for continued negotiations. The mediators then suggested arbitration of the difference between their own and the Paraguayan formulae. By 4 July a secret agreement was reached between the mediators and each litigant on what the final arbitral award would be.[20]

The Conference then offered a draft treaty (9 July 1938) which stipulated arbitration *ex aequo et bono* of zones where agreement had not, ostensibly, been reached. Asunción's objections to direct ratification were met by provision for a plebiscite thus lodging responsibility with the people. Báez and Diez de Medina accepted and recommended the agreement to their governments.[21]

The Treaty of Peace, Friendship, and Boundaries signed 21 July 1938 established peace and provided for arbitration by the presidents of the six mediator Republics. The littoral south of the Otuquis was exempted from consideration. Paraguay guaranteed Bolivia ample free transit, especially through Puerto Casado where La Paz might establish a customs zone, depots, and warehouses. War claims were reciprocally renounced.[22]

The Bolivian legislature ratified the treaty in secret session by a vote of 102 to 7. In Paraguay the plebiscite supported the peace 135,385 to 13,204. The designated arbitrators delegated their responsibility to their ambassadors to the Conference, who then received the respective cases and constituted an advisory military commission to fix geographic coordinates and render a report on the arbitration zone.[23]

The cases submitted were merely symbolic since, as the Bolivian *"exposición"* pointed out, the conclusion was already determined. Nevertheless, and sadly enough, Finot offered a review of the case which Bolivia had always hoped to lay before a legal arbitration. The Audiencia and the *cédulas* were cited, along with Cháves and Manso, the colonial Indian wars, Azara, and the domain of Chiquitos. Not omitted were the protests to the Hayes Award, and the assertion that *fortines* had been built only to contain Guaraní expansionism. Dealing with the present very narrow zone, Finot proved it had always been a *de facto* Bolivian possession. He pleaded for enough high ground below the Otuquis for a port, citing Bolivia's historic activities in that area, particularly Oliden. In conclusion, he succinctly summarized the broad case and called for a verdict favorable to Bolivia.[24]

Paraguay's "memorial" also included the full colonial cases—Mendoza's *capitulación,* expeditions, missions, *cédulas,* Fuerte Borbon, and the Province of Paraguay. The Hayes Award and subsequent developments were stressed as logical continuations of long possession. The natural-limits doctrine was asserted, and a verdict solicited based on security, military, economic, political, and geographic needs. The document failed to establish title to the arbitration zone for the simple reason that Paraguay had none.[25] It lay beyond her historic zone and fell into her grasp only as a result of Bolivia's failure to end the war at an earlier date. Her rights to the region as a consequence of the war were well known and required no enumeration.

The Conference handed down its verdict on 10 October, fulfilling the formality that the Chaco dispute had been solved by arbitration. The ignorant hailed Paraguayan recognition of the swampy Petropolis cession as giving Bolivia a useful corridor to the river. The war left the latter so exhausted and so poor, however, that it would not have been possible for her to build and defend a sovereign port for many, many years. More important for La Paz was barring of Paraguay from the oil zone, a necessity for which Busch would have paid £400,000 had it been required.[26]

At Villa Montes on 28 December 1938 the military commission declared that each side's territory had been delivered in accordance with the arbitral award. When the Peace Conference dissolved 23 January 1939, the Chaco dispute passed into history, almost sixty years from the time of Antonio Quijarro's first journey to Asunción in search of a peaceful diplomatic solution.[27]

A very probable factor in bringing a peace treaty in 1938 was the transport agreement signed on 25 February between Bolivia and Brazil. A railroad from Santa Cruz to Corumbá was to be built with the £1,000,000 still owing La Paz under the Petropolis Treaty; Brazil agreed to provide the additional funds at 3½ per cent. Besides giving Bolivia a better link with the Rio Paraguay, this project (completed in November 1954) provided a Brazilian market for the oil of the Andean anticlines. It thwarted Saavedra Lamas' old desire to acquire exclusive control of Bolivian oil for Argentina.[28]

Time has proved the validity of Eusébio Ayala's views in other ways. In July 1949, Yacuiba and Santa Cruz were linked by an Argentine-financed railroad, providing an additional transportation outlet for the Bolivian *oriente*. With Puerto Suárez improved, and its channel deepened with United States credits, Bolivia began a maritime shipping venture on the Rio Paraguay in late 1958, connecting her territory with Buenos Aires by vessel. Perhaps most significant was a December 1956 agreement

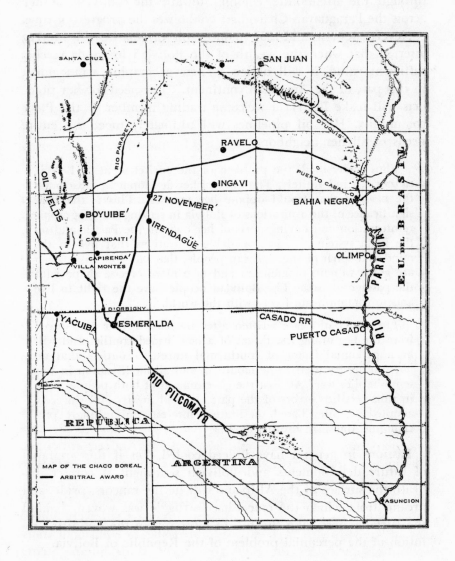

MAP OF THE CHACO BOREAL
——— ARBITRAL AWARD

between the former enemies for a trans-Chaco oil pipe line. Probably the road presently being pushed from Villa Hayes through the Mennonite colonies toward the Bolivian border across the Paraguayan Chaco best symbolizes the progress of time.

Nevertheless, a mid-1959 monograph originating in La Paz asserted that when the wealth of the Bolivian lowlands reaches sufficient value, it will oblige a "new geographic arrangement in this part of the American continent." The need for her products will make Bolivia a welcome trading member of the Plata community. Her oil pipelines will ultimately meet the entire needs of all her neighbors.

> Thus understood, the problem of the encirclement of Bolivia cannot last indefinitely. The force of her development must burst the barriers that would oppose her progress. This is the bare significance of the aspirations of Bolivia in seeking her geographic reintegration and having ports of her own on the Pacific and on the Plata system . . . irreconcilable aspirations that live in the mind and spirit of the Bolivian people, that far from dissipating are going to gain momentum and take more precise shape with the passage of time. The Bolivian people have the right to live and to communicate freely with the world. . . .

> The treaty of peace written after the Chaco War introduced from the beginning the threat of a new armed conflict and will be a perennial factor of continental unrest. 'Frontiers that do not suit are frontiers to be modified, and all modification in this sense implies war.' At least the governments of both peoples have in time rectified errors of the past . . . and loyally and sincerely adopted a policy based on mutual interest, unblushingly proclaiming American brotherhood.[29]

Passions in general have indeed cooled. Yet if this appraisal of future developments and Bolivian sentiment is correct, beneath the surface of the Altiplano still lie the rancors, pride, and dreams from which the epic Chaco struggle was woven. Behind the curtains obscuring the future must repose the definitive solution of the perennial problem of the Republic of Bolivia.

Notes

1. *Peace Conference,* 8, 55-57; *Conferencia,* 66; Toro, 339-342; U. S., *Foreign Relations,* 1935, IV, 91; República del Paraguay, *La Paz con Bolivia* (Asunción, 1938), 11-63.

2. *Peace Conference,* 14, 61-66; *Conferencia,* 73-159; Vacca, 20-69; U. S., *Foreign Relations,* IV, 95, 102, Saavedra Lamas, according to United States delegate Hugh S. Gibson, was openly pro-Paraguayan and supported demands that Bolivia pay reparations. He tacitly suggested that Chile reopen the Pacific question for Bolivia's benefit, and intended the United States to finance reconstruction of both countries, while Argentina benefited from increased flow of money in the Plata. As he informed Gibson and the Chilean of these views "his voice was shrill and at times hysterical"; U. S., *Foreign Relations,* IV, 98, 100, 112, quotation, 106. In 1939 Estigarribia, then Minister to the United States, secured credit to rebuild his nation.

3. *Peace Conference,* 16-17, 72-76; Saavedra, 154-188, U. S., *Foreign Relations,* 1935, IV, 114-124, 130.

4. Saavedra, 202-208; U. S., *Foreign Relations,* 1935, IV, 109, 114, 124-126, 128, 130.

5. *Peace Conference,* 77-81; *Conferencia,* 751-757.

6. U. S., *Foreign Relations,* 1935, IV, quotations, 155, 158.

7. *Ibid.,* 165-166.

8. *Ibid.,* quotations, 175-176; *Peace Conference,* 130-134; *Conferencia,* 768-773. In debate on the Protocol in June, the opinion was expressed in the Paraguayan Congress that the creation of a new status quo (by the Protocol) was a complete triumph, resting on the mapped line prepared by the military commission, and constituting a provisional frontier with Bolivia; Paraguay, *La Paz,* 16, 47-48.

9. *Peace Conference,* 125-130; *Conferencia,* 761-767; U. S., *Foreign Relations,* 1935, IV, 174.

10. U. S., *Foreign Relations,* 1935, IV, 171, 177-178.

11. *Ibid.,* 182-198; 1936, V, 36-39; *Peace Conference,* 83-86; Saavedra, 246-247; Paraguay, *La Paz,* 73-77. The sum received by Paraguay was very nominal indeed considering that the average prisoner was in her hands about fifteen months.

12. Artaza, 95-97, 101-118; Warren, "Political Aspects," 8-11; U. S., *Foreign Relations,* 1936, V, 858-862, 868-871. See also Juan Stefanich, *El Paraguay Nuevo* (Buenos Aires, 1943), 17.

13. *Peace Conference,* 19, 87-94; *Conferencia,* 162-282; U. S., *Foreign Relations,* 1936, V, 43-57.

14. U. S., *Foreign Relations,* 1936, V, 220-236, quotation, 221; Diez de Medina, *De un Siglo,* 355; Vergara Vicuña, *Bilbao,* quotation, 458.

15. *Peace Conference,* 99-122; *Conferencia,* 308-314, 348-440, 564-

572, 655-656; U. S., *Foreign Relations*, 1936, V, 58-77; 1937, V, 18-25; Juan Stefanich, *La diplomacia de la revolución* (Buenos Aires, 1945), 92-99. Stefanich (101-102) considered the agreement a fresh diplomatic triumph, regularizing the Paraguayan hold on the western Chaco.

16. *Peace Conference*, 24, 123-124; *Conferencia*, 657-664; note especially Paraguay, *La Paz*, 92, but see also Diez de Medina, *De un Siglo*, 357-358; Stefanich, *La diplomacia*, 104; U.S., *Foreign Relations*, 1937, V, 250-256, 263-264, 718-725. A major charge against Franco was his sale on 15 January 1937 to one Theovald G. Ehrich, a Jewish arms merchant, of a large number of weapons and trophies for £22,035; Artaza, 39-41.

17. *Conferencia*, 774-794; Stefanich, *La diplomacia*, 23-24; U.S., *Foreign Relations*, 1936, V, 77-105.

18. *Peace Conference*, 138-144; *Conferencia*, 823-825; U. S., *Foreign Relations*, 1937, V, 5; 1938, V, 93-122. Note Diez de Medina, *De un Siglo*, 361-362.

19. *Peace Conference*, 145; *Conferencia*, 834-840; U. S., *Foreign Relations*, 1938, V, 98, 129-130, 134; Diez de Medina, *De un Siglo*, 363.

20. *Peace Conference*, quotation, 26; *Conferencia*, 842-848; Diez de Medina, *De un Siglo*, 364-366; U. S., *Foreign Relations*, 1938, V, 108, 131-153, 158, 160.

21. *Peace Conference*, 27; *Conferencia*, 851-856; Diez de Medina, *De un Siglo*, 367-368; U. S., *Foreign Relations*, 1938, V, 154-167. *Ex aequo et bono*—according to what is right and good. Zubizarreta resigned rather than sign, and was replaced by the Paraguayan Minister to Washington, General José F. Estigarribia.

22. *Peace Conference*, 153-155; *Conferencia*, 857-861; U. S., *Foreign Relations*, 1938, V, 168-173.

23. *Peace Conference*, 154, 164-172; *Conferencia*, 873-877; Paraguay, *La Paz*, 71-72; Diez de Medina, *De un Siglo*, 375. Paraguay's Congress legally approved the treaty on 16 February 1939.

24. *Conferencia*, 886-925. See also the military commission's report, 976-1019.

25. *Ibid.*, 926-963.

. 26. *Ibid.*, 1033-1037; *Peace Conference*, 173-176; Diez de Medina, *De un Siglo*, 373-374; U. S., *Foreign Relations*, 1938, V, 174. See also *Time*, 24 October 1938, 16.

27. *Peace Conference*, 179-182; *Conferencia*, 1054-1056.

28. *Bolivia*, 1941, No. 3, 6-8; Diez de Medina, *De un Siglo*, 360; U. S., *Foreign Relations*, 1937, V, 40.

29. Ayala Moreira 94-95.

BIBLIOGRAPHIC ESSAY

With the exception of personal letters from actors in the Chaco drama, this book rests entirely upon published materials. Most of the important diplomatic records have been offered to the world, often by as many as four governments. Several of the major diplomatic battlers have prepared memoirs of varying worth; among these, Don Vicente Rivarola's is the most valuable. Any investigator quickly discovers an abundance of polemical accounts, but he must exercise his greatest care with works lying in the gray area between fact and fancy. Of these, Finot, Bautista Saavedra, and Stefanich are noteworthy authors.

Bolivian military accounts of the Chaco War appeared for the most part in the ten years immediately following the conflict. With exceptions, the finest Paraguayan works date from the last decade. This situation results, no doubt, from the compulsion of the defeated to explain their conduct, a pressure not felt by the victors. Consequently, impassioned Bolivian participants endeavored to lodge with one another the principal accountability, each blandly asserting that *he* spoke disinterested truth! Upon the student, therefore, rests the responsibilty of sifting and comparing contending accounts, and presenting what he deems factual explanations.

A basic Bolivian study is Vergara Vicuña's splendid, but wordy, *Historia de la Guerra del Chaco,* which consists mainly of documents interpersed with interpretation. Díaz Arguedas, the chief of the Bolivian Army's historical section, must be accorded respect. No history could be complete without use of the Salamanca documents edited by Arze Quiroga. The memoirs of the key officers—Moscoso, Rodríguez, and Toro—are essential. The only recent work is Ayala Moreira's startling *Por que no ganamos la Guerra del Chaco.*

For Paraguayan history, Fernández' projected five-volume work promises to be the finest contribution; to date only two books have been published. The method, careful approach, and intimate personal knowledge of this retired officer differentiates him from others. Of course, Estigarribia's memoirs, as edited by Dr. Pablo Max Ynsfran of the University of Texas, is a must. Caballero Irala and Delgado wrote significantly, but twenty years ago. As for recent Paraguayan material, importance need be attached only to Florentín, Ortiz, and Franco's small book of essays. Juan B. Ayala's vain attempt to polish his tarnished reputation with smooth words should be examined. The Rios account of Paraguayan military preparations is of the greatest value; it can be compared with González' two-volume rebuttal, *Preparación del Paraguay . . .* , a contentious and often shallow work. (Encouraged by President Alfredo Stroessner, Colonel Manuel W. Chaves of the Historical Section of the Paraguayan Ministry of National Defense presently has in progress several document collections and a memoir.)

A few propaganda items have been cited because of their unique merit as representative of psychological warfare techniques and devices. Periodical literature dealing with the Chaco question is almost invariably worthless. All that emerged during the war era was colored, and rarely in accord with the facts which have since been revealed.

BIBLIOGRAPHY

I. Source Materials
   A. Government Publications

   1. Argentina
Ministerio de Relaciones Exteriores y Culto. *La Conferencia de Paz del Chaco 1935-1939*. Buenos Aires: E. L. Frigerio e Hijo, 1939.

La Neutralidad Argentina en el Conflicto Boliviano-Paraguayo. Buenos Aires: Jacobo Peuser, Ltda., 1933.

La Política Argentina en la Guerra del Chaco. 2 vols. Buenos Aires: Guillermo Kraft, 1937.

   2. Bolivia
Mensaje del Presidente de la República de Bolivia al Congreso Nacional. (Titles vary slightly.) 38 vols. 1880-1935.

Ministerio de Guerra y Colonization. *Memoria del Ministerio.* (Titles vary slightly.) 8 vols. 1920-1930.

Ministerio de Relaciones Exteriores y Culto. *Actas y Documentos de las Conferencias de Plenipotenciaros Bolivianos y Paraguayos.* La Paz: Escuela Tipográfica Salesiana, 1929.

Boletín del Ministerio de Relaciones Exteriores. La Paz: Talleres Gráficos Renacimiento, January 1929-December 1937.

Bolivian-Paraguayan Conflict. La Paz: Imprenta Electra, 1932.

La Conferencia de Mendoza y el Conflicto del Chaco. La Paz: Imprenta Electra, 1933.

Documentos Relativos a la Agresión del Paraguay contra el Fortín Boliviano Vanguardia. La Paz: Editorial Renacimiento, 1929.

Las Fronteras de Bolivia. La Paz: Editorial Universo, 1941.

Memoria del Ministro de Relaciones Exteriores y Culto al Congreso Ordinario. (Titles vary slightly.) 40 vols. 1885-1934.

Notas y el Memorandum de Bolivia contra el Tratado de Arbitraje Argentino-Paraguayo de 1876. La Paz: Escuela Tipográfica Salesiana, 1929.

La Reintegración Marítima de Bolivia. La Paz: Imprenta Artistica, 1929.

Tratados Vigentes 1825-1925. 3 vols. La Paz: Litográfias e Imprentas Unidas, 1925.

Díaz Arguedas, Julio (Colonel). *Los Elegidos de la Gloria*. La Paz: Imprenta Intendencia General de Guerra, 1937.

——————. *La Guerra con el Paraguay*. La Paz: Imprenta Intendencia Central del Ejército, 1942.

——————. *Historia del Ejército de Bolivia*. La Paz: Imprenta Central del Ejército, 1940.

Mujía, Ricardo. *Bolivia-Paraguay. Anotaciones a la Réplica del excelentisimo Sr. Ministro plenipotenciario especial del Paraguay Don Fulgéncio R. Moreno*. La Paz: Editora de El Tiempo, 1916.

——————. *Bolivia-Paraguay. Exposición de los titulos.* . . . 3 vols.; annexes, 5 vols. La Paz: Empresa Editora de El Tiempo, 1914.

Nogales Ortiz, Edmundo (Captain). *Nuestra Caballeria en la Guerra del Chaco*. La Paz: Imprenta Intendencia General de Guerra, 1938.

3. Brazil
Debarros, Jayme. *A Política Exterior do Brasil*. Rio de Janeiro: Departmento de Imprensa e Propaganda, 1941.

4. Great Britain
Foreign Office. *British and Foreign State Papers*. 38 vols. London: William Ridgway, 1852-1889.

5. Mexico
González Roa, Fernando. *Comisión de Investigación y Conciliación*. Mexico, D. F.: Imprenta de la Secretaria de Relaciones Exteriores, 1930.

6. Paraguay
Cámara de Senadores de la República del Paraguay Sesiones del Periodo Legislativo del Año 1896. Asunción: Tipográfia de La Opinion, 1896.

Congreso Nacional. *Protocolo de Paz*. Asunción: Imprenta Nacional, 1935.

——————. *La Paz con Bolivia ante el Poder Legislativo*. Asunción: Imprenta Nacional, 1939.

Ejército. *Guerra del Chaco. Los partes del conductor*. Asunción: Ayudantía General Sección Historia e Imprenta, 1950.

Mensaje del Presidente de la República del Paraguay al Honorable Congreso Nacional. (Titles vary.) 9 vols. 1913-1932.

Ministerio de la Defensa Nacional. *Breve resumen de la campaña del Chaco*. Asunción: Imprenta Militar, 1935.

Paraguay-Bolivia. Aspectos de la Guerra del Chaco. Asunción: Imprenta Militar, 1934.

Ministerio de Economía. *Las Colonias Mennonitas en el Chaco Paraguayo*. Asunción: Imprenta Nacional, 1934.

Ministerio de Relaciones Exteriores. *Archivo Diplomático y Consular del Paraguay.* Asunción: Tipográfico de El Civico, 1908.

Cuestión de Límites con Bolivia. Negociaciones diplomáticos 1915-1917. 2 vols. 2d ed. Asunción: Imprenta Nacional, 1928.

Informe del Plenipotenciaro Dr. Dominguez acerca de Negociaciones Domínguez-Cano. . . . Asunción: Imprenta Nacional, 1929.

Libro Blanco. Documentos Relativos a las Conferencias de Buenos Aires. . . . Asunción: Imprenta Nacional, 1928.

Libro Blanco. Documentos Relativos a la Conferencia de Washington para el estudio de un Pacto de No Agresión. . . . Asunción: Imprenta Nacional, 1933.

Libro Blanco. Documentos Relativos a la Actuación de la Comision Especial de la Sociedad de los Naciones. . . . Asunción: Imprenta Nacional, 1934.

Lista de Ministros de Relaciones Exteriores del Paraguay. Asunción: Imprenta Nacional, 1943.

Memoria del Ministerio de Relaciones Exteriores Presentada al Honorable Congreso. (Titles vary slightly.) 7 vols. 1879-1902.

Paraguay-Bolivia. Cuestión de Límites. Asunción: Imprenta Nacional, 1924.

Paraguay-Bolivia. Protocolos y Notas cambiadas. Asunción: Imprenta Nacional, 1927.

Paraguay-Bolivia. Tratados y Protocolos. Asunción: Imprenta Nacional, 1927.

Aceval, Benjamín. *Chaco Paraguayo. Memoria presentada al arbitro.* Asunción: H. Kraus, 1896.

————. *Appendix and Documents Annexed to the Memoir filed by the Minister of Paraguay.* New York: n. p., 1878.

Amarilla Fretes, Eduardo. *La Liquidación de la guerra de la Triple Alianza contra el Paraguay.* Asunción: Imprenta Militar, 1941.

————. *El Paraguay en el primer cincuentenario del fallo arbitral del Presidente Hayes.* Asunción: Imprenta Nacional, 1932.

Audibert, Alejandro. *Cuestión de Límites entre El Paraguay y Bolivia.* Asunción: Escuela Tipográfia Salesiana, 1901.

————. *Los límites de la antigua provincia del Paraguay.* Buenos Aires: Imprenta La Económica, 1892.

Ayala, Eusebio. *Ante el Pais.* Asunción: Imprenta Nacional, 1932.

Báez, Cecilio. *Historia diplomática del Paraguay.* 2 vols. Asunción: Imprenta Nacional, 1931-1932.

Domínguez, Manuel. *Bolivia atropello el statu-quo y sus reconocimientos del laudo Hayes.* Asunción: Imprenta Nacional, 1935.

————. *Nuestros Pactos con Bolivia.* Asunción: Imprenta Nacional, 1928.

7. United States

Department of State. *Papers Relating to the Foreign Relations of the United States.* 32 vols. 1907-1938.

The Chaco Peace Conference. Washington: Government Printing Office, 1940.

Proceedings of the Commission of Inquiry and Conciliation Bolivia and Paraguay. Baltimore: The Sun Book and Job Printing Office, Inc., 1929.

Moore, John Bassett. *History and Digest of the International Arbitrations to which the United States Has Been a Party.* 6 vols. Washington: Government Printing Office, 1898.

8. League of Nations

Armaments Year-Book. 12 vols. 1927-1938.

League of Nations Publications, Political, 1934, VII, No. 1, *Dispute between Bolivia and Paraguay. Report of the Chaco Commission.*

No. 2, *Dispute between Bolivia and Paraguay. Communication from the Paraguayan Representatives.*

No. 5, *Dispute between Bolivia and Paraguay. Memorandum from the Bolivian Government dated February 12th, 1934 and Memorandum from the Paraguayan Delegation dated March 8th, 1934.*

No. 6, *Dispute between Bolivia and Paraguay. Observations of the Paraguayan Government on the Chaco Commission's Report.*

No. 7, *Dispute between Bolivia and Paraguay. Statement of the Paraguayan case submitted to the Assembly by the Paraguayan Government.*

No. 9, *Dispute between Bolivia and Paraguay. Statement of the Bolivian Government's case communicated in virtue of Article 15, paragraph 2, of the Covenant.*

No. 13, *Dispute between Bolivia and Paraguay. Report as provided for under Article 15, paragraph 4, of the Covenant.*

League of Nations Official Journal, Special Supplement No. 124, *Dispute between Bolivia and Paraguay. Appeal of the Bolivian Government under Article 15 of the Covenant.*

Special Supplement No. 132, *Dispute between Bolivia and Paraguay. Records of the Special Session of the Assembly.*

Special Supplement No. 133, *Dispute between Bolivia and Paraguay. Appeal of the Bolivian Government under Article 15 of the Covenant.*

Special Supplement No. 135, *Dispute between Bolivia and Paraguay. Records of the Special Session of the Assembly.*

B. Memoirs and Document Collections

1. Diplomatic

Alaiza, Miguel (Colonel). *Los Derechos de Bolivia sobre el Oriente y el Chaco Boreal.* La Paz: Imprenta Unidas, 1928.

Baptista, Mariano. *Obras Completas.* Vol. IV, *Asuntos Internacionales.* La Paz: Editora Renacimiento, 1932.

Benites, Gregorio. *Exposición de los derechos del Paraguay.* . . . Asunción: Tipográfica La Opinion, 1895.

Diez de Medina, Eduardo. *De un Siglo al Otro. Memorias de un Hombre Público.* La Paz: Alfonso Tejerina, 1955.

Finot, Enrique. *Nuevos Aspectos de la Cuestión del Chaco.* La Paz: Editora Renacimiento, 1931.

Ichaso, Telmo. *Antecedentes del Tratado de Límites Celebrado con la República del Paraguay.* Sucre: Tipográfia El Cruzado, 1894.

Iraízos, Francisco. *El sudeste de Bolivia.* La Paz: Sociedad Geográfica de La Paz, 1901.

Quijarro, Antonio. *Bolivia. Política Internacional.* Buenos Aires: Imprenta de Jacobo Peuser, 1887.

————. *La Cuestión de Límites entre Bolivia y el Paraguay.* Buenos Aires: Compania Sud-Americana de Billetes de Banco, 1901.

Ramírez, Juan Isidro. *La Paz del Chaco.* Buenos Aires: Imprenta Ferrari Hnos, 1942.

Rivarola, Vicente. *Memorias diplomáticos. El Paraguay en el litigio de límites con Bolivia.* 3 vols. Buenos Aires: Editorial Ayacucho, 1952-1957.

Saavedra, Bautista. *El Chaco y la Conferencia de Paz.* Santiago: Editorial Nascimento, 1939.

————. *La Cuestión Fronteriza con el Paraguay.* La Paz: Talleres La Prensa, 1908.

Stefanich, Juan. *La Diplomacia de la Revolution.* Buenos Aires: Editorial El Mundo Nuevo, 1945.

2. Military

Aponte B., Leandro (Major). *Cincuenta años de aeronautica en el Paraguay.* Asunción: El Arte, 1957.

Arze Quiroga, Eduardo, ed. *Documentos para una Historia de la Guerra del Chaco.* 2 vols. La Paz: Editorial D. Bosco, 1951, 1952.

Ayala, Juan Batista (General). *La Guerra del Chaco hasta Campo Via.* Buenos Aires: Artes Gráficas Aconcaque, 1958.

Ayala Moreira, Rogelio (Colonel). *Por que no ganamos la Guerra del Chaco.* La Paz: Talleres Graficos Bolivianos, 1959.

Barrientos Gutiérrez, Pablo H. (Major). *La contraofensiva del Parapetí.* Santiago: Imprenta General Díaz, 1936.

Caballero Irala, Basiliano (Lieutenant Colonel). *Nuestros Zapadores en la Guerra del Chaco.* Montevideo: Editorial Libertad, 1939.

Delgado, Nicolás (General). *Historia de la Guerra del Chaco.* 2 vols. Asunción: Imprenta Nacional, 1943.

Díaz Arguedas, Julio (Colonel). *Como fue derrocado el hombre símbolo.* La Paz: Editora Universo, 1957.

Fernández, Carlos José (Colonel). *La Guerra del Chaco.* 2 vols. 2d ed. Buenos Aires: Impresora Oeste, 1956.

Florentín, Heriberto (Colonel). *La batalla de Strongest.* Buenos Aires: Editorial Asunción, 1958.

————. *Lo que he visto en Boquerón.* Buenos Aires: Editorial Asunción, 1957.

Franco, Rafael (General). *Dos batallas de la Guerra del Chaco.* Buenos Aires: Editorial Yegros, 1959.

González, Antonio E. (Colonel). *La Guerra del Chaco.* Sao Paulo: Tipográfia Cupolo, 1941.

————. *Preparación del Paraguay para la Guerra del Chaco.* 2 vols. Asunción: Editorial El Gráfico, 1957.

Guerrero, Julio C. (Lieutenant Colonel). *La Guerra en el Chaco.* Lima: Imprenta T. Scheuch, 1934.

Macías, Silvio. *La Guerra del Chaco.* Asunción: n. p., 1936.

Manchego, Tomás (Lieutenant). "El Asalto Paraguayo al Fortín Vanguardia," *Revista Militar,* Nos. 100-101. La Paz: Imprenta Militar, 1930.

Melean, Aurelio. *La Sanidad Boliviana en la campaña del Chaco.* Cochabamba: Imprenta de la Universidad, 1938.

Moscoso Gutiérrez, Oscar (Colonel). *Recuerdos de la Guerra del Chaco.* Sucre: Escuela Tipográfica Salesiana, 1939.

Oliver, Manuel Maria. *La Guerra en el Chaco Boreal.* Buenos Aires: Editorial Castany, 1935.

Olmedo, Natalício. *Pitiantuta.* Asunción: Talleres Gráficos Estado Major General del Ejército, 1933. 2d ed., 1959.

Ortiz, José Antonio (Colonel). *La batalla de Strongest.* Asunción: n. p., 1959.

Pol, Hugo René (Major). *La Campaña del Chaco.* La Paz: Editorial Fenix, 1945.

Rios, Angel F. (Major). *La Defensa del Chaco.* Buenos Aires: Imprenta Ayacucho, 1950.

Rodríguez, Angel (General). *Autopsia de una Guerra.* Santiago: Ediciones Ercilla, 1940.

Taborga T., Alberto (Major). *Boquerón.* La Paz: n. p., 1956.

Toro Ruilova, David (General). *Mi actuación en la Guerra del Chaco.* La Paz: Editora Renacimiento, 1941.

Torres Ortiz, Humberto (Captain). *Campo Via.* La Paz: Editorial Fenix, 1937.

Urioste, Ovidio. *La Encrucijada.* Cochabama: Editorial Canelas, 1941.

————. *La Fragua.* . . . n. p., n. d. [1933].

Vacca, Juan Esteban. *Notas de la pasada Guerra del Chaco.* Buenos Aires: Círculo Militar, 1938.

Vasconsellos, Cándido A. (Lieutenant Colonel). *Guerra Paraguay-Bolivia. Mis memoria de la sanidad en campaña.* Asunción: La Colmena, 1942.

Vergara Vicuña, Aquiles (Colonel). *Historia de la Guerra del Chaco.* 7 vols. La Paz: Imprenta Unidas, 1940-1944.

Vidaurre, Enrique (Colonel). *Acciones Militares en Toledo y Fernández*. n. p., 1940.

————. *El 41 de Infanteria*. La Paz: Escuela Tipográfica Salesiana, 1936.

————. *El Material de Guerra en la Campaña del Chaco*. La Paz: Escuela Tipográfica Salesiana, 1942.

Vysokolán, Dr. Stephan (Brigadier General). *Batalla de Nanawa*. Asunción: Imprenta Militar, 1958.

Wewege-Smith, Thomas (Lieutenant). *Gran Chaco Adventure*. London: Hutchinson & Co., Ltd., 1937.

Ynsfran, Pablo Max, ed. *The Epic of the Chaco: Marshal Estigarribia's Memoirs of the Chaco War 1932-1935*. Austin: University of Texas Press, 1950.

II. Selected Secondary Materials

A. Diplomatic and Political

Alvéstegui, David. *Bolivia y el Paraguay*. La Paz: Imprenta Renacimiento, 1926.

Andia, Ernesto Daniel. *En el Pais de los Heroes*. Buenos Aires: El Ateneo, 1947.

Antokoletz, Daniel. *La Cuestión del Chaco Boreal*. Montevideo: Impresora Uruguayo, 1934.

Artaza, Policarpo. *Ayala, Estigarribia y el Partido Liberal*. 2d ed. Buenos Aires: Editorial Ayacucho, 1946.

Ayala Queirolo, Victor (Colonel). *El Carmen*. Asunción: Imprenta Militar, 1959.

Bejarano, Ramón César (Colonel). *Antecedentes de la Guerra con Bolivia*. Asunción: Editorial Toledo, 1959.

Benítez, Justo Pastor. *Bajo el signo de Marte*. Montevideo: Impresora Uruguaya, 1934.

Díaz Machicao, Porfirio. *Historia de Bolivia. Salamanca, La Guerra del Chaco, Tejada Sorzano, 1931-1936*. La Paz: Gisbert, 1955.

Finot, Enrique. *Nueva historia de Bolivia*. Buenos Aires: n. p., 1946.

Fretz, Joseph Winfield. *Pilgrims in Paraguay*. Scottdale, Pa.: Herald Press, 1953.

Gondra, César. *La diplomacia de los tratados Paraguay y Bolivia*. Buenos Aires: Imprenta Didot, 1906.

Grey, C. G. and Leonard Bridgman. *Jane's All The World's Aircraft*. London: Sampson Low & Co. 12 vols. 1925-1936.

La Foy, Margaret. *The Chaco Dispute and the League of Nations*. Ann Arbor: Edwards Brothers, 1946.

Loza, Leon Martínez. *El Laudo Hayes; su ineficacia en el litigio Boliviano-Paraguayo*. La Paz: Editorial Renacimiento, 1936.

Mercado Moreira, Miguel. *El Chaco Boliviano*. Cochabamba: Editorial López, 1928.

————. *El Chaco Boreal.* La Paz: Imprenta Velarde, 1920.

Ostria Gutiérrez, Alberto. *La doctrina del no-reconocimiento de la conquista en America.* Rio de Janeiro: Birsoi & Cia., 1938.

Ramírez, J. Isidro. *Alrededor de la Cuestión Paraguayo Boliviana.* Lima: Imprenta Minerva, 1930.

Rios, Cornelio. *Los Derechos de Bolivia sobre el Chaco Boreal.* . . . Buenos Aires: n. p., 1925.

Rodas Equino, Justo. *La Guerra del Chaco.* Buenos Aires: Bernabe y Cia., 1938.

Stefanich, Juan. *El Paraguay Nuevo.* Buenos Aires: Editorial Claridad, 1943.

Virreira Paccieri, Alberto. *Bolivia-Paraguay. 5 de Diciembre de 1928.* La Paz: Imprenta Electrica, 1922.

Zook, David H., Jr. *The Evolution of the Chaco Dispute.* Ann Arbor: University Microfilms, 1959.

B. Economic

El Banco Central de Bolivia durante la Guerra del Chaco. La Paz: Editorial America, 1936.

C. Propaganda

Colle, Elio M. A. *El Drama del Paraguay.* Buenos Aires: Editorial Claridad, 1935.

Gandía, Enrique de. *Historia de Santa Cruz de la Sierra.* Buenos Aires: Talleres Gráficos Argentinos de L. J. Rosso, 1935.

Hinojosa, Robert. *El Condor Encadenado.* Monterey, N. L.: n. p., 1941.

Marof, Tristan (pseudonym of Gustavo A. Navarro). *La Tragedia del Altiplano.* Buenos Aires: Claridad, 1934.

Samaniego, Roque (Major). *Problemas Nacionales. El Paraguay frente a Bolivia.* Asunción: n. p., 1932.

Saona N., Carlos Napoleon (Captain). *Bolivia: Apuntes geográficos.* . . . Quito: Editorial Labor, 1936.

Sofovich, Manuel. *La Tragedia Boliviano.* Buenos Aires: Noticias Gráficas, 1932.

Terán Gómez, Luis. *Bolivia Frente a los Pueblos del Plata.* La Paz: Imprenta Arno Hnos, 1936.

D. Biography

Aponte B., Leandro (Major). *General Garay.* Asunción: El Arte, 1956.

Benítez, Justo Pastor. *Estigarribia. El Soldado del Chaco.* 1st ed., Buenos Aires: Editorial Difusam, 1943. 2d ed., Buenos Aires: Ediciones Nizza, 1958.

Bray, Arturo. *Hombres y Epocas del Paraguay.* Buenos Aires: Editorial Difusam, 1943.

Cardozo, Efraím. *Tres Heroes del Paraguay.* Buenos Aires: Ayacucho, 1952.

Guerrero, Julio C. (Colonel). *Peñaranda.* . . . La Paz: Intendencia Central del Ejército, 1940.

Vergara Vicuña, Aquiles (Colonel). *Bernardino Bilbao Rioja.* La Paz: Imprenta Unidos, 1948.

E. Newspapers and Periodicals

Bolivia. A Quarterly Survey of Bolivian Activities. New York: The Bolivian Consulate. 1926-1938.

New York Times. 1927-1936.

The Times (London). 1927-1932.

Time. 24 October 1938.

F. Articles

Kain, Ronald Stuart. "Behind the Chaco War," *Current History,* XLII (April, 1935), 468-474.

Morris Robert M. "Bolivia," *Bulletin of the Pan American Union,* LXX (February, 1936), 169-171.

Schor, P. S. "Dust in the Chaco," *Living Age,* CCCIL (October, 1935), 151-159.

Warren, Harris Gaylord. "Political Aspects of the Paraguayan Revolution, 1936-1940," *Hispanic American Historical Review,* XXX (February, 1950) , 3-21.

INDEX

INDEX